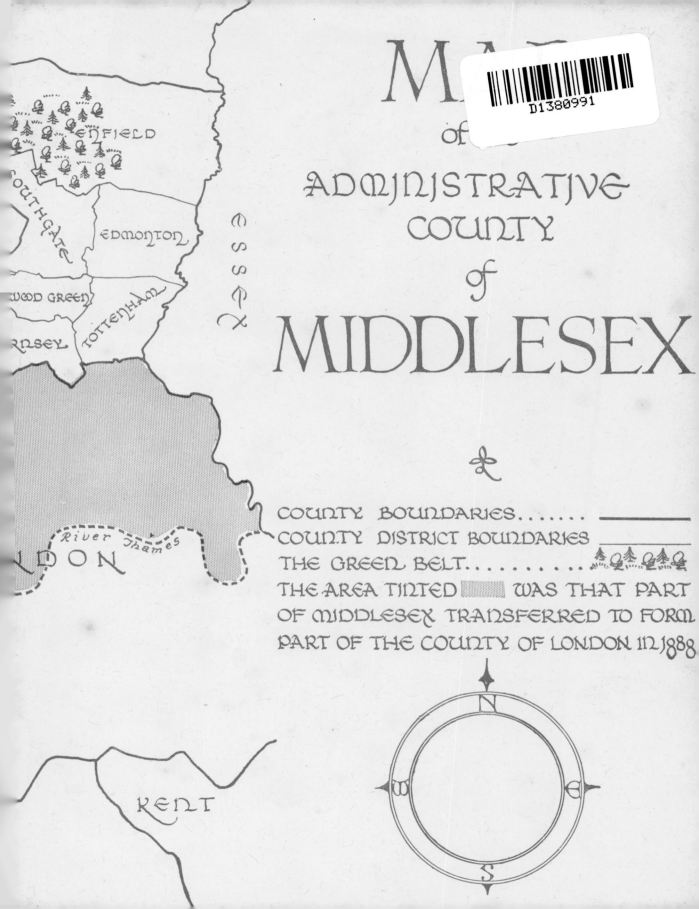

MAP
of the
ADMINISTRATIVE
COUNTY
of
MIDDLESEX

ENFIELD

SOUTHGATE

EDMONTON

WOOD GREEN

TOTTENHAM

RNSEY

ESSEX

KENT

River Thames

DON

COUNTY BOUNDARIES........
COUNTY DISTRICT BOUNDARIES ____
THE GREEN BELT..........
THE AREA TINTED ▓▓ WAS THAT PART
OF MIDDLESEX TRANSFERRED TO FORM
PART OF THE COUNTY OF LONDON IN 1888

N
W E
S

MIDDLESEX

THE JUBILEE OF THE COUNTY COUNCIL
1889–1939
✦

THE
ARMORIAL
BEARINGS
OF THE
MUNICIPAL
BOROUGHS
WITHIN THE
COUNTY

MIDDLESEX

THE JUBILEE OF THE COUNTY COUNCIL
1889–1939

BY

C.W. RADCLIFFE

CLERK OF THE PEACE &
CLERK & SOLICITOR
TO THE COUNTY
COUNCIL
✠

EVANS BROTHERS LIMITED LONDON

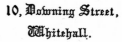

10, Downing Street,
Whitehall.

The Middlesex County Council has done well to
publish this Jubilee Celebration Book, for it is an
inspiring record of the work of the County Council during
the fifty years since it was formed.

It will enable the school children and their parents
to appreciate how the Council's work has grown from small
beginnings to the wide ramifications of to-day, extending
over the whole field of the social services and all the
branches of public health. It brings to their attention not
only the activities for which the Council itself is
responsible, but also its relation to those conducted by the
district authorities. It thus brings out clearly how the
administration of the county area rests on the support and
structural framework provided by the County Council.

The passages on the value and dignity of civic duties
should serve to inspire men and women of ability and public
spirit to participate in the responsibilities of local
administration and to bear their part in service to their
fellow citizens.

Neville Chamberlain.

MAGNA CARTA

The famous Charter of Liberties, was granted to the English people by King John at Runnymede in June, 1215.   In the words of a modern historian : " The whole of the constitutional history of England is a commentary on this Charter."

MAGNA · CARTA

WILLIAM D'ALBINI · ROGER BIGOD · HENRY LE BOHUN · HUGH BIGOD · RICHARD de CLARE

GILBERT de CLARE · ROBERT FITZWALTER · JOHN FITZROBERT · WILLIAM de FORTIBUS · WILLIAM de HARDELL

WILLIAM de HUNTINGFIELD · JOHN de LACYE · WILLIAM de LANVALEI · WILLIAM MALET · GEOFFREY de MANDEVILLE

ROGER de MONTBEGON · RICHARD de MONTFITCHET · RICHARD de PERCY · WILLIAM MARSHALL · ROBERT de ROOS

SAIR de QUINCEY · GEOFFREY de SAYE · WILLIAM de MOWBRAY · EUSTACE de VESCI · ROBERT de VERE

SHIELDS · OF · THE · SIGNATORY · BARONS

INTRODUCTORY NOTE

IN June, 1937, the County Council agreed that I should prepare a book, in accordance with the following communication:—

"17th June, 1937.

DEAR MR. CHAIRMAN,

I have, for many years, felt that the County school-children should be afforded a greater opportunity of studying and taking a really live interest in the vast and multifarious municipal activities of the County and I have, on many occasions, discussed this subject with the Secretary to the Education Committee.

The senior boys and girls in the County Schools should, in my opinion, be encouraged to understand the machinery of Local Government so that they might be equipped with the necessary knowledge to enable them eventually to take their share in the responsibility of the administration of their County, either as elected representatives or as officials.

With regard to the latter, I think that the organization of specialist courses in Local Government for senior pupils has much to commend it and is worthy of careful consideration by the Education Committee, particularly as such classes would form a most useful recruiting ground for the municipal service. A series of lectures on various aspects of the work, by County experts with many years' practical experience, accompanied by appropriate illustrative films of the main County roads, rivers, bridges, drainage works, open spaces, small holdings, and places of historical interest in the County, together with the interior working of County offices, hospitals, institutions, schools, court-houses, &c., supplemented by visits, would I am sure be of invaluable interest to the pupils.

The field of County administration is necessarily a very wide one and I am encouraged by the widespread success and appreciation of the County Coronation book and by the forthcoming Jubilee of the County Council to suggest that I should write a descriptive book, for presentation to all the senior school-children, on the history and growth of the County ; dealing, in simple language and with illustrations, with all the various phases of the County work. A book of this kind would, I feel, kindle an enthusiastic interest, form the nucleus of the specialist classes and induce a more detailed study of work of such national importance.

It was apparent from the great number of letters of appreciation of the Coronation souvenir book that the book had also attracted the attention of parents and, in my opinion, the cultivation of a greater civic interest in the County and its administration is desirable.

I am, my dear Sir,
Your obedient Servant,
C. W. RADCLIFFE,
Clerk of the County Council."

The local government machinery to-day is such a mass of complexity that it has been found a somewhat difficult task to cover such a wide field in phraseology which will be readable and understood by children in their last year at the elementary and secondary schools of the County.

The once rural county of Middlesex, known for its intensive agricultural interests, has had a phenomenal growth and is now the most densely populated "dormitory" area outside the metropolis.

INTRODUCTORY NOTE

In 1888 the population was less than 500,000—to-day it is over 2,000,000. The rateable value in 1888 was £2,900,000—to-day it is over £20,250,000. The main road mileage in 1888 was approximately 100 whereas to-day it is over 375. There were 214 schools in the County in 1888 whereas to-day there are 788. Similar comparative statistics showing the rapid growth of the administration could be furnished for all the multifarious public social services of the County.

The post-war period has, of course, been the most intensive of any. A 1*d*. rate in 1920 produced approximately £35,000—to-day it produces approximately £85,000.

I have always felt how instructive it would be for the children in our schools if only they could see for themselves how gigantic schemes (to give only one instance, the world's greatest sewerage purification work in West Middlesex) grow stage by stage from the preliminary report.

Lectures and visits of inspection might, with great advantage, be encouraged, and it is hoped that this small book will also be of some assistance to the teachers in our schools and assist them to inculcate in the child mind the immense interest and importance of the County's local government work.

An effort has been made to make the work both interesting and instructive and it is hoped that the section dealing with the numerous and varied careers open to the youth of to-day in the local government service will be of assistance and value to both the teachers and the children.

Apart from the children and their teachers for whom it is primarily designed, it is hoped that the parents will take the opportunity of reading this work.

A former Minister of Health, the Rt. Hon. Sir Kingsley Wood, addressing the County Councils Association on March 23rd, 1938, said:

" Your work and that of other local authorities touches, I suppose, the lives of men and women more frequently, and its results, whether they be successes or failures, are felt much more intimately than is perhaps the more remote interest of Parliament itself. . . . I have been particularly struck, when on so many occasions I have met members and officers of local authorities up and down the country and have examined their work, by the excellence of what they are doing, and I think that, above everything else, we want to see that this work of local government of ours particularly captures the interest and the sympathy of the younger generation. I believe that there is an urgent call to this honourable service in our country to-day and a real need of recruits, particularly from the younger generation, and I hope that in all that we do and in all the work which inspires us, we may be able to inspire others."

I have received great assistance from the heads of the various Departments. I am especially indebted to Messrs. W. Le Hardy, J. Goldberg, and J. B. Stephens. My sincere thanks are also due to Miss J. Heddle for reading manuscripts and proofs and for many valuable suggestions, to Mr. A. Bartholomew for his great help in the preparation and collection of the illustrations and to Messrs. H. Rider and E. Railton for additional illustrations.

C. W. R.

Middlesex Guildhall,
Westminster.

January, 1939.

COAT ARMOUR OF LORD LIEUTENANTS OF MIDDLESEX 1714 — 1926

1714 The Duke of Newcastle
1762 The Duke of Northumberland
1794 The Duke of Portland
1868 The Duke of Wellington
1842 The Marquess of Salisbury
1884 The Earl of Strafford
1898 The Duke of Bedford

FROM THE STAINED GLASS WINDOWS IN THE GUILDHALL

CONTENTS

PART ONE

THE HISTORICAL DEVELOPMENT OF MIDDLESEX

PART TWO

THE ESTABLISHMENT OF COUNTY COUNCIL ADMINISTRATION

PART THREE

COUNTY SERVICES

CONTENTS

PART FOUR

CAREERS AND PROFESSIONS IN THE COUNTY SERVICE

LUCEM·SPERO

COAT ARMOUR OF
THE LORD ROCHDALE
✠
LORD LIEUTENANT &
CUSTOS ROTULORUM
MIDDLESEX

THE HISTORICAL DEVELOPMENT OF MIDDLESEX

MIDDLESEX BEFORE THE NORMAN CONQUEST

VERY little is known of prehistoric life in the area which was afterwards to be known as Middlesex, and it is probable that the low-lying sections of the County were mere swamps, while the clay sub-soil that constituted the greater part of the County was covered with impenetrable forests. The remains of a camp have been found at Enfield and of a mound at Ruislip, while others at Kingsbury and Hounslow were reported to have existed before building development obliterated all traces. Air photography has been responsible for locating some evidence of early occupation in Stanwell and East Bedfont. Traces of Grims Dyke are found along a line running northeast from Cuckoo Hill, west of Pinner, to Weald Wood, west of Stanmore, and at one time it was thought that this marked the boundary of the Catuvellauni tribe. More recent excavations, however, have shown that it could not have been dug earlier than the fifth century.

THE INVASION OF JULIUS CÆSAR

The invasion of the English coast by Julius Cæsar fifty-five years before the birth of Christ was merely in the nature of a raid, and the Roman forces did not penetrate far inland. In the following year, however, Cæsar marched his army northwards towards the Thames. Whether he crossed at Lambeth or at Brentford is a point on which much controversy has raged, but in any event he must have traversed the County in order to reach the capital of the Catuvellauni, known as Oppidum Cassivelauni and said to be situated near Wheathampstead in Hertfordshire.

After his notable victory over this powerful tribe, Cæsar imposed a heavy tribute and withdrew his army back to Gaul, leaving traces of his occupation at Laleham and Shepperton, and allowed Britain to look after its own affairs.

There is no evidence that the tribute which Cæsar imposed was ever paid, and we may imagine that the country lived in comparative peace for over a century.

Whether London existed at all at this date is open to some doubt though, as the name has a distinctly Celtic origin, it is probable that some sort of settlement had been established, perhaps merely consisting of fishermen.

REMAINS OF ANCIENT BRITISH STAKE FROM BED OF THE RIVER THAMES AT BRENTFORD
Now preserved in the Middlesex Guildhall.

Changes which had an important effect on the development of London, and incidentally on the County of Middlesex, were brought about by the removal of the capital of the Catuvellauni from Verulamium to Colchester, where the town of Camulodunum had been established before Cunobelinus (the Cymbeline of Shakespeare) became the chief of the tribe. As a result of this change, the roads leading from the Kentish ports, which crossed the Thames either at Lambeth or farther west, were diverted to a ford or possibly a bridge at Southwark, and so led eastwards to Colchester. London was thus left in the apex of a triangle formed by these roads, and no doubt this situation encouraged its development.

THE ROMAN CONQUEST OF BRITAIN

In A.D. 43 the famous Roman Emperor, Claudius, sent Aulus Plautius with a well-equipped army of 40,000 men to undertake the conquest of Britain. His campaign was entirely successful, and before long he had subdued the whole area south of the Humber and east of the Severn. During this campaign, Prasutagus, king of the people living in Norfolk and Suffolk who were known as the Iceni, submitted to the Roman rule without joining contest, and as a reward was allowed to retain his kingdom. On his death he bequeathed half his possessions to the Roman Emperor and half to his daughters. The Roman ruler in Britain was not satisfied with this arrangement and endeavoured to obtain the whole of the kingdom of the Iceni, which so infuriated the warlike Boadicea, widow of the late king, that in A.D. 60 she raised an army and sacked Colchester. Flushed with success, she marched on to St. Albans, while fortunately for her, Suetonius, the Roman general, was with his army in Wales and before he could reach the south London was already in the hands of the victorious British Queen.

Her success was short-lived, for when Suetonius reached the south with a large portion of his forces, he completely overthrew the rebellious tribe and slew their gallant leader. Nobody can say exactly where this action took place, but all the authorities seem to agree that the borders of Middlesex and Hertfordshire were the most likely places. Two places have been known as " Boadicea's grave ", one between Hampstead Ponds and Highgate Ponds, and the other near Bentley Priory in Harrow Weald, but excavations have failed to establish the claim of either of these places.

For two centuries after these events England flourished under Roman rule and the City of London began to take shape. According to the earliest-known description of London, given to us by Tacitus, the Roman historian, it was, in A.D. 61, " a city teeming with merchants and busy with the trafficking of wares ".

THE ROMANS CAME TO ENGLAND IN SHIPS SUCH AS THESE

In Middlesex much was done, no doubt, to reclaim the swampy ground and to cut down some of the forests. As London grew, so did the neighbouring agricultural area prosper. Roads were rapidly built and improved, and to-day Watling Street and Ermine Street form the foundation of our great arteries to the north-west and north-east, while the Via Trinobantica, which ran from Staines (then known as Pontes from the fact that it crossed the Colne and Thames by bridges) to the west, is followed by the route of the old Bath Road.

The position of London prevented the growth of any big towns in the County at this time, and Staines and Sulloniacæ at Brockley Hill are the only places which can warrant such a description. Traces of Roman settlements have, however, been found at Harmondsworth, Kingsbury, Acton, Chiswick and at Bentley Priory in Harrow, with others at Harefield, Hanwell and Ealing which are not quite so easy of identification.

The raids by the Franks and by the Saxon pirates in 285, their defeat in 296, and the incursions of the Picts, Scots, Saxons and Attocotti during the fourth century must have made their effect felt on the County, as more often than not London, the principal stronghold of the defenders, was the objective of the intruders.

AFTER THE ROMANS LEFT BRITAIN

When the Roman empire was threatened with destruction at its centre, the Roman troops were gradually withdrawn from Britain and the natives were bidden to defend themselves. Their plea to Rome for help in 496 against the invasion

The Shield of ST. EDWARD THE CONFESSOR. The Shield of WILLIAM THE CONQUEROR.

of Hengist and Horsa was disregarded, and a Jutish kingdom was set up in Kent. We know little of the events which occurred during the next century until Middlesex emerges in 527 as part of the East Saxon Kingdom. Its overlordship changed from time to time but from 664, except for a brief period after the battle of Burford in 752, it remained under the King of Mercia until that kingdom was merged with the Kingdom of England under King Egbert in 827.

The county system was not introduced into England until 900, but nearly two centuries earlier the first reference to

Middlesex is found in a charter in 704, when the King of the East Saxons granted a piece of land in Twickenham " in the Province which is called Middelseaxon ".

MIDDLESEX UNDER THE DANES

It is probable that the County also suffered under the Danes in 851, when London was burned to the ground, and in the campaign waged by Alfred to avenge this defeat in 871, but after this brave monarch had accomplished his object the County must have lived under peaceful conditions until 1002, when the Danes, led by their king, Sweyn, successfully attacked our shores. Although Sweyn was elected King of England in 1013, he died the following year and the English recalled Ethelred, who ruled until his death three years later. Edmund Ironside, his son, was then elected king by the citizens of London, but Canute landed on the east coast with a large force and immediately set siege to Ironside and his supporters within the walls of the city. After the gallant Ironside had repulsed many attacks he eventually escaped and was able to collect his army, which had been in Wessex. With these he returned towards London and defeated Canute at Brentford, though only to survive a short time before meeting death by murder at Oxford. After this Canute managed to persuade the people of England to elect him king, no doubt by virtue of his marriage with good Queen Emma, widow of Ethelred, and he continued in power until his death in 1035.

During the rule of Harold and Hardicanute, both sons of Canute, the County appears to have remained unmolested, and on the latter's death in 1042 Edward, the son of Ethelred and Emma, was elected to the throne. Better known as St. Edward the Confessor, he had great influence over the people of Middlesex and was responsible for the building of the original Westminster Abbey. His death in January 1066 led to the invasion and conquest of the whole country by William of Normandy, better

HOLDING A SAXON COURT UNDER A THORN TREE

known as William the Conqueror, whose reforms will be dealt with in the next chapter.

THE INTRODUCTION OF CHRISTIANITY

Christianity had been introduced into England as early as the second century, and it is related that Lucius built a church in Cornhill in A.D. 179, when London was created a bishopric. It is probable, however, that the Faith was not generally adopted until about seventy years later, when the Roman Emperor decreed that persons throughout the empire should be allowed to consecrate buildings for the purpose of carrying on their religious worship. But Christianity did not proceed along easy paths, and the martyrdom of St. Alban just outside Verulamium illustrates the opposition which had to be overcome.

The Council at Arles in 314 was attended by the Bishop of London, who signed the canons which were drawn up on that occasion.

We know little further about the development of Christianity in England until the arrival of St. Augustine in 596, when for a few years converts from paganism are supposed to have been numerous. During this revival Saebert,

king of the East Saxons, is reputed to have begun the building of St. Paul's Cathedral, but on his death in 616 the County relapsed into its former pagan condition. Sigebert III, who had previously been converted, restored the Christian religion, and in 656 appointed a Bishop of London, but the diocese cannot be considered as permanently established until the consecration of St. Erkenwald in 674.

From this date onwards it seems clear that Christianity became generally widespread and there is no reason to suppose that the County of Middlesex failed to follow the general trend of opinion. In his *History of Middlesex*, written in 1810, Daniel Lysons refers to evidence of Saxon work being found in many of the churches in the County, but in the recent survey by the Royal Commission on Historical Monuments, no reference is found to buildings of a date earlier than the twelfth century.

As far as is known no monasteries or priories were established in Saxon times within the boundaries of the present County, although the great Abbey founded by King Offa at St. Albans, Westminster Abbey, Canterbury and St. Paul's Cathedrals all held large areas of land within the confines of the County.

NORMAN AND MEDIÆVAL MIDDLESEX

THE development of the County during the Saxon régime had no doubt been considerable, and probably vast areas of swamp had been regained, more roads had been built, and forests had been cleared, while London in particular had grown into a large and flourishing city.

As has been the case in succeeding centuries, the City of London dominated the development of Middlesex, for by the nature of its situation London has always formed the market for Middlesex, both in regard to supplies and labour.

WILLIAM OF NORMANDY INVADES BRITAIN

When William of Normandy landed at Hastings in 1066, Middlesex was a typical agricultural area and possessed no town of any importance.

The news of William's victory at Hastings over the Saxon forces of Harold spread quickly to London, where a council of state was at once called. By this time the northern army, which Harold had left when he hastened south, was rapidly approaching the city, and neighbouring inhabitants sought the protection of its walls, as was their custom in times of danger. Two courses therefore presented themselves to the chief men in the city: either to admit the victory of William and submit to him, or to fight it out. They decided on the latter course, and elected Edgar, the grandson of Edmund Ironside, as their King.

On the approach of William's forces, the Saxons made an unsuccessful attempt to dislodge them from Southwark, but even this small success did not tempt William to make the fatal error of a frontal attack on the city, and he led his army westwards to a crossing of the Thames at Wallingford, between Reading and Oxford. The Conqueror's army then turned eastwards and marched through Hertfordshire and Middlesex, laying waste the country on its way. The news of the strength and efficiency of the invaders and their rapid approach towards the city influenced the inhabitants to call another council early in December to reconsider the position, and at this the vital decision was made to accept William's claim to the throne.

Leaving his army at Barking, William and his staff made for Westminster, where Edward the Confessor had already built his abbey and palace, and on Christmas Day, 1066, he was crowned in Westminster Abbey amidst the applause of both Saxons and Normans. In fact so enthusiastic were these shouts that the Norman guards outside the Abbey mistook them for a hostile outburst and caused a riot among the crowd assembled outside, which almost resulted in the complete destruction of the neighbouring houses.

Soon after his coronation, William proceeded to secure his position, and his first step in this direction was to build the Tower of London so as to protect him from the raids of the Norsemen, and at the same time to overawe the citizens and their neighbours. He also ousted the Saxon landowners and divided the country among his own faithful followers.

This task having been accomplished, he set in motion the compilation of one of the most remarkable books in history, that is to say the Domesday Book. This book —or rather books, for there are two of them—is still in existence, and may be seen at the museum of the Public Record Office in Chancery Lane. It was a complete survey of such parts of England as had submitted to his rule, and sets out the name of the holder and the approximate area of each manor, its value, and the name of the previous holder in the time of Edward the Confessor.

MIDDLESEX AND THE DOMESDAY BOOK

From a study of the part which relates to the area of the present County of Middlesex, we are able to form a fairly clear idea of its condition at this date.

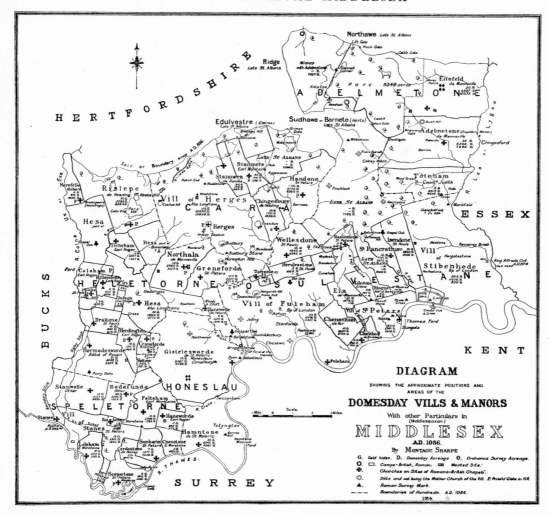

DIAGRAM

SHOWING THE APPROXIMATE POSITIONS AND
AREAS OF THE

DOMESDAY VILLS & MANORS

With other Particulars in
(Middlesaxan.)

MIDDLESEX

A.D. 1086.

By MONTAGU SHARPE

The County was divided up into six Hundreds just as it is to-day, with the exception that the Hundred of Isleworth was then called the Hundred of Hounslow.

The following places are mentioned by name: Hornsey, West Twyford and Willesden in the Hundred of Ossulstone; Harrow, Hendon and Stanmore in the Hundred of Gore; Hampton and Isleworth in the Hundred of Hounslow; Edmonton, Enfield and Tottenham in the Hundred of Edmonton; Colham, Cowley, Cranford, Dawley, West Drayton, Greenford, Hanwell, Harefield, Harling-ton, Harmondsworth, Hayes, Hillingdon, Ickenham, Kingsbury, Northolt and Ruislip in the Hundred of Elthorne; and Ashford, Bedfont, Charlton, Feltham, Hanworth, Kempton, Laleham, Shepperton, Staines, Stanwell and Sunbury in the Hundred of Spelthorne.

It is probable that Acton, Brentford, Chiswick and Ealing fell within the large area of Fulham, while South Mimms formed part of the Manor of Enfield; Finchley was joined with Hornsey, Edgware probably belonged to Harrow, Heston to Isleworth, Norwood to Hayes,

GREENFORD AND HANWELL
Facsimile copy of entry in Domesday Book.

ville was by far the most important, and held Northolt, Perivale (Greenford Parva), Edmonton, Enfield, Hadley and Ickenham ; Roger, Earl of Arundel, held Colham, Dawley in Harlington, Hillingdon and Ickenham ; William Fitz Ansculf held Cranford ; Richard Fitz Gilbert, Earl of Brioux, held Harefield ; Ernulf de Hesding held Kingsbury and Ruislip ; Walter Fitz Other held East Bedfont and the overlordship of West Bedfont and Stanwell ; Roger de Rames held Charlton and Little Stanmore or Whitchurch ; Earl Mortain held Feltham, Laleham, Kempton and Great Stanmore ; Walter de St. Waleric held Hampton and Isleworth ; Judith, the widow of Waltheof, held Tottenham. This Waltheof was the son of Saward, Earl of Northumberland, who defeated Macbeth, the usurper of the crown of Scotland, immortalized by Shakespeare ; when Gospatric, who had been created Earl of Northumberland by William I, was deprived of his title, the Conqueror granted this earldom, together with the earldoms of Huntingdon and Northampton, to Waltheof, but he was arrested for a conspiracy against the King and beheaded at Westminster.

Littleton to Laleham, Teddington to Staines, and Uxbridge to Hillingdon.

THE CHIEF LANDOWNERS

The chief landowners were the Bishop of London, who owned Ealing, Finchley, and Hornsey ; the Abbot of Westminster, who held Ashford, Cowley, Greenford, Hanwell, Staines, Shepperton, Sunbury, Hendon and certain privileges in Laleham ; the Dean and Chapter of St. Paul's, who had West Drayton, West Twyford and Willesden ; the Abbot of Holy Trinity, Rouen, in Normandy, who held Harmondsworth ; the Archbishop of Canterbury, who owned Hayes and Harrow ; whilst of the lay lords, Geoffrey de Mande-

A DESCRIPTION OF MIDDLESEX

A study of the Domesday Book shows that the majority of the County was arable land or pasture, with large areas of wood along its western and northern boundaries. Isolated wooded areas were also found at Isleworth, Northolt, and Hanwell, while vineyards are mentioned at Colham, Hillingdon, Harmondsworth, Kempton, and Staines.

Except for the Domesday survey very little is recorded in regard to the County during the reign of the early Norman kings. An important meeting of the bishops took place at Hayes in the house of Anselm, Archbishop of Canterbury, as a result of which the Archbishop refused to give way to William II in regard to the recognition of Urban II as Pope and compelled the King to make his peace with the Church.

Many of the parish churches which are now standing still show evidence of Norman work, notably at East Bedfont, Cowley, Harefield, Harlington, Harmondsworth, Harrow, Kingsbury, Laleham, Norwood and South Mimms, but

NORMAN DOORWAY   HARLINGTON CHURCH

other churches which undoubtedly were in existence then have since been rebuilt.

Whilst there are now no traces left of early domestic architecture, it is known that the Archbishop had a house at Harrow in addition to his Hayes residence, and that the Bishop of London had a house at Hornsey. Lands in Ruislip, Hillingdon, Cranford, Sunbury, Feltham, Hampton and Stanmore were granted to various religious houses early in the twelfth century.

The only known fortified house in Middlesex was at Enfield and was owned by members of the de Bohun family, who had inherited the Mandeville estates on the marriage of the Mandeville heiress, Maud, with Humphrey de Bohun.

Some of the Norman landowners who are mentioned in Domesday gave up their English possessions and returned to France, some died without heirs so that their estates returned to the ownership of the King, and others sold off parts of their estates. Consequently by the end of the twelfth century we may visualize the County with its village communities well established; the church, the manor house, the rectory or vicarage, and a few cottages scattered about to house those tenants who did not live within the Hall.

TROUBLED EVENTS AFTER THE CONQUEST

The peaceful development of the land received a setback in 1135, when the accession of Stephen was hotly disputed by the daughter of Henry I, the Empress Maud. Civil wars raged throughout the majority of the reign, and whilst no actual battle is recorded as having taken place within the County, it suffered much from constant devastation as the opposing armies marched through on their way to the citadel of London.

One of the principal actors in this grim drama was Geoffrey de Mandeville, grandson of the great Norman landowner mentioned in Domesday Book. He was Constable of the Tower and endowed Walden Abbey in Hertfordshire with the churches of Enfield, Edmonton, South Mimms, and Northolt. The treacherous support which he gave to both sides resulted in his ultimate downfall, and in 1144 he was slain at the siege of Burwell Castle in Cambridgeshire.

Shortly after King John was forced by his barons to accept the terms of the Great Charter at Runnymede, it is recorded that a tournament was held on Hounslow Heath. Two years later, also

KING JOHN RECEIVING MAGNA CARTA
From frieze over entrance to Guildhall.

at Hounslow, the Dauphin of France presided over the conference between Henry III and his barons, which led to the Treaty of Lambeth. During the later troubles Simon de Montfort stayed with the King's brother, Richard, at his Palace at Isleworth, while his adherents encamped in the Park, though shortly afterwards Richard went over to the King's side, and a large party of Londoners, led by Hugh Despenser, laid waste the whole of the Manor of Isleworth and burnt the Palace, for which they were subsequently fined 1000 marks. The faint-hearted Earl of Gloucester shortly afterwards brought his forces to Hounslow Heath but on the arrival of the King's army its opponents mysteriously disappeared.

Middlesex witnessed the climax of the Peasants' Revolt, for on the morning of June the 13th, 1381, Jack Straw marched on Highbury with his army and set fire to the Hospital of St. John at Clerkenwell. Two days later the insurgents at Mile End demanded an interview with young Richard II, who with his mother rode

out and granted their requests, but this was not sufficient for the other party of the insurgents at St. Bartholomew's Church, who demanded that the King should meet them also. As the King approached, Wat Tyler rode forward to press the grievances of his followers, but after a short altercation he was struck down with a dagger by William Walworth, Mayor of London. The luckless Richard of Bordeaux during the last days of his reign rode out to Hornsey to meet the Duke of Gloucester in battle, but when he had come within range his army deserted him.

Henry IV married the de Bohun heiress, and consequently became possessed of the original Mandeville estates, which had passed into the de Bohun family as noted above. Part of these estates, consisting mainly of forest land, became the favourite hunting-ground of successive kings of England.

No actual battle was fought within the confines of the County during the Wars of the Roses, though Middlesex must have suffered considerably by the passage of troops, especially before and after the battles of St. Albans and of Barnet, and it may be supposed that many of her sons took part in the contests.

The County witnessed the tragic passage of the boy King Edward V, when he was brought by his uncle Richard ostensibly to join his mother, but actually to meet his death by murder in the Tower. On that occasion the Mayor and many citizens of London came out and greeted him at Hornsey.

After the short reign of Richard III, Henry Tudor (the direct descendant of John of Gaunt, Duke of Lancaster, third son of Edward III) acceded to the throne as the first monarch of the house of Tudor.

MIDDLESEX UNDER THE TUDORS AND STUARTS

THE peaceful reign of Henry VII encouraged the development of domestic life in England which the troublous times of previous reigns had scarcely permitted, and Middlesex gradually took upon itself an appearance not unlike that known to its inhabitants of a century ago.

The greatly increased trade of London was having its effect on the population, and the City became so overcrowded and unhealthy that merchants who could afford the luxury of country residences within easy reach of their place of business looked to Middlesex to supply these amenities.

THE DEVELOPMENT OF ARCHITECTURE

Such circumstances encouraged domestic architecture, which during the sixteenth and seventeenth centuries attained a standard which has perhaps never been surpassed. The recently-published report on historical monuments in Middlesex, with its beautiful photographic illustrations, provides ample evidence of those specimens of the builders' craft which may still be found in the County in spite of modern building developments.

Many of the interesting churches that we know to-day had been altered or rebuilt before the beginning of the sixteenth century, and in spite of modern restoration their outward appearance to-day is not unlike that presented to the Tudor inhabitants. In many cases the interiors were adorned with those large artistic monuments which became so fashionable during the next two centuries.

The Royal Palace of Westminster and other royal residences in the County and its surrounding districts attracted the passage of courtiers, politicians, and lawyers through Middlesex, which resulted in the development of the village inns, of which many interesting examples are still to be found.

A SIXTEENTH-CENTURY PICTURE OF MIDDLESEX

In writing this short account of Middlesex, it has been necessary to extract such items as relate to the County, up to the middle of the sixteenth century, from the general history of England, but from the year 1549 the records of the Quarter Sessions have been preserved by the County authorities, and from these a very human picture of the life in the County can be obtained.

The largely increased population of London provided the inhabitants of Middlesex with a ready market for their produce, and it may truly be said that by the end of the seventeenth century the whole County was being cultivated for market-gardening and agricultural or dairy produce. The roads were exceedingly bad, and consequently transport became difficult and expensive, and large teams of horses or oxen were required for drawing even the lightest loads. The highways were infested with robbers, and travelling was not only uncomfortable but highly dangerous, while the highway taverns were the haunt of card-sharpers or pickpockets.

THE TWO TUDOR QUEENS

To tell of the historical events during the reigns of Mary and Elizabeth would be to write the history of England, and

A 17TH-CENTURY HOUSE   STANWELL

only a few events peculiar to Middlesex can be mentioned.

The rebellious army of Sir Thomas Wyatt, in an endeavour to oust Mary from the throne after her intended marriage with Philip of Spain had been announced, crossed the river at Brentford and began a march to Hyde Park. The Lord Mayor, however, got news of it and dispatched an army which routed Wyatt's forces.

On her visits to her sister, Elizabeth once stayed the night at the house of the founder of Highgate School, and on another occasion at the George Inn at Colnbrook.

In 1586, Anthony Babington, a Jesuit who had conspired to murder Elizabeth, took refuge at Uxendon near Harrow but was discovered there, arrested, and afterwards beheaded. It was found that Mary Queen of Scots was implicated in this plot, and this discovery led to her execution a short time later.

In 1588 the whole country was haunted by the dread of an invasion by the Spanish Armada, and the trained bands of Middlesex, together with those of Warwickshire and Leicestershire, had the honour of supplying a bodyguard to the Queen. The beacon on Hampstead Heath was one of the chain of flares which was lighted throughout the length and breadth of the country, after the Armada had been sighted.

MIDDLESEX AND THE STUARTS

On his journey to London, James I of England and VI of Scotland passed through Middlesex, and later in his career, when Theobalds Park became his favourite place of residence, his passages through the County must have been numerous. James had destroyed the Palace at Enfield and used the materials for beautifying Theobalds.

Enfield played an important part in the Gunpowder Plot, for Garnett, one of the conspirators, had his lodgings there, and a few days before Parliament was due to assemble Guy Fawkes visited White Webbes, a house in Enfield Chase, to make the final arrangements. The Earl of Northumberland was fined £30,000 for the part he played in the plot and tried to compound by offering Isleworth Manor to the Crown, but the King would not accept it.

Middlesex probably followed the example of the City of London in opposing the demands of Charles I for ship money and other levies, and these led to disorders which occasionally necessitated the calling out of the trained bands. Apart from these incidents, Middlesex saw no actual fighting, but Hounslow Heath, Colnbrook, and Uxbridge were favoured camping-grounds for the Parliamentarian Army, and the Earl of Essex reviewed his forces in Finsbury Fields in 1643.

THE CIVIL WAR

The Civil War hovered round the borders of Middlesex, but the County suffered little more than the burden of the passage of troops through its area. Brentford was the scene of one of Prince Rupert's most brilliant cavalry charges, but owing to the time wasted by his troops in pillaging, his opponent, Essex, managed to collect all his forces in and around London, and by sending Hampden to attack the enemy's flank at Acton, succeeded in turning what was at first a serious defeat of the Parliamentarian forces into a victory. It is thought by many that if Charles had followed up the initial success of Prince Rupert, it would have had a considerable effect on the whole war.

In April 1646, Charles I made good his escape from Oxford in disguise and reached Harrow, but made off again to Southwell in Nottinghamshire. Later, when he was held prisoner at Hampton Court, he was allowed to receive visits from his children,

THE TREATY HOUSE   UXBRIDGE

who had been put in charge of the Earl of Northumberland at Syon House, and during this time Cromwell, who was living at Putney, also visited the King at

A 16TH-CENTURY HOUSE   HILLINGDON

Hampton. In October 1647 he was persuaded to make his escape, but was recaptured after a short period of freedom. In July 1647 Fairfax's army reached Uxbridge, and after a conference had taken place at Syon House the famous Cromwellian general, together with about a hundred members of Parliament, reviewed the Parliamentarian army.

Many of the more influential inhabitants of the County sided with the King, among them Sir Francis Rouse of Headstone Manor in Harrow, Sir Henry Wroth of Durants, Sir Henry Spiller of Laleham, Sir Robert Fenn and his son, and Sir John Page. As a result of their Royalist tendencies these wealthy land-owners suffered considerably from the financial demands afterwards made on them by the Commonwealth, and their tenants suffered also by the breaking up of their estates.

Almost before the death of the King the opinions of the inhabitants of Middlesex seem to have veered towards the Royalist cause, and these feelings may have been intensified when Parliament tried to break up Enfield Chase and distribute it to Parliamentarian soldiers who had fought in the war.

The arrival of the Scottish Army at

Barnet in August 1651 caused some consternation in the County and the militia was called up, but the timely victory of Cromwell at Worcester soon restored normal conditions.

In February 1660, General Monk marched with his army from Barnet to the City on his way to open up negotiations for the restoration of Charles II.

THE END OF THE STUARTS

Mainly with the idea of overawing the country, James II established a large camp on Hounslow Heath and there reviewed 15,000 men in 1686. His repeated visits to this camp and the attendant gaieties caused Hounslow Heath to be looked upon as a sort of pleasure resort, but the waning support of the King caused the gradual disaffection of the troops, with the result that this camp became a menace rather than a security.

The rebellion of the Duke of Monmouth left the County unscathed, as did the bloodless revolution on the arrival of William of Orange and his Queen, Mary, daughter of James II, and actually the inhabitants of London and Middlesex welcomed their new King and Queen with a glad heart. Both these monarchs, as we shall subsequently see, became much attached to Hampton Court and undertook the building of the famous Wren wing.

The Dutch friends of the King formed a colony in Middlesex, and when the Duke of Schomberg was given an English title he chose that of Earl of Brentford.

When a breach occurred in the friendship between Queen Mary and her sister Anne, the Princess of Denmark was forced to leave Hampton Court and to take up her residence at Syon House. On her accession, however, she returned and made Hampton Court her residence during the majority of her reign.

An attempt on the life of William III by Sir George Barclay was hatched at Turnham Green, and was to have been made whilst the King was crossing the ferry at Brentford on his way to hunt at Richmond. The conspiracy became known before it could be put into execution, and Barclay escaped to France.

LIFE IN TUDOR AND STUART TIMES

The Middlesex records throw much light on the local administration of the County during the period of the Tudor and Stuart kings. The justices, who were of course selected by the King, had in some instances much wider powers than those of other counties, as many of them held commissions similar to those now given to assize judges, and consequently had the power of life or death over the prisoners who were brought before them. They sat more often than those in other counties, and besides administering justice they made orders for the well-being of the community.

Every parish elected its own constables, and each hundred had one or more high constables. These officers were given very wide powers, and beside their responsibility for keeping order in the streets and open spaces, had the right to enter any house where irregularities were suspected. They would then obtain a warrant from one of the justices, arrest the culprits, and take them to the county gaol or nearest " house of correction ".

The streets, as we have learned, were in a deplorable condition, and such maintenance as existed was undertaken by the freeholders within each parish, who were bound to supply so many men and so many carts, according to the rateable value of their properties.

Rates were collected as and when the money was needed, and were raised for a particular object; as, for instance, to support a poor family which had become chargeable to a parish, or to build a bridge for which the parish was responsible. The more important bridges were a county charge, and a rate for their repair was raised upon the whole County.

A scale of wages payable throughout the County in the case of each trade was drawn up by the justices, and any person paying more or less than the rate was liable to a heavy fine. Unemployment was illegal and the justices arranged that every man should have a master. If a man refused employment he became a vagabond and was dealt with accordingly.

The dissolution of the monasteries by Henry VIII probably affected Middlesex less than some other counties, for such monastic buildings as existed within it were of minor importance, but the subsequent rules laid down by law for the observance of religion as established by the Church of England brought hardships and inconvenience to those whose conscience dictated otherwise. If any inhabitant refused or neglected to attend his parish church he was brought before the Court and was condemned as a "recusant".

Puritanism, though exercised with great vigour during the Commonwealth, was not so rabidly followed in Middlesex as in some of the neighbouring home counties.

Various references are found to plagues, but the Great Plague does not seem to have seriously attacked the rural areas outside London and Westminster.

We find no mention in the records that the Fire of London had any great effect on the County as it is to-day, though no doubt many whose homes in the City had been destroyed must have taken refuge in Middlesex.

MIDDLESEX UNDER THE HANOVERIANS

SLOW DEVELOPMENT OF MIDDLESEX

THE history of Middlesex after the accession of George I seems to lose much of its individuality, and this is mainly due to the tremendous development in building which occurred during the eighteenth century in the City of Westminster and in the parishes immediately surrounding the City of London. Stepney, Stoke Newington, Hackney, Marylebone, Islington, Chelsea, Fulham and Kensington were rapidly losing their rural appearance, and even Hampstead and Hornsey were falling a prey to the builders. Consequently the area now comprised in the County of London dominated the situation. The remainder of the County, representing roughly the area as now administered by the Middlesex County Council, retired into its rural shell, and its inhabitants profitably devoted their time to the production of provisions to satisfy the ever-enlarging appetite of London.

It was unlikely that the local towns should develop when London provided so ready a market and was so accessible for those who wished to purchase what the village store did not stock. Edgware, Edmonton, Brentford, Highgate, Hounslow, Uxbridge and Harrow were the only towns worthy of the name, and these actually consisted of nothing more than a main street where shops and inns were built to provide for the needs of wayfarers on their journey to London.

Although more work was being done on the roads throughout the country, traffic was increasing enormously, and consequently transport remained as difficult and expensive as it had been a century earlier. These conditions contrived to develop the agricultural potentialities of Middlesex to an even greater degree than hitherto, as its accessibility to London allowed its produce to be delivered to the markets at a minimum of expense.

TURNPIKE ROADS AND BRIDGES

The eighteenth century saw the establishment of the turnpike road. Under this scheme the main roads were leased out to companies known as Turnpike Trusts, which were responsible for their upkeep, and in return charged heavy tolls to cover the cost. In some cases good work was done by these trusts, but more often than not the promoters, possessing as they did a monopoly, preferred to increase their dividends rather than improve their roads.

Rates raised in the County must have increased considerably during the century, for quite apart from the cost of administering the poor law, greater sums were required for repairing or rebuilding bridges to bear the increased traffic. In June 1739 the state of Brentford Bridge was examined, and it was found that a new one was essential. The old bridge was built obliquely to the road, and it was recommended that the new one must be constructed in a straight line with it. While the new bridge was being built under the supervision of Labelye, a Swiss architect who had built Westminster Bridge, a temporary one was constructed. The building of the new bridge was handicapped by weather conditions and by labour troubles, but to get over the latter the justices informed the workmen that if they did not work harder they would themselves have to bear the extra charges! The cost amounted to over £4,000, but the architect, who had put in three years' work, received only £20 for his expenses and a fee of £120.

THE DAWN OF SOCIAL REFORMS

The opening of the century witnessed the dawn of social reforms which have been extended yearly even to the present day. These began with an investigation into conditions in Newgate and in the houses of correction within the County. These apparently were appalling, and were to a large extent reformed by order of the justices. No gaol or house of correction existed within the area of Middlesex at the time, and in fact Newgate and the New Gaol were the only prisons for the use of Middlesex and London prisoners. The gaol-keepers received little or no salary, but made what profits they could from the work done by the prisoners, who had to pay for most of the food they ate.

In 1741 a committee of justices was appointed to investigate the conditions at the Clerkenwell house of correction. They found that inquests were seldom held on persons who died there, owing to the demands for fees made by the coroner and the jurors, which the gaoler had to find from his own pocket. An exception was the case of Matthew King, " one of Turpin's gang ", who was shot in the breast before he was arrested. Owing to the fact that the coroner happened to be holding another inquisition near by, he consented to examine the cause of death of Dick Turpin's friend without fees.

PRISON REFORM

Prisoners committed to hard labour could earn anything from $1\frac{1}{2}d.$ to $3d.$ a day, and in return the keeper allowed them a quartern loaf among eight prisoners and " good water ". Those committed for want of bail received no food or drink at all " except what he sometimes sent them to keep them from starving ".

Sometimes the " Quakers' Workhouse " took pity on the prisoners and sent them broth. The condition of many of those serving sentences was " near unto starving ", and they were so faint or ill from want of food that they were obliged to be discharged. On one occasion the keeper of the Bridewell had boiled some beans and left the water " in the kettle " ; some of the prisoners discovered this and a fight ensued to dip their bread in the bean water. They were even glad to eat pea-shells. As a result of the investigation it was decided that a penny a day should be allowed to each prisoner. If expended on necessary food " and not on gin ", this amount, in the opinion of the justices, would be sufficient.

THE REPAIR OF PARISH CHURCHES

Rates were raised for the repair or rebuilding of parish churches, and one such case is found in 1733, when Ealing Church was rebuilt. " The existing edifice " was then of brick and stone " of very great antiquity ", and was so ruinous that the parishioners " durst not assemble

"Paying Toll"

there ", while the tower had fallen down five years previously. In place of the old church, no doubt a building of beauty, the parishioners had built a " Tabernacle wherein to worship ".

APPRENTICESHIPS

The disputes concerning apprenticeships appear to diminish as the century progresses, and this may indicate that the custom of apprenticing was passing out of favour. In one case an apprentice complained that his master compelled him to wear a " girdle of quicksilver " in order to destroy the vermin on his body.

GAMING, DRINKING AND BULL-BAITING

Tremendous activity was exercised by the justices in stopping unlawful gaming not only in the taverns, but even in the houses of the nobility; and also in the suppression of theatres and music-halls. Actors and actresses were dealt with as " rogues, vagabonds and sturdy beggars ", and were consequently subject to the punishment of being " stript naked from the middle up and beaten on their backs till they were bloody ". The haunts of vice which are enumerated in the records

lay outside the present area of the County, and were mainly to be found in Clerkenwell, Mayfair and Chelsea.

The drinking of gin had greatly increased during the middle of the eighteenth century, and the justices took every step in their power to suppress it, apparently without much success. To such an extent had the habit developed that shopkeepers would give their clients " a dram of gin " to encourage them to become reckless in their purchases.

Bull-baiting at Edmonton in 1746 resulted in the injury of many of the spectators, and the justices issued their orders that constables were to suppress this form of entertainment throughout the County.

ATTEMPTS TO CHECK CATTLE DISEASE

Outbreaks of cattle disease, the same as, or forerunner of, foot and mouth disease, were first reported in the County about the middle of the eighteenth century, and in 1747 overseers were appointed to inspect " distempered cattle " and to see that regulations were enforced to prevent the disease from spreading.

INFLUENCE OF THE JACOBITES

In order to hold office and avoid suspicion of being a Jacobite, it was advisable to obtain a certificate that one had received the Blessed Sacrament, and among such certificates are found some interesting names, including those of Sir Christopher Wren, Sir Isaac Newton and Sir Godfrey Kneller.

Little mention is found of the 1715 Jacobite rising, except that orders were made for the billeting of soldiers and the prosecution of those who went about singing seditious ballads. The wearing of white roses on the Pretender's birthday was prohibited.

The victory of the Young Pretender at Prestonpans in 1745 and his subsequent march on London, caused much excitement in the County. London was in a panic and there was a run on the Bank of England; all business was suspended and shops were shut. The alarm was fortunately shortlived, for in April 1746 the army of George II successfully shattered the Pretender's hopes at Culloden Moor. During this period of alarm the militia was embodied and other voluntary forces were raised in the County.

THE EARTHQUAKES OF 1750

Another event which disturbed the tranquillity of the inhabitants was the series of earthquakes which occurred in the early part of 1750. The first shock occurred in January, and in exactly a month to a day, a second and more severe one followed. Even the most unsuperstitious became alarmed, and it only needed the publication of a pamphlet by a trooper in the Guards, predicting a far worse shock a month later, for the inhabitants of London to indulge in a panic which has fortunately never been equalled or surpassed. All roads out of London were thronged with every kind of conveyance, many filled with fashionable people. The more rural districts of Middlesex must have reaped a profitable harvest, for fabulous sums were paid for

beds and shelter outside what was considered to be the danger zone. The less wealthy made for the open spaces. Nothing occurred, and the citizens somewhat shamefacedly returned to London the following morning.

Nevertheless, the trooper was not an entirely false prophet, for in the following April a third shock did occur, but with no serious result. The Bishop of London was not slow to take this opportunity of pointing out that these shocks were visitations of the Almighty as a warning of what might happen if Londoners did not mend their ways, and the justices ordered that copies of this sermon should be bought and distributed to every parish.

THE CLOSE OF THE CENTURY

The Gordon Riots in 1780, while chiefly affecting London, had no doubt some repercussions on the more rural parts of the County, but the records of this date have not been examined in sufficient detail for particulars to be given.

During the Napoleonic wars, the number of militia men, which had been scarcely 300 in 1802, was raised to over 2,000 in 1808 and to 12,000 in 1812. Several " Loyal Associations " were also formed in the County, and the Hadley and South Mimms Volunteers were among the forces reviewed in Hyde Park by George III in 1799. Cavalry corps were raised at Uxbridge, Twickenham, Edmonton, Ealing and Brentford.

At the close of the eighteenth century we reach a period when the ancient records of the County need no longer be consulted, but before passing on to the period immediately before 1888, reference should be made to the notable buildings which made the County famed, and some of the celebrities who lived within its boundaries. Brief descriptions are also given of the administration of justice, and the Guildhall and its predecessors, from which the County has been controlled from the time from which our earliest records exist.

MIDDLESEX GUILDHALL

Jubilee Decorations, 1935.

MIDDLESEX GUILDHALL
AND SESSIONS HOUSES OF THE PAST

THE building which stands opposite the north side of Westminster Abbey and faces Parliament Square, and is probably familiar to all, is known as the Middlesex Guildhall, and is the administrative centre of the County of Middlesex.

You may well ask why this county hall should be in the City of Westminster and in the County of London, but the answer is to be found in the Local Government Act passed fifty years ago. This Act, among other things, established the County of London, which was formed out of parts of Middlesex, Surrey and Kent.

Before the passing of this Act the County of Middlesex had stretched right up to the boundaries of Essex and of the City of London, and was bounded on the south by the Thames. Within it there was a separate jurisdiction, known as the Liberty of Westminster, which really embraced the original area under the jurisdiction of the Abbot of Westminster. This jurisdiction had from early times had its headquarters adjacent to the Abbey, whilst the County of Middlesex was administered from buildings in Clerkenwell.

On the establishment of the County of London, it was not thought convenient

C

THE SESSIONS HOUSE   CLERKENWELL

for the Middlesex justices to remove their County Hall into the newly-restricted confines of the County, and consequently it was agreed that the Middlesex justices should surrender their headquarters in Clerkenwell while the newly-formed County of London should hand over the Guildhall site in Westminster to be the headquarters of the Middlesex County Council.

THE ORIGINAL ASSEMBLY OF THE COUNTY JUSTICES

Before dealing with the history of the present Guildhall, it will keep our story

THE SANCTUARY

in its chronological sequence if the original headquarters of the justices of Middlesex is described in the first place.

Little is known of the place of assembly of the County justices before the middle of the sixteenth century, but from that date the records give us a continuous story. Before 1613 the Court assembled at " The Castle ", Clerkenwell, a tavern in St. John Street, which must have been ill-suited for the important business which was transacted within its walls. In 1613 Sir Baptist Hicks, a wealthy mercer and a justice of the County, who assisted James I as his financial adviser, built a hall near " the Castle " for the use of the justices. This was in future to be known as Hicks Hall, and was continued as a place of Sessions until it was closed in 1782. A new Sessions House was then built on Clerkenwell Green, and opened in the same year with great pomp. The new building continued to be used until the year 1892, when the justices moved to the Guildhall at Westminster, as a result of the arrangements made under the Local Government Act of 1888. The Sessions House at Clerkenwell is still standing, but is now used for commercial purposes.

In addition to the Quarter Sessions which were held at Clerkenwell, general Sessions of the Peace were held twice yearly at Westminster Hall or in the Exchequer Court at Westminster, and other Sessions were occasionally held at Finsbury, Holborn, Highgate and Turnham Green, as circumstances demanded.

The more serious crimes were tried by the Justices of Gaol Delivery, who invariably sat at the Old Bailey.

The Sessions for the Liberty of Westminster were held at the Gate House, originally the principal entrance to the precincts of the monastery which stood where the memorial to Westminster boys who fell in the Crimea is now erected, until it was demolished in 1777. The Court room was built over the gateway, and the cells for the prisoners were in the basement.

About the year 1763, the Duke of

Northumberland, who was Lord Lieutenant of the County, gave to the Justices of the Liberty of Westminster for use as a Guildhall a building on the west of King Street, a street now abolished, which used to run parallel to Parliament Street direct to the Sanctuary; but it does not appear to have been in use for many years, for in 1777 an Act of Parliament was passed authorizing the building of a new Court House or Guildhall for the use of the Liberty, by which Act large sums were allowed to be raised for the purpose. The site selected probably closely adjoined the building given by the Duke of Northumberland, and on it for many centuries had stood the Old Belfry of the Abbey of

CRYPT OF THE OLD BELFRY

Westminster, until it was partially demolished on the dissolution of the Abbey by Henry VIII, and converted into a tavern to be known as the " Three Tunns ". It was of very massive dimensions, and originally held two bells which were renowned throughout the world. They were rung on the occasion of coronations and tolled at royal funerals. " Their ringings ", men said, " sowered all the drinke in the town." Owing to its strength, the building appears to have been constantly used by those seeking sanctuary within the precincts of the Abbey.

THE WESTMINSTER MARKET

In 1750 the tavern was demolished to make room for the Westminster Market. but the destruction of the foundations proved so formidable that eventually it was decided to build the market over the top. The market remained until shortly after the year 1800, when the site was taken over by the justices and a new Guildhall was built on the site which had been thus enlarged. This Guildhall was a one-storey building of stone, and a drawing of it appears on p. 38. When this was built in 1805 the foundations of the Old Belfry still defied destruction, and were converted for use as a wine-vault and for the accommodation of prisoners. Under an Act of 7 and 8 Victoria (1845), the

A COMPOSITE DRAWING SHOWING SANCTUARY CHURCH WITH BELFRY

(Continued on p. 39)

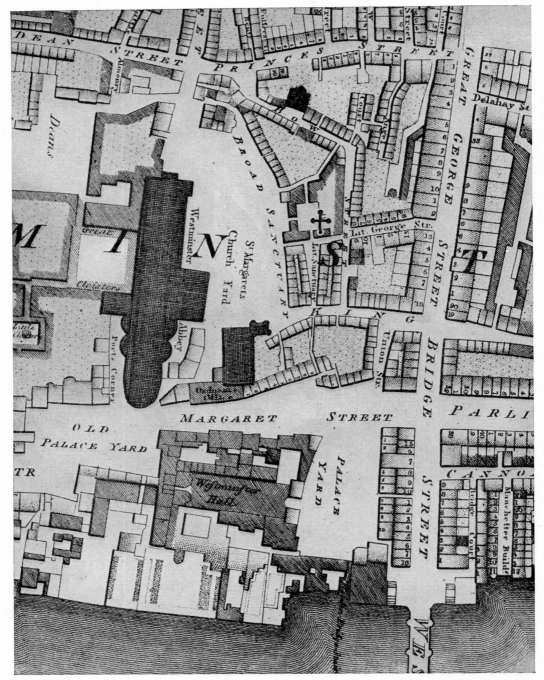

PORTION OF AN OLD MAP OF THE PRECINCTS OF THE MIDDLESEX GUILDHALL (CIRCA 1789).   GUILDHALL
MARKED THUS ✝

PARLIAMENT SQUARE   1807

LITTLE GEORGE STREET, SHOWING GUILDHALL   1807

THE GUILDHALL   *1805–1892*

THE GUILDHALL   *1892–1911*

PARLIAMENT SQUARE   1939

Sessions House was transferred to the jurisdiction of the Middlesex Justices. This Court House was demolished in 1892, and a new building begun; but even then the builders decided not to attempt the destruction of the old foundation, and it was not until the building of the present Guildhall was started in 1911 that this was finally destroyed. Under the crypt was a raft of rubble five feet thick and seventy-two and a half feet square, built on oak piles driven into the primeval

FUTURE PARLIAMENT SQUARE, NEW PLAN   After demolition of Westminster House.

OAK PILES   See page 39.

sand of Thorney Island. Explosives had to be used, and one of the piles has been preserved and is now on exhibition in the Guildhall.

THE PRESENT GUILDHALL

The foundation stone of the present building was laid in 1912 by the Duke of Bedford as Custos Rotulorum and Lord Lieutenant of the County, and was opened on the 19th of December, 1913, by His late Royal Highness Prince Arthur of Connaught, K.G., G.C.V.O., accompanied by Her Royal Highness Princess Arthur of Connaught. It cost over £111,000. The site is one of the finest in London, and provides an excellent grandstand for the historic ceremonies which take place at the Abbey; at the Coronation of King George VI the building was used as a broadcasting station for the whole world. Around the front entrance, just below the first-floor windows, is a frieze carved in stone depicting the granting of Magna Carta by King John, Henry III granting a charter to the Abbey of Westminster, the Great Hall at Hampton Court, and Lady Jane Grey accepting the Crown of England from the Duke of Northumberland at Syon House.

The present Guildhall contains two Court rooms where Quarter Sessions are held, committee rooms, a large council chamber and ante-room, and accommodation for the ever-increasing staff.

ART TREASURES

Some very fine pictures are to be seen in the Guildhall, and amongst others may be mentioned those of Sir Baptist Hicks, the donor of Hicks Hall (attributed to the Flemish artist, Paul van Somer); the 11th Duke of Bedford, Lord Lieutenant of the County, 1898–1926 (by John Collier); two of Sir Ralph Littler, chairman of Quarter Sessions, 1888–1908 (by Herkomer and Beatrice Offer); Sir Montagu Sharpe, chairman of Quarter Sessions, 1908–1934 (by G. Spencer Watson); two of Sir John Fielding, the blind magistrate and prison reformer (by Nathaniel Hone 1773 and W. Peters); two of Earl Hugh Percy, 2nd Duke of Northumberland, Lord Lieutenant of the County (by Ramsdyke and Thomas Sainsbury); the 2nd Duke of Wellington, Lord Lieutenant of the County; the Marquis of Salisbury, Lord Lieutenant of Middlesex, 1876 (by Eddis); the Earl of Northumberland, Lord Lieutenant of the County (by Sir Joshua Reynolds); Henry Pownall, Chairman of Middlesex Sessions, 1861 (by Eddis); Sir Francis Brockman Morley, Chairman of Middlesex Sessions, 1878 (by John Collier); William Mainwaring, Chairman of Middlesex Sessions (by Thomas Gainsborough); the 3rd Earl of Strafford (by Percy Bigland); William Regester, Chairman of Quarter Sessions, 1909–1919 (by Collier), and numerous water-colour views and prints of Middlesex as it was before the recent developments took place.

REMINDERS OF AN EARLIER PERIOD

In the basement are built about one hundred waiting-rooms for prisoners and accommodation for warders, police and others, boilers and heating apparatus, and the remaining space is used for the storage of documents, including the very valuable collection of records which have been constantly referred to in this account.

In the courtyard of the basement is a stone doorway removed from the old Westminster Bridewell, and in the wall is set the old tablet on which is an inscription which reads:—

> " *Here are several Sorts of Work*
> *For the Poor of this Parish of St.*
> *Margaret's, Westminster,*
> *As also the County, according to*
> *LAW, and for such as will Beg, and*
> *Live Idle in this City and Liberty*
> *of Westminster. Anno 1655.*"

In addition to the Newgate Gaol, there were houses of correction or bridewells at Clerkenwell (built 1614); at Tothill field (built in 1618), which was converted into a prison in the reign of Queen Anne and in 1826 removed to the Vauxhall Bridge Road; and the Gate House prison already described.

The justices of Middlesex were placed also on the Commission of the Peace for Westminster until 1888, when the separate commission for Westminster ceased and the Westminster justices were transferred to the County of London. The Westminster justices wear a special badge, which was authorized by George III. Sir Montagu Sharpe, the late Chairman

THE SPECIAL BADGE WORN BY THE WESTMINSTER JUSTICES, AUTHORISED BY GEORGE III

of the Quarter Sessions, and still serving on the Bench, is the last of the active justices of the Liberty of Westminster to wear one of these badges.

THE ADMINISTRATION OF JUSTICE

IN dealing with this subject it will not be possible to differentiate the dates when various laws came into force, and the object of the survey is merely to give a general view of justice as it was administered during the sixteenth, seventeenth and eighteenth centuries.

THE APPOINTMENT OF JUSTICES AND CONSTABLES

As has already been stated, the justices of Middlesex were appointed not only to maintain the peace, but in many cases were commissioned to the Gaol Delivery also, which sat regularly at the Old Bailey and had powers to deal with the cases which in other counties would have come before the judges of Assize.

Constables were elected by each parish and high constables for each hundred. These persons had very wide powers and were able to enter any house where irregularities were suspected. If any breach of the law was discovered, the local justice would issue his warrant, and the prisoner would be brought before him and enter into a bond that he would appear at the next Sessions. He would of necessity have to name at least two sureties who would stand bail for him. Witnesses had also to bind themselves to appear and give evidence.

If the crime was of a serious nature, the person would be imprisoned in Newgate and await his trial at the next Gaol Delivery. Every inhabitant was bound to assist the constables in the execution of their duties and to answer a " hue and cry " if raised. That is to say, that if a prisoner escaped or ran away from justice, a constable could raise the cry in the King's name, and anybody standing near would be compelled to join in the chase.

Each parish would also appoint night-watchmen, who were responsible for patrolling the streets by night.

THE UPKEEP OF ROADS AND BRIDGES

In addition to the detection of crime the local constables were responsible for reporting roads and bridges which were in need of repair; whether their stocks were in good order; and that their archery grounds or butts were in proper condition.

Roads were maintained by the local landowners under orders from the justices, and each holder of land was bound to provide so many men and so many carts, according to the rateable value of the property.

Carriers and others who overburdened their carts, or who had too many horses or oxen to draw them, were fined by the justices.

Bridges as a rule were either repaired by the County—or in the case of those over the Thames jointly with the adjoining county—or by the lord of the manor, according as custom decreed, and it is not difficult to imagine that they were often much neglected.

Permission to stop up or divert foot-paths and highways was within the jurisdiction of the Court, and those who did so illegally were dealt with by the justices.

CRIMES AND THEIR PUNISHMENT

Early in the seventeenth century, houses of correction were built in which vagabonds, insolvent debtors and persons charged with minor crimes were placed. They had to provide their own food and were compelled to work.

As the Sessions were held regularly, few prisoners were left in gaol for any length of time, and they would either be convicted and put to death, otherwise punished, or discharged. Those who for any reason had to spend any length of time in gaol usually died of gaol fever.

The most severe punishment awarded was to be hanged, drawn and quartered. This was the punishment usually imposed upon persons convicted of high treason. The traitor was laid upon a hurdle and drawn along the ground to the gallows and there hanged by the neck, but so that his neck was not broken. He would then be cut down while still living, and his entrails would be pulled out of his stomach and burnt before his eyes; his head was afterwards cut off and his body divided into four parts. His head was then hung up in some prominent place where the King should command.

For coining or falsifying money of the realm, although adjudged high treason up to a comparatively recent date, the culprit was drawn on a hurdle and hanged only.

It was petty treason for a servant to kill his master or mistress, or a husband his wife, or a clergyman his prelate, and for this the culprit was merely hanged by his neck until he was dead.

For a woman who had committed high or petty treason, the punishment was to be drawn and burnt alive.

Nearly all other crimes were adjudged felonies, and for this a prisoner was hanged by the neck until he died and all his possessions were forfeited.

PLEADING TO FELONIES

There were, however, exceptions to this rule. If a criminal wished to preserve his possessions for his successors, it was open to him to refuse to plead, which was known as " standing mute ", and he was then awarded the punishment known as the " *Peine forte et dure* ". In

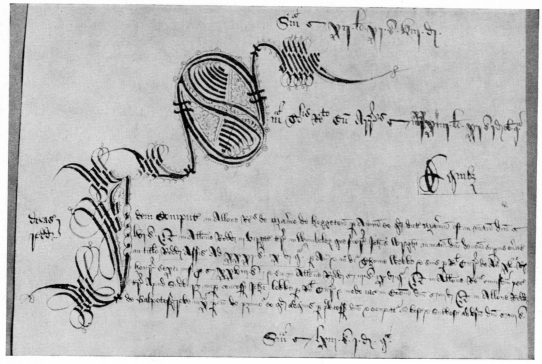

FACSIMILE FROM HARROW COURT ROLL, HENRY VII See p. 62.

this case he was returned to prison and laid on his back naked in some low, dark room upon the floor, and his arms and legs were drawn with cords to the four corners of the room. Large weights of iron and stone, which were increased day by day, were then placed on his body. He was allowed barley bread and foul water on alternate days, and so he remained until he died. There are many cases to be found in the records of even women undergoing this terrible torture

In all cases of felony it was possible for the accused to " plead benefit of clergy ", that is to say he could demand to be given the Bible, and the justices would select a verse for him to read. If he could read this successfully, he was branded with a hot iron on the left hand and discharged. If he could not read, or if it was found that he had already been branded, he suffered death by hanging in the usual way.

PRIMITIVE FORMS OF PUNISHMENT

A verdict of petty larceny was returned in cases where the goods stolen were not of the value of 12*d.* or over, and we constantly find instances in the records where the value of the goods has obviously been reduced by the justices in order to bring the crime within the bounds of petty larceny. For this the punishment was whipping. The prisoner was generally committed to the house of correction, and on a given day, generally a market day, was taken out, stripped to the waist and tied to the back of a cart. He would then be whipped along the street for some considerable distance. In earlier days the convict would sometimes lose an ear instead of being whipped.

For forgery, stealing, libelling, using false weights and measures, forestalling the market and offences against the baking and brewing laws, a person would usually be sentenced to sit in the stocks, and the nature of the crime was written on a piece of paper nailed over his head.

For striking in the King's Court, whereby blood was drawn, the criminal

ANCIENT STOCKS, OLD HIGH STREET, ACTON

had his right hand cut off in Court, and we find a case of this in the County Sessions Records of 1610, when Robert Allaley had been charged with house-breaking at Kingsbury. He stood mute, and was sentenced to the *peine forte et dure*, but as the gaoler was leading him from the Court he turned round and struck him. The Court promptly ordered that his right hand should be cut off there and then, and that he should lose the benefit of standing mute and be hanged, whereby he forfeited all his estates.

Drunkards, vagabonds, profane swearers, loose, idle and disorderly persons, night-walkers and the like, were put into the stocks for varying periods of time.

SCOLDS

A scold—that is, a woman who spread scandalous rumours about her neighbours —was condemned to the ducking-stool. This consisted of a chair tied to a board placed on a pedestal, after the fashion of a see-saw, over the village pond, or other convenient water. The culprit would then be tied into the chair and the chair ducked so that the prisoner was totally immersed. The victims of her slander no doubt looked on with righteous satisfaction.

TRANSPORTATION

Although it had been introduced in the reign of Queen Elizabeth, transportation to the colonies for life, or for a term of years, did not become a common punishment until early in the eighteenth century. The culprits were placed in hulks in the Thames and sent out to America or one of the other colonies. The worst part of this punishment was the journey out, and the conditions in the hulks were appalling. Strange to say, it seems almost possible that some persons deliberately committed crimes in order to be transported at the expense of the country. When the convict reached the colony he was handed over or sold to a master, and his subsequent enjoyment of life depended naturally on the character of his master.

LAWS AGAINST NONCONFORMISTS

When the Church of England was established in this country after the separation from Rome, persons who followed the old religion were looked upon with the gravest suspicion. Anybody who had not been to his or her parish church regularly and who had not attended Holy Communion for more than a month, was brought before the justices as a " recusant ". When once convicted as such, a recusant was bound to report every month to a justice and to conform with other vexatious regulations. Failure to comply entailed a heavy fine.

Persons accused of any form of nonconformity were likewise subjected to various types of persecution.

LAWS REGULATING TAVERNS AND VAGRANCY

Inns and taverns were licensed by the justices, and if misbehaviour was reported, the proprietors lost their licences.

Rates were raised, as has already been observed, when occasion demanded and in some cases assessments were made for the purpose of restoring or rebuilding the parish church, while the conveyance of vagrants and the maintenance of bastard children caused a constant drain on the ratepayer's pocket.

When a person was unable to support himself, he was transported to his " place of legal settlement ", which was in most cases his birthplace ; but naturally every parish fought against taking on the burden of supporting the pauper, and consequently a sort of game of shuttlecock took place, whereby the wretched vagabond would be sent from parish to parish until in some cases he eventually died.

On his second conviction of being a vagabond, an accused person would be burnt in the gristle of the right ear, but on his third conviction he would be hanged.

So strong was the feeling against gypsies that in 1594, when certain inhabitants of Hounslow were seen " in the consort or society of vagabonds commonly called Egipcians ", they were sentenced to be hanged.

REGULATION OF WAGES AND APPRENTICESHIP

The wages of servants were fixed by the justices, and the relations of masters and employees were arranged by the Court. Apprenticeship deeds were also registered by the justices, and any infringement of the terms of those agreements by either party was brought before the Court.

BUILDING AND FOOD REGULATIONS

During the reign of James I, strict regulations as to building of houses were enforced, and under these no house was allowed to be erected unless it was surrounded by four acres of land. No inhabitant was allowed to take in lodgers or inmates without permission of the justices.

Meat was not allowed to be sold in Lent, nor on days on which fish only was ordered to be eaten, and the justices saw that these regulations were enforced.

PRISON SHIP AT DEPTFORD   From an old engraving.

The price of various commodities was fixed by the justices, and the parish constables were responsible for seeing that bread was of the right measure and beer of the correct strength.

One of the most unpopular schemes was that by which purveyors to the royal household were allowed to demand supplies whenever the King or Queen was resident within the " Verge ". This was an area of twelve miles around any royal residence. As the monarch was generally residing in Middlesex, the County suffered considerably, and, to make matters worse, these purveyors were often of an unscrupulous character, and kept the people from whom they had demanded supplies waiting a long time for their money.

SOME INTERESTING CASES

It will, perhaps, be of interest to quote some of the more unusual cases which are recorded in the printed calendars of the Sessions Records.

On the 1st August, 1561, John Grysley of South Mimms, with other honest persons, was shooting with bows and arrows at the butts when, unaware of the presence of Thomas Mosse, he drew his bow and sent from it a shaft that by mischance, striking the same Thomas in the neck, killed him. It was found to be involuntary homicide, and the accused received the Queen's pardon.

In 1569 Matthew Vincent of Ickenham, who did not possess goods to the value of 40s., unlawfully kept dogs for coursing hares, and at Hillingdon he broke into the warren of Edward, Earl of Derby, and hunted his rabbits.

Several cases of witchcraft are found: Elizabeth Ducke of Harmondsworth enchanted an ox in 1575; Helen Beriman bewitched four calves at Laleham in 1576; Joan Barringer of Harrow Weald practised her detestable arts on Rose Edlyn, whereby she died, in 1584; Elizabeth Roberts was held responsible for the death of four persons in 1601; Agnes Godfrey was accused of the like practices at Enfield in 1610 and again

in 1613; and Ann Beaver at Edmonton in 1612 and again in 1625. Most of these persons were discharged.

During the Civil Wars, the Commonwealth, and immediately after the Restoration, many persons were charged with speaking insulting words either against Charles I, Charles II or against the Parliamentarian leaders in accordance with the changing politics of the justices.

Any game except archery was held to be illegal, mainly, no doubt, because the practice of such pastimes would prevent persons from becoming proficient at the butts. During a game of football at South Mimms in 1585, one of the players went to kick the ball, but kicked another player instead and caused his death.

Duels were of fairly frequent occurrence, but the survivor was generally brought before the justices, and often condemned to death.

Eleanor Trevener gave a dish filled with " pieces " mixed with ratsbane (or arsenic) to her mistress at Enfield in 1591 with a view to murdering her; and John Pemmer of West Drayton administered poison in the form of powdered hellebore roots " in a potion " to the sick wife of Robert Fisher of Harlington. In 1633 Sarah Braynt of Heston mixed a pancake of flour and water, into which she put ratsbane and gave it to her husband; she was condemned to be burnt to death.

In 1599 John Smithe, described as a gentleman, entered the parish church at Ruislip and there " disturbed and molested Henry Studley, clerk ", when he was about to administer and celebrate the Divine Sacrament, and " threw down and abused the blessed sacrament "; Edward Backhouse was charged with molesting, disturbing and disquieting Mr. Prichard, minister of West Drayton, while he was preaching a funeral sermon in 1658; and in 1662 John Ketch was arrested for " the riotous and forcible breaking of the church doors of Ashford ", and for speaking " opprobrious " words against the government " and in derogation of the Book of Common Prayer."

The observance of Sunday was strictly

enforced, and any one found drinking in a tavern during Divine Service was brought before the justices.

A curious case arose in 1649, when Anne Curtyn was arrested on the charge of being a Jewess, and the case was referred to " the Assembly of Divines." After their finding that she was " obstinate " in her profession of a Jew, the Court decided that it was entirely an ecclesiastical matter, and she was discharged from prison.

When William Hide, " Master of the Free School at Harrow Hill ", was chosen by the Court Leet as " Headborough " for the Manor of Harrow, he appealed to the justices that his " time was required among his scholars " and he was discharged from the execution of this office.

Many cases of cruelty towards apprentices are to be found, and the case of Matthew Nicholas, who was apprenticed to William Lovejoy of Uxbridge, may be quoted as typical. Lovejoy used to send his apprentice on Sundays " sometymes two, three, four, fyve or sixe myles from home " to gather wood and fuel, and misused him by fastening " a lock with a chaine to it, and tyinge and fetteringe him to the shoppe ". On other occasions he and his wife used to whip him until he was " very blooddy and his flesh rawe over a great part of his body, and then salted him and held him naked to the fyre, beinge soe salted to add to his paine ". This occurred in 1655.

Cases of abduction are occasionally to be found, as in 1591, when Richard Lylliard and Anthony Walden took Mary Burton aged thirteen from her lawful guardians with a view to obtaining her inheritance, which she would receive on her marriage; and in 1608, when Joan and Christopher Ward were charged with attempting " to take away a young gentlewoman from her parents by night ".

Ralph Shakespeare of Isleworth was bound over in 1666 " for refusing to appear on shipboard in the fleet ", he being impressed to serve the King " in this famous expedition ". The expedition referred to was that by General Monk against the Dutch commanded by de Ruyter and van Tromp. At this period the press gang was no doubt active throughout Middlesex, as it was in other counties.

The plot initiated by Colonel Danvers in 1666 to overthrow the Government and to put Charles II to death does not seem to have affected inhabitants within the present area of the County, though many residents in Westminster appeared before the county justices charged with being accomplices therein. Less than two years after this plot had been discovered John Rathbone, late a colonel in the Commonwealth army, was arrested for being responsible for other outbreaks of violence, but again this disturbance did not interfere with the peace of the County.

Likewise it would seem from an examination of the Sessions Records that no inhabitants of the County were embroiled in the popish plots of Titus Oates and others during those critical years 1678–1681, although many in the neighbourhood around London were tried and executed.

The attempted introduction of the Dutch loom-engine into this country caused wild rioting among the Spitalfields weavers, but appears to have been confined to that area, and not to have affected any part of the present County of Middlesex.

This survey ought not to be closed without some reference to the practice of kidnapping, which was prevalent in and around London during the close of the seventeenth century. Persons were snatched from their homes or from the streets and placed on board ship in the Thames; they were then transported to America and sold as slaves. Rural Middlesex does not appear to have suffered from this scandal in the same manner as did the more thickly populated area around the City, but several cases were brought before the justices, and it is not difficult to imagine that many who practised this nefarious trade escaped beyond the reach of the arm of the law.

FAMOUS COUNTY PERSONALITIES

TO attempt an account of all the well-known people connected with Middle-sex would be to write a volume in itself, as there can have been few notable personages who at one time or another have not lived or stayed within its hospitable boundaries. Kings, queens, foreign princes and courtiers visited the royal palaces within the County, and attention has already been drawn to some, whilst much has been written in reliable histories to enable those with imagination to conjure up the gorgeous scenes of tournaments, masques and other State functions which took place within the County.

It will be sufficient if some of the more notable characters in different walks of life are recorded.

After the death of Henry VIII, his widow, Catherine Parr, married Sir Thomas Seymour, brother of the " Protector Somerset ", and had charge of the infant Princess Elizabeth. It was at their house at Hanworth that Sir Thomas was alleged to have forced his attentions on the young princess with a view to marriage, when he had conveniently disposed of the Dowager Queen. It has also been suggested that it was his behaviour which influenced Elizabeth to remain a spinster throughout her life.

Meinhardt, last Duke of Schomberg, the famous German soldier who became a British general and commander-in-chief of the English auxiliary forces in the wars of the Spanish Succession, built a mansion at Little Hillingdon and died there in 1719.

Maria, who succeeded her father as Queen of Spain in 1833 when only three years old, lived during her minority with the Earl of Lucan at Laleham House. George Bingham, the third Earl of Lucan,

gave the order for the charge of the Heavy Brigade which followed the more famous charge of the Light Brigade at Balaclava, and for his action was severely censured by Lord Raglan.

Francis Scott, second Duke of Buccleuch, lived at Hillingdon Heath in 1746, and Henry, Lord Paget, a courtier and politician, took the title of Uxbridge when elevated to an earldom. The third Lord Burlington, a well-known patron of the arts, built Palladian Villa at Chiswick in 1736. Henry Bennett, who figured as a member of the Cabal Ministry, was born at Harlington, and was subsequently created Earl of Arlington. His daughter married the natural son of Charles II, and thus became Duchess of Grafton. The royalist officer and politician, Francis, Earl of Bradford, lived at Richmond House, Twickenham; and Henrietta, Countess of Suffolk, mistress to Charles II, lived at Marble Hill, Twickenham, where she entertained a circle of distinguished men of letters.

Richard Boyle, Lord Shannon, the hero of the Battle of Vigo in 1702, lived in Hillingdon; and Lord Heathfield, the defender of Gibraltar during the siege from 1779 to 1783, had a house at Turnham Green. Sir William Waller, the famous Parliamentarian general, occupied Osterley for some years before his death in 1668.

Several persons who rose to high civic rank were inhabitants within the County, and among them may be mentioned Sir Nicholas Raynton, who was Lord Mayor of London in 1646; there is a monument to his memory in Enfield Parish Church.

When Archbishop Tillotson was Dean of St. Paul's, he favoured Edmonton as his

A TOURNAMENT

country residence and occasionally returned there after he had been consecrated Archbishop in 1691. Archbishop John Gilbert died at Twickenham in 1761. Cuthbert Tunstall, Bishop of London and later of Durham, was at one time Rector of Harrow, and Richard Terrick, who held the see of London two centuries later, was Vicar of Twickenham.

Several well-known judges and lawyers lived in Middlesex, and among them may be mentioned Sir Samuel Dodd, Chief Baron of the Exchequer, who owned Colham Manor in Hillingdon; Sir John Bankes, Lord Chief Justice during the Civil Wars, who lived at Stanwell; Sir Matthew Hale, another Lord Chief Justice and a famous jurist, had a house at Acton; Lord Chief Justice Popham resided at Friern Barnet, and Lord Chief Justice Cholmeley lived at Renters in Hendon. The Lord Chancellor Bacon died at the Earl of Arundel's house at Highgate in

1626, and Sir Orlando Bridgeman was buried at Teddington in 1674.

The Newdigate family lived at Harefield; John Lenthall, Speaker of the House of Commons during the Commonwealth, was born at Twickenham; and Joseph Ayloffe the famous antiquary lived at Hendon.

The arts are especially well represented: Hogarth lived at Chiswick, Sir Godfrey Kneller and J. M. W. Turner at Twickenham, and John Norden, the surveyor and cartographer, at Hendon; while of poets, Jonathan Swift, John Gay, Alexander Pope, Sir John Suckling, Paul Whitehead and Alfred Tennyson were all residents at Twickenham. This riverside resort also housed Mrs. Pritchard and Catherine Clive, both well-known actresses. The stage was represented elsewhere in the county by John Rich, the pioneer of the pantomime and inventor of the Harlequinade, who was buried at Hillingdon; Barton Booth, a celebrated tragedian, at Cowley; Elizabeth Barry at Acton; Charles Mallory, playwright, at Edmonton; and Mrs. Porter and Charles Johnson at Hendon. There is a monument to Peg Woffington in Teddington Parish Church, and David Garrick lived for a while at Hendon before moving to Hampton, where he was buried.

William Hobbayne lived at Hanworth, where he founded a charity and school; the famous Mayor of London, Richard Whittington, founded the almshouses at Highgate; and Thomas Arnold, headmaster of Rugby, started a school in his house at Laleham where his son Matthew was born.

William Penn the Quaker and colonist lived at Teddington in 1688, and Sir William Berkeley, Governor of Virginia, was buried at Twickenham in 1677.

While only a few of the most famous characters in history have been mentioned, their names are sufficient to show what the County has produced, and to foster a hope that under the efficient educational facilities provided by the County, coming generations may add equally distinguished names to its future history.

D

SOME HOUSES OF HISTORICAL INTEREST

THE first impression of a foreigner viewing the County of Middlesex from the air before his arrival at Croydon or Heston would probably be that of an extensively built-up area, and would give him no idea of the wealth of beauty and interest still to be found within its bounds. Yet one has only to turn over the pages of the volume published by the Historical Monuments Commission * to appreciate that the County is as rich as, if not richer than, most other counties in buildings of beauty and of historic importance.

HAMPTON COURT

Hampton Court, by its size, its associations and its preservation, must perforce overshadow all other domestic buildings in the County, and it is with this Palace that this account will deal in the first place.

The land on which Hampton Court is built was granted to the Knights Hospitallers of St. John of Jerusalem early in the thirteenth century, and remained in their hands until shortly before the dissolution of the religious houses, when it passed by exchange to Henry VIII in 1531.

The monastic building was, no doubt, a commodious place, for records show that important guests, on their visits to the Palace of the Black Prince at Kempton, were housed at Hampton, while visitors to Henry VII at Richmond likewise enjoyed the hospitality of the Knights. In 1514 Cardinal Wolsey obtained from the Prior of the Order a lease of the manor of Hampton Court for ninety-nine years, on condition that he could rebuild or alter the house in whatever way he chose, and the advantage he took of this clause is evident to-day, for a bell in the chapel alone remains as a memento of the Hospitallers'

* *Middlesex: A Survey and History by the Royal Commission on Historical Monuments*, p. 66 (H.M. Stationery Office).

house, which was practically destroyed when the Cardinal's new building was begun. By 1516 the new building was sufficiently advanced for Henry VIII to pay his first visit, but it was probably not until 1520, on his return from the "Field of the Cloth of Gold", that this luxury-loving monarch cast envious eyes upon the amenities of the palatial new house.

The pomp in which the Cardinal lived probably exceeded anything hitherto seen in royal palaces, and ambassadors from all countries were entertained within its walls. During these visits the most gorgeous and lavish spectacles were witnessed, and one in particular, which was held in 1519, is recorded in some detail. After many masques had been performed, the guests sat down to a supper of countless dishes of confections and other delicacies, and when supper was ended, "large bowls filled with ducats and dice were placed on the tables for such as liked to gamble". When the party was tired of gambling, the tables were removed, and dancing was enjoyed until "long after midnight".

Again in 1527 Wolsey entertained the "grand master and marshal of France" and their retinue of over one hundred of the wealthiest of their compatriots. Never before had such extravagance in the entertainment of guests been seen. Every bedroom was provided with "a bason and ewer of silver, some gilt or parcel gilt and some two great pots of silver in like manner, and one pot at the least with wine and beer, a bowle or goblet and a silver pot to drink beer in, a silver candlestick or two and a staff torch". Such functions were bound to influence the jealous King, but although the Cardinal surrendered his lease before his downfall, this generous action, as we know, did not save him from disgrace.

From 1529, when Henry VIII took possession of Hampton Court, it continued to be a popular resort of the reigning monarchs until the death of

HAMPTON
COURT
PALACE

E. RAILTON

SYON HOUSE, ISLEWORTH

George II's consort, and although from that date to the present time it has remained as a possession of the Crown, it has never again been a royal residence.

Early in 1530 Henry VIII, Queen Catherine and the Princess Mary took up their residence at Hampton, and Anne Boleyn was also given lodgings there, so that when, before long, Henry sent Catherine away, he was able to continue uninterruptedly his courtship of Anne in the Palace and its beautiful grounds.

On the birth of Prince Edward in 1537, so elaborate a pageant was enacted that the excitement of it is said to have caused the death of his mother, Jane Seymour.

Henry's love of sport is exemplified by the tennis-court which was built shortly after his arrival and still exists, while there were ample facilities for archery and hunting close at hand. After the dissolution of the monasteries had been effected, whereby much adjoining property came into the King's hands, an " Honour of Hampton " was created to include Hanworth, Kempton, Feltham and Teddington, and many manors in Surrey, which were preserved for the King's hunting.

Henry spent most of his married life with Catherine Howard at Hampton, whence that ill-fated consort was sent to Syon House before her execution on the 13th of February, 1542. The haunted gallery is so called from the fact that Catherine's ghost is said to run shrieking along it.

Edward VI lived at Hampton during most of his short reign, and in 1549 the Palace was put into a state of defence on

THE TEMPLE AND DAVID GARRICK'S HOUSE AT HAMPTON

account of the plot against the Protector Somerset.

Hampton Court continued to be the popular residence of Queen Mary, and subsequently of Queen Elizabeth, who, however, in 1562 nearly succumbed to a serious attack of smallpox there.

James I usually arranged to spend Christmas at the Palace, when great revelries took place, and his son Charles I also enjoyed prolonged visits there. When taken prisoner by the Parliamentary army, he was permitted to use Hampton as his place of imprisonment, and his children were allowed to visit him. He eventually escaped from there in 1647.

In October 1651, Cromwell installed himself at Hampton, though two years later the property was sold to John Phelps. It was, however, re-conveyed to Cromwell in 1654, and until his death the Protector constantly used the Palace as his place of residence. In 1657 a plot was

hatched to murder him, and the accomplices decided to carry out their nefarious act while he was travelling between Whitehall and Hampton, but the plot was discovered before it could be put into action.

On his restoration, Charles II undertook many alterations to the Palace, which he made his permanent home, and it was there that his honeymoon with Catherine of Braganza was spent. The untoward scenes which were witnessed when the King insisted on introducing the notorious Lady Castlemaine into the Household are vividly depicted by contemporary diarists and historians.

The Palace does not appear to have been a popular resort of James II, but William of Orange and his Queen, after his accession, immediately decided to rebuild it. The work of Christopher Wren now stands as a monument to these joint monarchs but, in order to

53

SUNBURY PLACE, POSSIBLY ON THE SITE OF THE ROYAL PALACE

effect these alterations, over half the Tudor buildings had to be destroyed. The Queen took the greatest personal interest in arranging the elaborate decorations which may still be seen, although unfortunately she died before she could enjoy the full benefits of her work, and William III only survived two years before a riding accident, which occurred in the Park, resulted in his death in Kensington Palace a fortnight later.

The heavy expenditure on rebuilding, necessitated Queen Anne taking over her inheritance heavily encumbered with debt, but she enjoyed as much time as possible there, and held many of her council meetings in the " Cartoon Gallery ".

Hampton Court appealed especially to George I but, during his absence in Hanover, the Prince of Wales and his Princess entertained on so lavish a scale that the Palace fell somewhat into dis-

repute, and George II only spent the early years of his reign in residence there. On the death of Queen Caroline in 1737, he gave up residence, and shortly afterwards it was turned into apartments for persons who had done good service to the Crown or State.

The building as it stands to-day provides perhaps the most perfect example of Tudor architecture, combined with Wren's domestic work at its best. The pictures which are to be seen there are sometimes criticized, but the ceilings, fireplaces, doorways and other fittings are some of the most beautiful of their kind to be found anywhere.

OTHER NOTABLE BUILDINGS

Inhabitants of the County must not for one moment think that Hampton Court is the only building which is worthy of attention, as nearly every township and village still possesses some features of historic interest. Indeed, there are other interesting houses at Hampton itself and, of these, Faraday House and the Old Court House, built by Wren, are especially notable. The Temple erected in honour of Shakespeare by David Garrick opposite his house at Hampton has recently been taken over for permanent preservation. St. Albans, which stands on the river bank, is said to have been built for Nell Gwyn, the favourite of Charles II, or for their son, the first Duke of St. Albans.

In Kempton Park, not far away from Hampton, lay the Royal Palace already mentioned of which no trace is now to

be seen. It was built in the thirteenth century, and remained a royal residence until after 1461. It was sold to Sir Robert Killigrew in 1631, and towards the end of the last century the famous race-course was laid out in part of the grounds.

Staines is historically notable as marking the site of one of the earliest bridges built in this County, though there are no traces of it now to be found. A seventeenth-century monument, called "London Stone", on the bank of the river, marks the limits of jurisdiction of the City of London over the River Thames, and it is probable that a similar stone has been in existence at this spot from Norman times. Duncroft House,

THE LONDON STONE, STAINES

near the church, bears evidence of seventeenth-century work, and contains some early panelling.

Another royal property within the County was Hanworth Manor. This was granted by Henry VIII in 1572 to Anne Boleyn, and subsequently was enjoyed by many other royal consorts. Lady Jane Grey frequently visited Queen Catherine Parr and her second husband, Lord Thomas Seymour, and it was here that Elizabeth spent much of her early youth. It was destroyed by fire in 1797, but a few traces of the old building can still be seen in the present manor house, which was built by the first Duke of St. Albans.

At Teddington, the manor house built in 1602 by Lord Buckhurst and renovated in the eighteenth century, and Udney House, which was at one time owned by Robert Udney, a famous collector of pictures, and subsequently by Lord Athlone, were the most important residences.

Part of the Manor of Twickenham was given to the monks of Canterbury, in whose hands it remained until the dissolution, after which it became the property of successive consorts. Queen Anne, while Princess of Denmark, lived at Twickenham, in a house which was subsequently occupied by the unfortunate Queen Caroline. In the same parish is York House, which was the residence of the famous Lord Clarendon, Lord

TWICKENHAM PARK

KNELLER HALL, TWICKENHAM

Chancellor to Charles II, and subsequently of his son, Lawrence, Earl of Rochester. Charles II probably resided there, as did his brother, James II, when Duke of York. Prince Stahremberg, Envoy Extraordinary from the Court of Vienna, lived there at the beginning of the last century, and in 1864 it was occupied by the Comte de Paris, nephew to the Duc d'Aumale. The house is now used as municipal offices.

Twickenham Park was the home of Edward Bacon, third son of the Lord Keeper, and it was here that Sir Francis Bacon entertained Queen Elizabeth, and presented her with a sonnet in praise of the Earl of Essex.

One of the most remarkable houses in the County must indeed be Strawberry Hill, which was originally built by the Earl of Bradford's coachman in 1698, and was sold by him to Colly Cibber, the famous actor and dramatist. In 1747 Horace Walpole (afterwards Earl of Orford) bought it, and in 1753 began to refashion it in what was to become the latest craze of Gothic architecture.

It is still standing, an example of a bad style which was unfortunately copied by countless architects in the last century.

Another Twickenham landmark is Kneller Hall, in which the famous artist, Sir Godfrey Kneller, lived. It was converted in 1856 into the Royal Military School of Music, and still survives as such. In the grounds the remains of an old moat are to be found. Orleans House was the residence of Louis Philippe in 1800, and was subsequently occupied by his descendant, the Duc d'Aumale.

At Feltham, the Manor House, once occupied by Lord Cottington, Chancellor of the Exchequer in 1634, and an ardent Royalist, shows traces of its seventeenth-century rebuilding.

The amazing determination of Henry VIII to satisfy his desires is exemplified by a story told in regard to the old Manor House at Stanwell. For many generations the family of Windsor had possessed this property, until one day a messenger called on Andrews, Lord

Windsor, announcing that the King would dine with him that night. At dinner Henry expressed his delight with the house and his resolution to possess it. In spite of the protestations of Lord Windsor, a deed of surrender was produced, which he was compelled to sign, and he was ordered to leave immediately. Lord Windsor had laid in his Christmas store, but such was his courtesy that he refused to take it away, and it was left for the King's household to enjoy. It

must have been extremely galling to him to find that the King never took advantage of his easily acquired possession, as he granted it to Lord Knyvet shortly after it had come into his hands. The School House at Stanwell, built by the foundation of Thomas Lord Knyvet in 1624, is still standing and is worthy of notice.

Traces of ancient work are to be seen at Harmondsworth, where there was a priory of the Benedictine Order, which was a cell to the Abbey of the Holy Trinity of Rouen in France. Much property in this parish was given by William of Wykeham for the foundation of Winchester College, though in 1544 it was exchanged with the Crown for other estates.

The Manor House of Cranford St. John bears traces of its Tudor existence, but it was considerably altered by James, Earl of Berkeley, Vice-Admiral of Great Britain, in 1722.

Perhaps one of the most notable private residences in the County is Osterley Park, in the parish of Heston, now occupied by the Earl of Jersey. This was built by Sir Thomas Gresham, the founder of the Royal Exchange, and finished about the year 1570, though it was extensively altered by Robert Adam in the eighteenth century. The Manor of Osterley had been given to the Prior of Syon, but on the dissolution of the monasteries it was granted to the Marquess of Exeter, who was attainted. The Duke of Somerset, the next owner, suffered a like fate, and it was then granted to Augustine Thaier, from whom it passed to Sir Thomas Gresham. Heston was renowned for the wheat which was grown there, and in Elizabethan times it was reserved for the Queen's Household.

During the visit of Queen Elizabeth to Osterley Park in 1576, two women broke into the park " for the keeping, feeding and preservation of deer and other wild animals ", while the Queen, " with divers magnates and honourable men of the Privy Council ", with many " other wealthy men and servants ",

SCHOOL HOUSE, STANWELL

Old plaque on wall : above are the arms of Lord Knyvet, impaling the arms of his wife, the Lady Elizabeth Hayward.

THE SCHOOL HOUSE, STANWELL

were present in the house, and tore up and threw down some of the paling and burnt it. Their trial is fully recorded in the records of the Quarter Sessions preserved at the Guildhall, Westminster.

The Bridgettine Abbey which was founded by Henry V at Twickenham moved to the site of Syon House in Isleworth in 1432, but was dissolved in 1539, when the property passed to John Dudley, Duke of Northumberland. After his attainder, Queen Mary restored the nunnery which was, however, soon dissolved by Queen Elizabeth, who in 1604 granted the property to Henry Percy, Earl of Northumberland. The house was restored in 1659, but incorporated much of the old abbey. It was reconstructed in 1760 by Robert Adam, and re-cased and substantially altered in 1826. Syon House received the un-

fortunate Catherine Howard the night before her execution at the Tower; the body of Henry VIII rested there prior to his sumptuous funeral at Windsor; and Lady Jane Grey stayed there with her father-in-law immediately before her election as Queen.

At Brentford we find Boston House, which was re-built in 1622 by Mary, the wife of Sir William Reade, and contains some fine specimens of plaster ceilings and carved fireplaces.

Probably the most popular residential neighbourhoods two centuries ago were Chiswick and Ealing, although the Wells at Acton attracted fashionable visitors during the eighteenth century.

Chiswick House (successively the home of Lord Burlington, the Dukes of Devonshire and of Charles James Fox) and Hogarth House, reputed to have been built for the famous artist, are still to be seen.

At Ealing, the Duke of Kent, father of Queen Victoria, had a villa on Castle Bar Hill which had at one time belonged to the famous Mrs. FitzHerbert, and Gunnersbury Park House was purchased by Princess Amelia, aunt to George III, in 1761. This estate has now been bought by the Middlesex County Council and a lease of land adjoining it is preserved among the County archives.

Southall Manor in Norwood was built by the Ausiter family in 1587, and much of the original work still remains.

Dawley Manor Farm in Harlington was at one time owned by Charles, Earl of Tankerville, a great patron of farming, who is said to have paid an artist £200 to paint pictures of farm implements along the walls of his hall.

The old Gatehouse at West Drayton is all that remains of the house which belonged to William Paget, created Baron Paget, a famous ambassador and courtier of Henry VIII and Edward VI.

The manor of Colham in the parish of Hillingdon belonged for many generations to the family of the Earls of Derby, but the village is chiefly famous for the fact that Charles I stayed at the " Red Lion " there on his escape from Oxford before he made off for Barnet.

The Treaty House at Uxbridge, now the " Crown Hotel ", in which two of the original fireplaces are still to be seen, lies on the south-west side of the High Street and was used in 1645 by the Commissioners of the King and of Parliament in their attempts to arrive at some treaty by which further hostilities could be abandoned. As we know, these dis-

HAREFIELD PLACE

THE CANONS, EDGWARE

cussions proved abortive and the civil wars continued to take their drastic course.

One of the most famous of the lesser country houses to be found anywhere in England is Swakeleys in Ickenham. The property originally belonged to Robert de Swalclyne, later corrupted into Swakeley, and passed to Henry Bourchier, Marquess of Exeter, who conveyed it in 1532 to Ralph Pexall. In the seventeenth century it came into the hands of Sir Edmond Wright, Lord Mayor of London in 1641, who built the present house in 1638, and it passed a few years later to Sir Robert Vyner, another Lord Mayor. Except for some minor alterations in the eighteenth century, the house is as fine a specimen of unspoilt seventeenth-century domestic architecture as it is possible to find. It is mentioned in Pepys' Diary.

The Abbey of Bec Harlewin in Normandy held much property in this County, and one of its most important manors was Ruislip. The possessions of all " alien " Priories were seized by Henry IV, and Ruislip was granted as part of the foundation of King's College, Cambridge. Some of the sixteenth-century house is still standing, and in the grounds there is evidence of an ancient castle, probably built by Ernulf de Hesding, who gave the manor to Bec Abbey in 1096. The Hawtrey family held property in this parish, and Ruislip Church contains a number of beautiful memorials to that family, dating from the sixteenth to the eighteenth centuries.

Milton was a frequent visitor to Harefield Place, and there he witnessed a performance of his " Arcades ", enacted in the grounds by the grandchildren of the Countess of Derby. Brakespears, a sixteenth-century house about half a

WROTHAM PARK

mile to the east of Harefield Church, is said to take its name from the family of which the only English Pope (Adrian) was a member.

Harrow belonged to the Archbishop of Canterbury at the time of the making of the Domesday Survey, and there can be no doubt that a country seat existed there to which succeeding Archbishops resorted when their presence near London was essential, or when travelling northwards. A great deal of the Harrow property was surrendered by Cranmer to Henry VIII, who granted this to Sir Edward, afterwards Lord North, from whom it eventually passed to the ancestors of the late Lord Northwich. Quite recently a most interesting collection of old records has been handed over by the executors of Lord Northwich to the County Council, and may be seen and examined at the Guildhall. In 1170 Thomas à Becket spent a few days at Harrow on his way to Canterbury, where he was murdered.

Harrow School, where much of the original school-house is to be seen, was founded " for the releyffe of the poore " by John Lyon before his death in 1592. The original rules governing the school, which are still preserved, decreed that recreations were to be confined to " driving a top, tossing a hand-ball, running and shooting ". For the last-mentioned sport it was laid down that the parents were to provide " bowstrings, shafts and bresters ". Archery was regularly practised at the school until the beginning of the last century and the school coat of arms shows crossed arrows, no doubt in commemoration of the school's activities in this direction.

Two other properties in the neighbourhood which belonged to the Archbishop were Headstone, at which there are traces of a fourteenth-century farm, and Hayes, where a sixteenth-century house still stands.

Wembley belonged to the Priory of Kilburn, and on the dissolution of the Priory it was granted to Richard Page. His descendants enjoyed the property for many generations until, on the death of the last known male heir, the property became the subject of many claims.

Bentley Priory, in Harrow Weald, marks the site of an early Roman settlement to which attention has already been directed. It was near the existing house that George IV when Prince Regent, with the Emperor of Russia and the King of Prussia, met Louis XVIII on his way from his exile at Hartwell House in Buckinghamshire to ascend the throne of France.

Little Stanmore, which bears the alternative name of Whitchurch, originally belonged to the Priory of St. Bartholomew, but came in the eighteenth century to James Brydges, who was created Duke of Chandos, that " princely nobleman ", as he is described by contemporaries. In 1712 he started to build his great mansion at Canons at a cost of over £250,000, a sum which in these days would be worth over three times that amount. His living is said to have corresponded with the magnificence of his mansion but, such was the cost of its upkeep, that on his death in 1744 the buildings were pulled down and the materials sold by auction. The statue of George I which was removed from the grounds of Canons now stands in the centre of Leicester Square. The site was sold to William Hallet, whose grandson conveyed it to Dennis O'Kelley, the owner of the famous racehorse " Eclipse ",

SPRING GROVE HOUSE, ISLEWORTH, NOW A MIDDLESEX SECONDARY SCHOOL

STRAWBERRY HILL, TWICKENHAM

in honour of which one of the most valuable races is now run annually at Sandown Park.

Chandos was a great lover of music, and, having rebuilt the village church, he installed Handel as his " chapel master ", and it was during his occupation of this post that he wrote some of his best-known works.

Hendon belonged to the Abbot of Westminster, and it was here that Cardinal Wolsey rested for the night on his way north to Leicester Abbey, where he died.

Willesden belonged to the Dean and Chapter of St. Paul's, and passed in the last century from that body to the Ecclesiastical Commissioners, who still own the manor. Originally it was divided into many prebends, and the profits of each prebend went towards supporting one of the prebendaries of the Cathedral. Nearly all evidence of early buildings in this parish has been swept away, but some portions of eighteenth-century work can be seen in Old Oxgate Farm, the Grove, and the Grange at Neasden, and at Willesden Paddocks.

Highgate is another place which has been much favoured as a residential district for the last three hundred years. Cromwell House, on the north-east side of Highgate Hill, was probably built about 1630, and although a fire greatly damaged it in 1865, there are still sufficient examples of old carved woodwork left for one to appreciate its original beauty, and the staircase is one of the most remarkable examples of its kind in the country. Highgate School was founded by Sir Roger Cholmeley, Chief Justice of the Queen's Bench, about the year 1565, but none of the original buildings survive.

Tottenham seems to have specialized in housing claimants to the Scottish throne, for Robert de Bruce and John de Baliol both had residences within the parish, the manor of Bruses and the manor of Baliols afterwards called Dawbeneys. The house which stands near the site of the original Bruce Castle, and is now used as the Borough Museum, was built in the early part of the sixteenth century by William Compton, and it was in this house that Henry VIII met his sister Margaret, Queen of Scots, in 1516. Queen Elizabeth visited the Castle in 1578. The Sanctus Bell at Tottenham Old Parish Church is said to have been the alarm bell of the garrison at Quebec, and was taken from there at the siege in 1759.

The house on the site of the Priory at Tottenham was built by Joseph Fenton, and two of the rooms contain the original panelling and fireplaces, with ceilings dated 1620.

Edmonton is immortalized by Cowper's vivid description of John Gilpin's holiday jaunt, but those who go there with a hope of seeing the " Bell " where Mrs. Gilpin was preparing the lunch, will be disappointed, for no trace of it can now be found. The " Angel " apparently marks the spot where it stood. Although there were many important houses in Edmonton, few traces of these can be seen, except Pymmes Park, once owned by the famous Lord Burghley, and Salisbury House. Minchenden House, the home of the Dukes of Chandos, was in Southgate, which formed part of Edmonton,

and near by stood Cockfosters, which has recently become famous to Londoners by an extension of the tube railway to it. It is mentioned in the County records as early as 1613 as the residence of Edward Kendall.

Enfield was the site of the only fortified residence known to exist in the County. Humphrey de Bohun, who had inherited his estates from Geoffrey de Mandeville, had licence to fortify it in 1347. Queen Elizabeth spent some of her childhood in a house of which portions can still be seen. Another house of some interest which still stands there is " Forty Hall ", which was built by Inigo Jones about the year 1630. Enfield Chase was a royal hunting-ground, and the lodges on the estate were subsequently much in demand. An original lease dated 1753, granting South Bailey Lodge to William Pitt, is now preserved among the County records.

*   *   *

Space does not permit of a detailed reference to all the interesting old buildings and relics in the County and in addition to those which have already been dealt with there are, of course, many other ancient buildings, including churches and inns. In the following sixteen pages an endeavour has been made to collate a schedule of the outstanding items of interest in each district. This information has been taken from *A Survey and Inventory by the Royal Commission on Historical Monuments*, published by His Majesty's Stationery Office, and containing considerably more detailed information and many beautiful illustrations.

HISTORIC BUILDINGS AND MONUMENTS

ACTON

ST. MARY'S CHURCH, rebuilt 1865, contains earlier fittings, including 17th-century highly enriched plate.

BERRYMEAD PRIORY (now Constitutional Club), possible 16th-century origin, but extensively altered.

GEORGE AND DRAGON HOTEL, probably two early 17th-century houses, much altered.

ASHFORD

ST. MATTHEW'S CHURCH, rebuilt 1858, earlier fittings.

CLOCK HOUSE FARM, probably 17th century, much altered; two original windows.

FORD FARM, possibly 17th century, partly burnt 1716, since altered.

BEDFONT EAST

ST. MARY'S CHURCH, 12th-century chancel and nave, with later additions; original chancel arch and doorway, and mediæval wall-paintings of unusual quality.

PATES MANOR FARM, house and barn— house probably 16th century, with various additions on E. side; reset panels with Christ's Hospital arms (former owners) in porch; weatherboarded barn.

BENNETS FARM, probably early 18th century.

FAWNS, 17th-century house, much altered.

GREEN MAN INN, 17th century, largely rebuilt in brick.

BRENTFORD

ST. LAWRENCE'S CHURCH, has 15th century W. Tower and bell cast by William Culverden, *c.* 1510; font, *c.* 1500.

BOSTON HOUSE, apparently rebuilt 1622–3, and further works carried out in 1671, probably including N. wing and E. outbuildings; noteworthy ceilings, staircase, fireplaces, 17th-century hall-screen (see p. 59).

BEAUFORT HOUSE and CHATHAM HOUSE originally one late 17th- or early 18th-century house.

LINDEN HOUSE and COBDEN HOUSE, the same, but partly refronted.

Various other houses of similar period in The Butts and High Street.

OLD ENGLAND, site on the Thames bank bordering Isleworth parish, has yielded finds dating from Bronze Age downwards, and excavations indicate a Hallstart settlement of some size.

FERRY HOUSE, late 17th or early 18th century; interior modernized.

GROVE HOUSE (now N., Middle and S. Grove), same period, but much altered.

Various other houses of similar period.

CHISWICK

ST. NICHOLAS' CHURCH, W. Tower 1416–35, remainder rebuilt 1882; coffin-lid in churchyard 13th-century Purbeck marble slab; various 17th-century monuments, etc.

CHISWICK HOUSE, 16th century; existing Grosvenor wing added *c.* 1700; 1730–6 Palladian villa added; original house demolished, 1788; gateway ascribed to Inigo Jones (see p. 59).

CHURCH HALL, 1707, much altered.

Chiswick Mall.

WOODROFFE HOUSE, late 17th to 18th century.

BEDFORD HOUSE and EYNSHAM HOUSE, originally one 18th-century building with modern additions.

THAMES VIEW and LINGARD HOUSE, originally one 18th-century house, much altered.

RED LION HOUSE, *c.* 1700, modern attic-storey and refaced S.E. front; original fireplace and staircase.

WALPOLE HOUSE, probably dates mainly from late 16th century, but little more than main chimney-stack left; S.E. front and addition on N.W. side early 18th century, 17th- and 18th-century panelling, fireplace and staircase.

STRAWBERRY HOUSE and MORTON HOUSE, *c.* 1700, former re-fronted *c.* 1730.

SWAN HOUSE and CEDAR HOUSE, originally

A 15TH-CENTURY HOUSE, EDGWARE

one late 17th-century house largely refaced 18th century.

BOSTON HOUSE, late 17th century, large early 18th-century S.W. addition.

4, 5, AND 6, CHISWICK SQUARE, 17th-century houses.

LATIMER HOUSE and HOLLY HOUSE, late 17th-century house, refronted etc. 18th century.

HOUSE, E. SIDE OF CHURCH STREET, now three tenements, much altered and added to, probably 16th-century plastered timber-framing house.

BURLINGTON CORNER, late 17th to 18th-century weather-boarded, timber-framing house, containing reset early 16th-century linenfold panelling; later additions.

HOGARTH HOUSE, 17th century, with early 18th-century S. addition; some original fittings (see p. 59).

DUKE OF DEVONSHIRE'S ALMSHOUSES, *c.* 1700, and many other 17th-century houses.

Strand-on-the-Green

17th-century houses, many extensively altered, including BULLS HEAD INN, CITY BARGE INN and SHIP HOUSE.

COWLEY

ST. LAURENCE'S CHURCH, 12th century nave; chancel rebuilt, and probably widened 13th century; later and modern restorations and additions; palimpsest brasses; fragments of 15th-century tracery and early 16th-century popey-heads in modern screen; remains of moulded stone bowl 12th or 13th century in churchyard.

MANOR FARM, built *c.* 1600, later additions; 17th-century barns.

THE OLD COTTAGE, early 16th century.

BARNACRE, MAYGOOD FARM, PLUM-TREE COTTAGE, CROWN INN, THE OLD HOUSE, all 17th century, subject to certain alterations.

CRANFORD

ST. DUNSTAN'S CHURCH, 15th century, with later additions; bell probably cast by William Burford *c.* 1380; monument to Sir R. Aston, 1612; monument of Lady Berkeley, 1635 (said to have been made in Rome), palimpsest brass.

HOMESTEAD MOAT, site of Manor house of Stanford le Mote.

CRANFORD HOUSE, E. block of E. wing, possibly early 18th century; house largely rebuilt during 18th century; early 17th-century stables (see p. 58).

THE RECTORY, partly 17th century; brick-faced and added to 18th century; probably 17th-century barn.

SPRINGFIELD HOUSE (now flats), probably early 18th century, later additions.

MOATED MOUND, roughly circular, 80 yds., N.N.E. of bridge, mostly filled in.

DRAYTON, WEST

ST. MARTIN'S CHURCH, signs of 13th-century origin, but largely rebuilt 15th century, and later restored; elaborately carved 15th-century font; inscribed chalice and paten, 1507

THE GATEHOUSE of former Manor House, early 16th century, but with alterations (see p. 60).

THE VICARAGE, N.E. wing probably 17th century, with 18th-century additions and rebuilding.

SIX BELLS INN, 17th century, refaced and altered.

OLD OAK LODGE, 16th century.

THE COPSE, 16th century, refaced and added to in 18th century.

THE OLD HOUSE, late 17th to 18th century.

AVENUE HOUSE, 16th-century E. wing, remainder 18th century.

SOUTHLANDS, early 18th century, with barn probably 17th century.

OLD MEADOWS, probably 16th century.

THE FRAYS, possibly 15th century, but refaced.

EALING

ST. MARY'S CHURCH, rebuilt 1866; contains old fittings; 15th-century brass; 17th-century monuments and plate.

ROCHESTER HOUSE said to have been built 1712; subsequent S.W. addition.

EDGWARE

ST. MARGARET'S CHURCH, rebuilt 1764 and later reconstructed; W. tower probably 15th century; Elizabethan cup, 1562.

BROCKLEY HILL, records and traces of Roman settlement.

ATKINSON'S ALMSHOUSES, 1680.

NICOLL'S FARM, late 17th to 18th century, but refronted.

BURY FARM, probably early 17th century, later added to and altered.

EDMONTON

ALL SAINTS' CHURCH, chiefly rebuilt 15th century on site of 12th-century predecessor, with subsequent additions; early 16th-century tombs.

PYMME'S PARK, 16th-century house apparently entirely rebuilt early 17th century and again remodelled 18th century (see p. 65).

SALISBURY HOUSE, late 16th to 17th century with modern additions; 17th-century overmantels (see p. 65).

VICARAGE COTTAGE, LAMB'S COTTAGE and other 17th-century houses, several refaced or altered.

ENFIELD

ST. ANDREW'S CHURCH, chancel rebuilt 13th century, 14th-century arcades; altar-tomb of Joyce, Lady Tiptoft, 1446, with a brass and later canopy; monument to Sir Nicholas Raynton, Sheriff and Lord Mayor of London, 1646; oval wall-tablet by Nicholas Stone, 1617, etc.

HOMESTEAD MOATS: (1) on Enfield Golf Course, about 1 mile W.S.W. of church;

HENDON CHURCH

(2) CAMLET MOAT about 2½ miles W.N.W. of church; (3) DURANTS, 1¾ miles E. of church (practically all filled in); (4) PLANTATION FARM, 2¾ miles N.E. of church, S. arm filled in.

HOUSE on E. side of Gentleman's Row, practically rebuilt, but portions of early 16th-century work discovered and sent to British Museum; contains fittings from old Enfield Palace, including 17th-century ceiling.

GRAMMAR SCHOOL, mid 16th century, refitted 18th century and later.

FORTY HALL, built 1629–32 by Sir N. Raynton, design ascribed to Inigo Jones; repaired and modernized, 18th century; elaborate 17th-century ceiling and hall-screen.

DOWER HOUSE, 17th century, enlarged and altered 18th century.

WORCESTER LODGE and THE HERMITAGE, early 18th century.

ROSE AND CROWN INN, probably same period, but much altered.

KING JAMES AND THE TINKER INN, 17th century, refitted and altered 18th century.

GLASGOW STUD FARM, 17th century; noteworthy staircase.

VICARAGE (largely modern), E. and W. wings possibly 16th century.

CLARENDON COTTAGE, GENTLEMAN'S ROW, altered and remodelled in 18th century, retains 17th-century chimney-stack.

OLD PARK FARM, 17th century, some original mullioned and transomed windows, otherwise much altered.

EARTHWORK AT OLD PARK, 1,250 yds. S.W. of church; N. and W. sides clear; S. side much levelled; E. almost obliterated.

FELTHAM

ST. DUNSTAN'S CHURCH, rebuilt 1802, enlarged 1855–6; some earlier fittings.

MANOR HOUSE, reputed rebuilt after fire 1634 (see p. 57). BARN probably 16th to 17th century.

Also 17th-century cottages.

FINCHLEY

ST. MARY'S CHURCH, rebuilt 15th century, early 13th-century font.

ST. PAUL'S CHURCH (modern), late 14th-century bell from Hatford, Berkshire.

HOMESTEAD MOATS: (1) Bishop's Lodge on Highgate Golf Course, and (2) at Manor House, both fragmentary.

VERANDAH HOUSE, late 17th century or early 18th century.

SPANIARDS INN, 17th century, extensively altered, added to and refaced.

FRIERN BARNET

ST. JAMES'S CHURCH, retains 12th-century doorway, otherwise 19th century.

CAMPE ALMSHOUSES, erected 1612, restored and altered 19th century; five old stone panels on front.

GREENFORD

HOLY CROSS CHURCH, restored and altered 15th or early 16th century; two mediæval bells—(1) 14th century, uninscribed, (2) cast by William Culverden about 1510; 1450 brass, half-figure of priest; 17th- or early 18th-century baluster font with contemporary cover; best heraldic glass in County—arms of Eton and King's College.

THE GRANGE, probably early 17th-century timber framing, recased in brick 18th century; some original panelling.

BARN AT GREENFORD GREEN FARM, 17th century, with later addition; also 17th-century house S.S.W. of church.

HAMPTON

ST. MARY'S CHURCH, rebuilt 1829–31, contains many earlier fittings.

HAMPTON COURT PALACE, commenced in 1514, many 16th-century additions and alterations, 17th-century works by Wren, etc. (see p. 50).

FARADAY HOUSE, 18th century, extensively altered. 16th–17th century outbuilding on S.E. (see p. 55).

COURT COTTAGE, c. 1700, parapet later and back refaced.

THE OLD COURT HOUSE, early 18th century, leased to Wren (see p. 55).

HOUSE (two tenements) 25 yds. S. of Faraday House, possibly 16th century.

OLD MALT OR BREW HOUSE, c. 1700.

ST. ALBANS, possibly late 17th century, extensively altered (see p. 55).

OLD GRANGE, mid 17th century, much altered.

FEATHERS COTTAGE, probably 16th to 17th century; and many other 17th- and 18th-century houses.

HAMPTON WICK

WOLSEY'S COTTAGE, late 16th century; and other 17th-century houses.

HANWORTH

ST. GEORGE'S CHURCH, rebuilt 1812, with some 15th-century glass and various fittings; panel of arms of James I, 1625.

HANWORTH PARK, remains of fireplaces, walls and moat (S. and S.W. of church). The house, originally belonging to Henry VIII, burned 1797 (see p. 56).

HANWORTH HOUSE, partly c. 1600, much altered.

HAREFIELD

ST. MARY'S CHURCH, 13th-century window, 14th-century S. aisle; foreign communion rails with richly carved panels; late mediæval font; highly remarkable series of monuments mostly to members of the Newdigate family, including fine canopied and painted monument to Alice, Countess of Derby, 1636; Elizabethan Communion cup, 1561.

CHAPEL AT MOOR HALL FARM, early 13th century; later brick repairs.

HOMESTEAD MOAT, 350 yds. S.E. of

BRACKENBURY FARM, house, barn and moat: house 16th- to 17th-century work; 16th-century barn; moat, formerly surrounding house, complete on three sides.

HILLINGDON CHURCH

ALMSHOUSES, built 1600.

HAREFIELD PLACE, remains of 16th-century brick garden walls (see p. 61).

BRAKESPEAR, house possibly 16th century, practically entirely rebuilt 17th century; and early 17th-century dovecot (see p. 61).

WHITE HORSE INN, late 16th century and modern additions.

MANOR COURT, probably 16th century, much altered.

THE CRICKETER'S INN, 17th century, walls refaced, modern additions on W.

KING'S ARMS INN, 15th century, largely rebuilt in 17th century, and later additions.

WHITEHEATH FARM, 17th-century house and barn: house walls refaced, later additions.

MEADOW COTTAGE, 16th century with 17th-century alterations and additions.

CRIPPS FARM COTTAGE, house and barn; 16th century, with later additions to barn.

JACK'S COTTAGE, 17th-century chimney-stack surrounded by rebuilt timbers from earlier building and later brick-work.

BOURNE FARM and barns, 17th century.

HIGHWAY FARM, rebuilt, retaining 17th-century chimney-stack.

NEW YEARS GREEN POND FARM, late 16th or early 17th century; modern addition on E., and early 17th-century oven.

NEW YEARS GREEN FARM, 17th century, largely rebuilt.

CROWS NEST FARM, late 16th or early 17th century, later additions and front refaced.

SWAKELEY FARM, house and barns; house c. 1709, has later additions.

HARLINGTON

CHURCH OF ST. PETER AND ST. PAUL, 12th-century nave and doorway; chancel built or rebuilt *c.* 1340, early 16th-century timber porch; 15th- and 16th-century brasses; tomb recesses probably 14th century; 16th-century tablet memorials; palimpsest brasses. W. Tower late 16th century.

CHURCH FARM, 16th- or 17th-century barn.

DAWLEY MANOR FARM, 16th century (E. Wing extended 17th century), with original window with four mullion-shaped diamonds; timber-framed barns, probably late 16th century. MOAT on opposite side of road now filled in (see p. 60).

DOWER HOUSE, chiefly 16th century.

HARMONDSWORTH

ST. MARY'S CHURCH, 12th-century origin with later additions; 12th-century doorway and font (possibly slightly later); fairly extensive remains of late mediæval seating; 15th-century hammer-beam roof over N. chapel.

Unusually fine 14th- or 15th-century BARN and MOAT, remainder of alien priory (see p. 58). Moat retains W. arm, traces of N. and S. enclosure.

THE GRANGE, 17th century.

HARMONDSWORTH HALL, rebuilt or remodelled 18th century, but incorporates 17th-century chimney-stack.

FIVE BELLS INN, 17th century, much altered.

SUN HOUSE, probably 16th century, extended 18th century.

KING WILLIAM INN and OLD MAGPIE INN, 17th century, much altered.

PALMERS FARM, built *c.* 1600, largely refaced in brick.

PERROTT'S FARM, 17th century, cross wing at N. end.

HEATHROW FARM, house late 16th century with later additions and refaced; three barns, 16th and 17th century.

PERRY OAKS FARM, house probably late 16th century, later remodelled; barn N.W. of house probably 16th century; 17th-century pigeon-house.

COLLEGE FARM, 17th century, largely refaced; cross wing at E. end.

WHITE HORSE INN, 17th century, much altered and refronted.

WEEKLY HOUSE and barns, 17th century.

Also various 17th-century houses and cottages; EARTHWORK nearly 2 miles E. of Church.

HARROW-ON-THE-HILL

ST. MARY'S, a cruciform church, the most extensive example of 13th-century work in the County; 12th-century doorway, &c., in Tower; late 14th- and 15th-century brasses and palimpsest brasses; good 15th- or 16th-century door; 12th-century font with circular enriched bowl; Elizabethan cup, 1568; a handsome pulpit given in 1708.

HOMESTEAD MOAT, 1,150 yds. S.W. of church, formerly rectangular; part of S.E. arm now forms pond.

HARROW SCHOOL, founded 1571–2, first opened 1611; original building still survives; 17th-century fireplace (see p. 62).

THE OLD HOUSE, formerly the "Queen's Head", apparently largely rebuilt in 17th or early 18th century.

HARROW WEALD

GRIMS DYKE, earthworks (see pp. 15 and 77).

PRIORY HOUSE, rebuilt but incorporates base of 16th-century chimney-stack; 17th-century garden wall (see p. 63).

SEVEN BELLS INN and FARM COTTAGE, 17th century.

HAYES

ST. MARY'S CHURCH, boarded and panelled roof; timber porch, originally 16th century, reconstructed; timber lych-gate, probably early 16th century; 14th- and 15th-century brasses; 12th- or 13th-century font; late 16th-century altar tomb; monument to Sir E. Fenner, 1611–12; 13th- and 15th-century wall paintings; 13th-century piscina.

HOMESTEAD MOAT, at site of Old Manor House, 750 yds. W. of Church, practically filled in.

ISLEWORTH CHURCH

MANOR HOUSE, N.E. part early 16th century, S.E. slightly later, whole refaced in brick 17th or 18th century with modern additions (see p. 63).

HENDON

ST. MARY'S CHURCH, 13th-century chancel work; later Renaissance monument to John Wolstenholme, 1669; tablet memorials of note; very boldly carved heraldic slab of touch to Sir John Whichcote, 1677; remains of 13th-century decorative painting and 16th- or 17th-century black-letter texts; painting of royal arms (Stuart); rich, elaborate 12th-century font.

17th-century WELL in the Grove, N.W. of Highwood Hill.

COPT HALL, rebuilt 1624 and extensively altered.

FRITH MANOR, rebuilt 18th century, but with 16th-century stone fireplace; linenfold panelling from elsewhere.

BITTACY HOUSE (modern), contains woodcarving of arms of James I.

NICOLL ALMSHOUSES, built 1696, extensively repaired 19th century.

ROSEBANK, built 1678, altered 1719.

THE GROVE, late 16th or early 17th century; old panelling.

RISING SUN INN, 17th century, extensively altered.

CHURCH END FARM, 17th century.

Two 17TH-CENTURY COTTAGES at Model Farm and barn 80 yds. E.; also other houses of same period.

HESTON

ST. LEONARD HESTON CHURCH, has timber lych-gate; good 15th- or 16th-century door; interesting brasses.

OSTERLEY PARK, almost completely remodelled from Sir T. Gresham's house of 1577; stables probably originals, 1570–80, though altered; reconstructed by Robert Adam, 1761 (see p, 58).

OLD COTE, probably early 16th-century house. WHITE HOUSE retains part early 16th-century roof. ST. LAURENCE COTTAGE, 17th century.

HILLINGDON

ST. JOHN THE BAPTIST'S CHURCH, 13th-century chancel work; 15th-century brass with canopy, and fine figure of Lady Strange; 16th-century brasses; imposing monument to Sir Edward Carr, 1636–7; tower staircase with early 17th-century pilaster balusters.

CEDAR HOUSE, c. 1580, partly remodelled 18th century and with modern wing.

ENCLOSURE WALLS, 17th century, E. side of Harlington Road and Lees Road.

GARDEN WALL on W. side of Hubbards Farm; 16th-century brickwork.

KIMBOLTON HOUSE, 16th century, S. block (earliest) refaced in brick; HOUSE at Gould's Green, late 17th to 18th century.

HOUSE, early 16th century, 70 yds. W.S.W. of church.

THE COTTAGE, south of house, mid-16th century.

EARTHWORK forming E. boundary of Coney Green.

Also various 17th-century houses at West Hillingdon.

HORNSEY

ST. MARY'S CHURCH (demolished 1927), W. tower built c. 1500; modern top.

CHAPEL of Cholmeley's School, rebuilt 19th century, contains 17th- and 18th-century floor-slabs in crypt (see p. 64).

CROMWELL HOUSE, good example late 17th century; apparently built c. 1630, additions 17th and 18th century; later fire destroyed upper part; highly remarkable carved oak staircase, and good doors, fireplace and ceilings (see p. 64).

LYNDALE HOUSE, largely rebuilt c. 1730, has late 17th-century ceiling and panelled door.

128–130 HIGHGATE HILL, House, built late in 17th century, partly refitted 18th century.

ICKENHAM

ST. GILES'S CHURCH, partly late 14th century, has mediæval bell cast by T. Bullisdon; small effigy of unusual character of the infant R. Clayton, 1665.

SWAKELEYS, built by Sir Edmund Wright, 1629–38, largely unaltered with contemporary fittings; 17th-century STABLES, much altered, and DOVECOTE; late 16th- and early 17th-century panellings, well-known 17th- to 18th-century paintings; 17th-century ceilings and hall screen (see p. 61).

MANOR FARM, early 16th century with 17th-century staircase and later additions. MOAT formerly surrounding house now large outer enclosure and moat on N. side.

COTTAGE, 60 yds. E. of church, late 15th or early 16th century, with later additions on E. and N.

COACH AND HORSES INN, 17th century, much altered, but original window.

MILTON FARM, has 17th-century barn.

TIPPER FARM, 17th century, some original panelling.

IVYHOUSE FARM, 16th-century barn.

BEETONSWOOD FARM, 17th century, with some original window- and door-frames.

ISLEWORTH

ALL SAINTS' CHURCH, has late 15th-century W. Tower; nave rebuilt 1706–7; brass with tiny figure of Margaret Dely, Sister of Syon, 1561; and other 15th- and 16th-century brasses; 17th- and 18th-century monuments.

HOMESTEAD MOATS: (1) S.W. of WYKE FARM, (2) 350 yds. N.E. of (1), oval and cut through by railway (3) on N. side of road 1 mile W.S.W. of church, almost entirely filled in.

SYON HOUSE, original building 16th century; completely remodelled in 18th and early 19th centuries, principal first-floor rooms by Robert Adam, 1760–5; fine early 16th-century carved panels; remains of 15th-century undercroft; early 17th-century lodges to W. of house; 16th-century stable, much altered and rebuilt (see p. 59).

KINGSBURY CHURCH

FERRY HOUSE, possibly early 17th century, but almost entirely rebuilt early 18th century.

INGRAM ALMSHOUSES, 1664.

SILVER HALL, late 17th or early 18th century.

HOLME COURT; ROSE COTTAGES, WORTON ROAD, and many other houses of same period.

KINGSBURY

ST. ANDREW'S CHURCH, possibly dates from before the Conquest; contains earliest mediæval bell in County, probably mid 14th century, cast by Peter de Weston.

BLACKBIRD FARM, probably 17th century.

LALEHAM

ALL SAINTS' CHURCH, 12th-century nave-arcades; Purbeck marble slab altar with consecration crosses.

CHURCH FARM, late 17th century.

EARTHWORK about 850 yds. W. of White House, visible from air only.

LITTLETON

CHURCH OF ST. MARY MAGDALENE, S. arcade *c.* 1200, additions *c.* 1280; N. Tower and clerestory early 16th century, etc.; church of architectural interest, with noteworthy communion rails, small chest, much-restored chancel screen, 15th-century traceried stall-backs said to come from Winchester; fairly extensive remains late mediæval seating.

OLD MANOR HOUSE, partly 15th century, partly 16th century and later.

RECTORY, *c.* 1700.

SOUTH MIMMS

ST. GILES'S CHURCH, with chancel probably 13th, nave 14th to 15th century, W.

TIMBER FRAMED HOUSES

DIAGRAM SHEWING PERIOD TO WHICH THEY BELONG

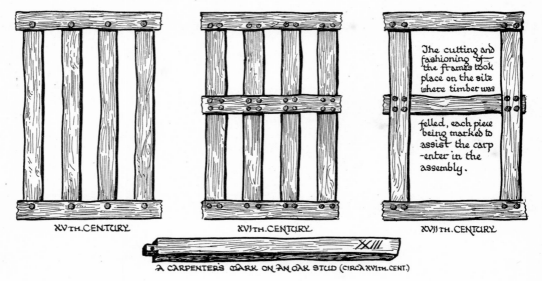

The cutting and fashioning of the frames took place on the site where timber was felled, each piece being marked to assist the carpenter in the assembly.

XVTH. CENTURY   XVITH. CENTURY   XVIITH. CENTURY

A CARPENTER'S MARK ON AN OAK STUD (CIRCA XVITH. CENT.)

Tower 15th century, northern arcade, chapel and aisle 16th century; 13th- or 14th-century chest, much early 16th-century glass (1526), but decayed; recumbent effigy—Frowyck—period doubtful, semi-Gothic but possibly more Renaissance; curious Renaissance canopy tomb, probably Henry Frowyck, 1527.

MOTTE AND BAILEY CASTLE, earthwork about 1 mile N.N.E. of church.

MIMMS HALL, probably early 16th-century house later cased in brick and altered on E. and S., fragments of MOAT which apparently surrounded house.

BLANCHE FARM, late 16th- or early 17th-century house; 17th-century staircase; 17th-century COTTAGE. MOAT originally surrounding house; filled on E. and W.

FOLD OR OLD FORD FARM, 17th-century house with later additions; 17th-century but much altered BARNS; MOAT S. of house, largely intact.

KNIGHTSLAND FARM, 16th century; 18th-century brick casing, notable wall paintings and linenfold panellings; 17th-century BARN.

MANOR FARM OR WYLLYOTS MANOR, house probably c. 1600, incorporated with W. part, originally 16th-century barn.

WHITE HART INN, late 17th or early 18th century, much altered.

BLACK HORSE INN, early 18th century.

SPARROW FARM, built c. 1500; 16th-century fireplace.

BRIDGEFOOT FARM and BENTLEY HEATH FARM, 17th century BARNS.

GREEN MAN INN, 17th century, much altered.

NORTHOLT

ST. MARY'S CHURCH, nave rebuilt c. 1300; brass—Henry Rowdell, 1452—and palimpsest brasses.

HOMESTEAD MOAT, N.E. of church.

DOWN BARNS, MOAT on W. side, house rebuilt late 17th or early 18th century; earlier massive chimney-stack on W.

PIGEON HOUSE AT ISLIP MANOR, probably 17th century, ruined.

ILIOTS GREEN, late 17th or early 18th century house.

MOAT FARM, house and barn, same period.

COURT FARM, house and barns, same period.

MEDLAR FARM, probably early 17th century, later additions at back, refaced at front; reset original window of four lights with moulded frame and mullions.

NORWOOD

ST. MARY'S CHURCH, nave probably 12th century; chancel probably added or rebuilt in 13th century; S. porch probably 15th century, but much altered; 15th-century font; 15th- to 16th-century glass; extensive restoration in 1824; 16th-century tombs and glass are noteworthy.

SOUTHALL MANOR HOUSE, 1587, with later additional wing and 18th-century extension; important example of timber-framed work with carved details of interest in hall; one of earliest over-mantels in County; 16th- to 17th-century panellings (see p. 60).

PERIVALE

PARISH CHURCH, chancel and nave may be late 13th century, but earliest surviving detail 15th century; late 15th-century font, with cover dated 1665.

HOMESTEAD MOAT, nearly 1 mile N.N.E. of church.

RECTORY, partly 15th century apparently, with 17th- and 18th-century additions.

PINNER

ST. JOHN THE BAPTIST'S CHURCH, early 14th-century chancel, nave, transepts, and aisles; consecrated 1321; 15th to 16th century and later additions.

HEADSTONE MANOR, part of archbishops' manor of Harrow; 14th- to 15th-century origin, added to or rebuilt 16th century and later; the original roof, etc.; BARN, c. 1600; MOAT, surrounding house.

EAST END FARM, late 16th century.

TUDOR COTTAGE, late 16th century, later added to.

CHURCH FARM, HOUSE and BARNS, 17th century, extended 18th century.

QUEEN'S HEAD INN, 17th century, later additions.

HOUSE 90 yds. W.S.W. of the inn, probably early 16th century; HOUSE 210 yds. W. of church, 16th century.

WAXWELL FARM, 17th century; one original window, etc.

PINNER PARK, site of former deer park.

GRIMS DYKE, only County earthwork of major importance (see p. 15).

RUISLIP

ST. MARTIN'S CHURCH, 13th-century nave and S. arcade; 15th-century additions and later; some interesting brasses; two large iron-bound chests probably 16th century; good 15th- or 16th-century door; interesting monuments and tablet memorials; traces of wall-painting of St. Christopher and of extensive wall-painted decoration of figures including St. Michael and the Virgin; Elizabethen cup dated 1595; 17th-century pulpit; remains of late mediæval seating.

HOMESTEAD MOATS: (1) over $\frac{1}{2}$ mile N.W. of church, (2) $1\frac{1}{4}$ mile N.E. of church and 150 yards W. of Eastcote Grange—fragmentary.

MANOR FARM, house probably early 16th century with later additions (see p. 61); the BARN is c. 1600; a second barn is being restored; the EARTH-WORKS consist of motte and bailey castle (probably 11th century) precinct; large enclosure and mound.

ALMSHOUSES, 17th century.

HOUSE, 1 AND 3 HIGH STREET, built c. 1500, extended N. 16th century and later.

OLD SWAN INN, has S. range of c. 1500; N. block adjoining c. 1600, and later addition.

GEORGE HOTEL, 17th century with modern additions.

THE OLD HOUSE, BURY STREET, 17th century, containing early 16th-century linenfold and later panelling.

MILL HOUSE, 17th century, largely modernized.

HILL FARM, FIELDEND FARM (house and barn); SHERLEY'S FARM; LITTLE MANOR FARM and WOODMAN'S FARM, all 17th century.

PLOUGH INN, has block on S. side of *c.* 1600 and remains of mediæval building with later additions.

YOUNGWOOD FARM, 17th century with later additions.

DUCKSHILL FARM, 17th-century house (refaced in brick) and BARNS.

NORTHWOOD GRANGE, has 15th-century block at W. end, some *c.* 1600 and modern additions.

GATESHILL FARM, CUCKOOHILL FARM, MISTLETOE FARM, HORNEND, CHENEY FARM: all originally 17th century.

ST. CATHERINE'S FARM, late 16th-century house and barn.

RAMIN, 17th century, with 16th-century barn.

EASTCOTE GRANGE, 16th century, with modern addition and 17th-century cottage.

EASTCOTE HOUSE, 16th to 17th century, later refaced and added to, and 17th-century stables.

EASTCOTE COTTAGE, late 16th century, much altered.

THE BARNS (house, 230 yds. S.E. of cottage) perhaps mediæval origin, much altered and added to.

PARK FARM AND SIGERS, 17th century.

FIELDEND LODGE, includes part 16th-century house.

FIELDEND FARM, 17th century, with modern additions and partly refaced; early 16th-century barn.

OLD BARN HOUSE, late mediæval, much altered.

FORE STREET FARM, 17th-century house (with later N. extension) and barn.

OLD CHENEY COTTAGE, IVY FARM (perhaps incorporating some mediæval work); CHERRY COTTAGE and HAYDEN HALL FARM: all 17th century.

SHEPPERTON

ST. NICHOLAS' CHURCH, rebuilt as a whole 1614, embodying 12th- or 13th-century work; earlier building reputed damaged or destroyed by floods; modern restorations and vestries.

RECTORY, late 15th to 16th century, remodelled and added to; 18th-century front.

IVY COTTAGE, 16th century, altered and partly refaced.

MANOR FARM BARN, late 17th century.

WHITE COTTAGE, late 16th century, refronted in brick.

SOUTHGATE

CHRIST CHURCH, founded 1615, rebuilt 1862; contains old fittings.

HOMESTEAD MOAT, N. side of Fords Grove and E. of New River; fragmentary.

STAINES

ST. MARY'S CHURCH, rebuilt 1828 with later additions; W. tower rebuilt 1631 and ascribed to Inigo Jones.

LONDON STONE, 260 yards W.S.W. of church, probably dates from 17th century (see p. 55).

DUNCROFT HOUSE, 17th century, extensively altered, interesting fittings.

BLUE ANCHOR HOTEL, 17th-century front rebuilt in brick *c.* 1700; contemporary fittings.

WHITE LION INN, 17th-century, extensive additions; other 17th-century houses.

STANMORE, GREAT

ST. JOHN'S CHURCH, 1849–50, near sites of mediæval and 17th-century predecessors, and contains many fittings from latter; 17th- to 18th-century baluster font and cover; imposing Wolstenholme monument, 1639, by N. Stone, and later monuments.

STANMORE, LITTLE

ST. LAWRENCE'S CHURCH, W. Tower early 16th century; remainder rebuilt 1715; noteworthy early 18th-century painted walls and ceilings, and fittings, including Handel's organ and the Chandos tomb (see p. 64).

LAKE ALMSHOUSES, founded before 1693.

WHITE HART INN, 17th-century front block, rebuilt 18th century.

TOTTENHAM CHURCH

CHANDOS ARMS (disused and condemned), probably 16th century with 17th-century additions—traces of royal arms painted on plaster.

BROCKLEY HILL FARM, 17th-century house (with early 17th-century panelling) and barn.

LYMES FARM, 17th-century house and barn.

STANWELL

ST. MARY'S CHURCH, arcades of nave 13th century; 14th-century chancel and tower; half figure brass of rector 1408; monument to Lord Knyvett, 1622; 14th-century sedilia forming continuation of wall arcading of chancel.

MOATED ENCLOSURE, 500 yards N. of church.

POYLE MANOR, rebuilt early 18th century; fragmentary MOAT.

SCHOOL-HOUSE founded 1624 and little altered (see p. 58).

THE CROFT, 17th century, much altered.

HAMMONDS FARM, c. 1700.

POYLE FARM, 17th century.

THE HOLLIES, 17th century, extensive later additions.

KING JOHN'S PALACE, late 16th- to 17th-century house, later extended.

STAR AND GARTER INN, 17th-century brick building.

WHITE HART INN, 17th century, largely rebuilt in brick 18th century.

SUNBURY

ST. MARY'S CHURCH, rebuilt 1752 and, except tower, in 1856, earlier fittings.

Fragmentary HOMESTEAD MOAT at Kempton Park over 1 mile N.E. of church.

IVY HOUSE, ROSSELL HOUSE, and THREE FISHES INN, late 17th to 18th century, with later additions.

HAWKE HOUSE, apparently 1703.

WILLSDON CHURCH

CLOCK HOUSE FARM, TWO BARNS, 17th to 18th century.

HARROW INN, 15th to 16th century, partly refaced in brick.

TEDDINGTON

ST. MARY'S CHURCH, largely rebuilt in 18th and 19th centuries; early 16th-century arch between N. chapel and aisle, and brick-built S. aisle with tiled roof.

Several 17th-century houses.

TOTTENHAM

ALL HALLOWS CHURCH, 14th-century tower and rebuilt old chancel and arcade naves; S. aisle largely rebuilt about 1500 and S. porch added. Later additions and restoration: early 17th-century Communion table; late 16th- to early 17th-century glass; various monuments (see p. 65).

HOMESTEAD MOAT, S. of R. Moselle and nearly ¾ miles S.W. of church.

TOTTENHAM HIGH CROSS, brick and modern stucco, brick probably replaced former wooden cross, *c.* 1600.

BRUCE CASTLE, house and tower, house now Borough Museum, structure appears to be late 16th century, later altered and added to (see p. 65).

TOWER, 16th century, use uncertain.

THE PRIORY (now Vicarage), *c.* 1620, later refaced and altered; 17th-century overmantels, ceilings (see p. 65).

ASPLIN FARM, early 17th century, later added to and altered.

DIAL HOUSE, GATEWAY (*c.* 1700), BROOK HOUSE, and other houses in High Road erected 17th century.

TWICKENHAM

ST. MARY'S CHURCH has restored 15th-century tower; mediæval bell (probably by J. Sanders, 16th century); 17th-century chest; 17th- or 18th-century baluster font.

KNELLER HOUSE, N. and W. arm of MOATED ENCLOSURE in grounds (see p. 57).

YORK HOUSE (now municipal offices), late 17th century with modern side wings and earlier staircase (see p. 56).

CAMBRIDGE HOUSE, largely rebuilt or refaced late 18th or 19th century; early or mid-17th-century fireplace; 16th-century foreign painted glass in staircase window.

FORTESCUE HOUSE (now school), early 18th century.

CROSSDEEP, c. 1700, with modern N. and S. wings.

RADNOR HOUSE, probably partly early 18th century, but completely refaced in 1847–8; 18th-century extensions and ceiling paintings; late 18th-century continental painted glass.

STRAWBERRY HILL (now St. Mary's College), part late 17th century now visible inside only, reconstructed by Walpole, mid 18th century (see p. 57).

INN, 32 KING STREET, 17th to 18th century, with some original panelling.

LIME TREE HOUSE, LONDON ROAD. 17th to 18th century; many other houses of same period.

TWYFORD

ST. MARY'S CHURCH, W. of Twyford Abbey, reputed rebuilt in 16th century, and pinnacles and W. Porch added 1808; interesting monuments.

UXBRIDGE

ST. MARGARET'S CHURCH has 15th-century hammer-beam roof over south aisle; monument to Lady Bennet, 1638, and others. Traces of late 14th-century work.

OLD TREATY HOUSE (now Crown Hotel), probably early 16th century, but greater part pulled down in 18th century (see p. 60).

THREE TUNS INN, probably late 15th or early 16th century, with 17th-century addition at back.

KING'S ARMS HOTEL, probably late 15th century; modern gables and exposed framing (mostly); 17th-century outbuilding.

GREAT WESTERN INN, early 16th century.

GEORGE HOTEL, c. 1576, refronted and much altered; reconditioned Guildhall or Court-Room on N. side of yard.

RED HOUSE, probably 16th century; front block rebuilt early 18th century.

QUEEN'S HEAD INN, probably late 15th or early 16th century; refaced in brick; also many houses of same period.

WEMBLEY

HUNDRED ELMS FARM, outbuildings early 16th century, part removed; some original windows; barn 17th century.

SUDBURY COURT and HILLSIDE FARM possibly 17th-century origin, greatly altered and enlarged.

LYON'S FARM, late 17th to 18th century (reputed birthplace of founder of Harrow School); back refaced.

MOOT-SITE OF THE HUNDRED OF GORE, 1000 yards N.E. of Lyon's Farm, identified by court-roll of 1445; triangular site raised about 3 feet above surrounding level.

WILLESDEN

ST. MARY'S CHURCH, 12th-century font indicates early foundation; earliest part of existing structure S. arcade of nave, mid-13th century; subsequent additions—noteworthy Communion table; cup dated 1606.

THE GRANGE, c. 1700 (see p. 64).

OLD OXGATE FARM, N. wing probably part of large 16th-century house, remainder 17th century (see p. 64).

THE GROVE (see p. 64) and THE COTTAGE, early 18th century, and later additions.

YIEWSLEY

THE GRANGE, 17th century with 18th-century additions.

PHILPOTS FARM, 17th-century BARNS.

RED COW INN, 17th century; originally timber-framed.

DE BURGH ARMS HOTEL, 17th century, extensively altered; some original mullion and transom windows.

CHAIRMAN AND CONVENERS OF THE COUNTY COUNCILS AT BUCKINGHAM PALACE, JUNE 23RD, 1897

[From original at Middlesex Guildhall.

PART TWO

THE ESTABLISHMENT OF COUNTY COUNCIL ADMINISTRATION

THE POSITION IN 1888

UNTIL county councils were established by the Local Government Act of 1888, a great part of the administrative work of the County of Middlesex was carried out by the justices. The duties of the justices did not, however, extend to all the administrative work, which is now undertaken by the Middlesex County Council. It may therefore assist the reader in forming a correct picture of the position of county government in 1888 if a reference is made to the method by which administrative duties, *other than those* per-

formed by the justices and now carried out by the County Council, were discharged. It must be remembered that in 1888, and indeed for quite a number of years after, the social services of the country had not been expanded to anything like their present extent.

The first and most important of these services is the Poor Law, or, as it is now generally called, " public assistance ". The history of the Poor Law goes back many centuries.

From ancient times, assistance to the

poor has always been regarded as a duty falling upon each individual according to his ability, and charity was a religious principle. It was not, however, until some 300 years ago that it was embodied in our laws to any extent. There had previously been efforts to supplement private charity. One of the earliest recorded is a law passed in Saxon times by Ethelred under which part of the tithe (certain revenues of the Church) was to be given to the poor and needy. The Norman Conquest and the consequent introduction of the feudal system did not improve conditions for the poor, in fact their lot became harder.

Unemployment is no new problem. From Norman times, particularly at the time of the Crusades, when the economic life of the country was disturbed, there were very many unemployed persons wandering about whose numbers had been increased by ex-soldiers from the Crusades or the constant " little wars". As time went on, the increase in the commerce of the country brought a corresponding weakening of the feudal system. Nevertheless, as those who remember their history will know, the years between 1300 and 1600 were full of trouble, in particular the Hundred Years War with France, the great pestilence called the " Black Death ", Wat Tyler's rebellion, the Wars of the Roses which followed the Hundred Years War, the disturbances caused by Lambert Simnel and Perkin Warbeck, further war with France, and the Spanish War and the Spanish Armada. It will not be surprising, therefore, that many of the population suffered poverty during these years. Many poor persons had been cared for by the various religious Orders, but the suppression of the monasteries by Henry VIII practically deprived them of this assistance.

Parliament had attempted to deal with the situation, but its legislation was directed rather to the punishment of vagrants and compulsory labour for the idle than to providing assistance with food and money. It is true that under some of the laws, the religious authorities were required to urge people to give alms, and one Statute even went so far as to render persons refusing to give charity liable to be brought before the justices at Quarter Sessions, but these Statutes brought about no improvement. Consequently in the closing years of the reign of Queen Elizabeth there was much poverty and want throughout the country.

THE POOR RELIEF ACT OF 1601

At last, towards the end of the sixteenth century, Francis Bacon introduced two Bills into Parliament, and several other Bills for relief of the poor were also under consideration. None of these Bills became law, but in spite of this discouragement other Bills were submitted to Parliament and ultimately, in the year 1601, the Poor Relief Act was passed.

You may be surprised to hear that many of the provisions of that Act remained in operation for over 300 years. As time went on, with the corresponding development in the standard of civilization, the administration of the Act of 1601 was modified and amended by Parliament, but until the early part of the nineteenth century the duties of relieving the poor devolved upon persons appointed for each parish, and called " overseers ".

THE POOR LAW AMENDMENT ACT OF 1834

A Commission was appointed to investigate the working of the Poor Law, and as a result of its report the Poor Law Amendment Act of 1834 established "Boards of Guardians", and many parishes were grouped together and called " Unions ", for which these guardians became responsible. The Unions were not, however, formed with strict regard to county boundaries, and it was not an uncommon thing to find a Union comprising parishes in three or more counties. For instance, the Edmonton Union included not only a considerable portion of north Middlesex, but also parishes in the counties of Hertfordshire and Essex. The Poor Law was being administered by these Boards of Guardians in the year

THEOBALDS PARK

Temple Bar, formerly in Strand.

1888, but they continued to function for over forty years thereafter. How the powers of the guardians were transferred to the county councils will be explained later.

THE EDUCATION SERVICES

In the early years of the nineteenth century there were a number of bodies formed (mainly connected with various religions) for promoting education, one of the most important being that connected with the Church of England, and commonly known as "The National Society".

About 100 years ago Parliament was asked to set up a Board of Education, but this request was unfavourably received. Queen Victoria, however, who took a great interest in this subject, was able to secure the establishment of a committee of the Privy Council to deal with education, and this body, called "The Committee of Privy Council on Education", was the predecessor of the Board of Education. It was not, however, until the year 1870 that a system of national education was established by Parliament. By the Education Act of that year "school boards" were established all over the country. These bodies were elected very much on the same lines as present-day councils. Their duties were to provide elementary education, irrespective of religion. The Church of England and other denominational bodies continued to carry on their own schools.

Towards the latter part of the nineteenth century various statutes were passed dealing with secondary and technical education, but only in a very modest way. In 1888, therefore, elementary education, so far as there was any municipal organization, was conducted by the school boards, which continued to exist until 1902.

THE PUBLIC HEALTH ACT OF 1875

A passing reference should be made to various services in connection with public health. By the Public Health Act of 1875, which incorporated and very largely extended the provisions of earlier Acts, a number of urban sanitary authorities called "local boards" were established in many parts of the country. These were concerned with such matters as the erection of new buildings, the laying out of new streets, the sanitary condition of property, the provision of means of drainage and other general health functions. Where a particular district had received a Charter of Incorporation—that is to say, was a municipal borough—it carried out the functions of the local board within its area. It might be useful to mention that local boards other than municipal corporations became in 1894 "urban district councils". In rural areas the functions of local boards were carried out by the guardians of the Union, but in the same year "rural district councils" were established and their members acted also as guardians. The borough councils and the urban and rural district councils have continued to act as sanitary authorities down to the present time, although the last of the rural districts in Middlesex became urbanized in 1934.

CONTROL OF THE POLICE FORCE

Another service calling for mention is the establishment and control of the police force. In Middlesex and certain areas adjacent to London (known as the Metropolitan Police Area) this duty has for many years been dealt with by the Government Department known as the " Home Office ". Outside the Metropolitan area, the control of the police in municipal boroughs generally devolved upon the " watch committee " of each corporation, whilst elsewhere it was in the hands of the justices, until the duty was transferred to the "standing joint committees ", of which mention will be made later.

DUTIES OF JUSTICES, 1888

Maintenance of highways was until comparatively recent times a responsibility of the parish and not the county. As time went on, increasing commercial and social progress called for better facilities, and many Local Acts of Parliament were passed authorizing the construction of roads by bodies of commissioners appointed for that purpose. Some of the important roads which served as through routes were designated " turn-pikes ". These turnpike roads were almost invariably toll roads, at any rate for a period of years after their construction, the money received in tolls being used for the upkeep, such as it was, of the roads.

The Highways Act of 1878 created a new class of highway called " main roads ", which included many of the turnpike roads. The cost of maintaining the main roads was raised partly by the justices out of the county rates and partly by the local " highway authority " out of its rates.

The Local Government Act of 1888 transferred the liability for the repair and maintenance of these main roads to the county councils, which were given the powers of highway boards.

Apart from any ancient custom in a particular locality, no person was obliged by law to make a bridge, and this statement is embodied in Magna Carta. At common law, that is, by the immemorial custom of the country, the repair of bridges forming part of a highway was generally the liability of the inhabitants of the county or of some particular division of it.

In the reign of Henry VIII, the Statute of Bridges was passed embodying the common law liability. Liability for the repair of a bridge included that of repairing the approach roads for a short distance on each side.

The responsibilities of justices in quarter sessions were accordingly extended to matters affecting county bridges,

COURT HOUSE, TOTTENHAM

and by the Statute of Henry VIII were authorized to levy rates on the inhabitants of the county to meet the cost of repairs.

The Bridges Act of 1740 gave the justices in quarter sessions power to purchase land for the purpose of building or repairing bridges. The general county liability to repair was modified by the Bridges Act of 1803, which excepted new bridges erected by private individuals if the county surveyor was dissatisfied with the work. All these powers and duties were transferred to county councils by the 1888 Act.

It should be borne in mind that not every bridge which carries a highway is a "county bridge". Certain of these bridges were made by private bodies or individuals who remain responsible for their maintenance.

By various Acts of Parliament relating to the care and maintenance of poor lunatics of unsound mind, and in particular by the Lunatic Asylums Act, 1883, the justices were required to arrange for the provisions of asylums for accommodation of such lunatics. This duty was to be exercised through a committee of visitors (afterwards called the Visiting Committee), and on which was conferred the necessary powers.

By two Statutes passed in the year 1866, certain duties were given to county justices in regard to the provision of reformatory industrial schools. To these schools were sent juveniles who had committed some minor offence or who for some other reason should be removed from the care of their parents.

The county justices also gave effect to a number of miscellaneous Statutes on subjects such as protection of wild birds, diseases of animals and the verification and inspection of weights and measures.

The justices controlled the granting of licences for music and dancing in London and Westminster, and within a radius of twenty miles thereof.

In regard to other social services which have not been particularly mentioned in the foregoing pages, it may be said that, generally speaking, and in so far as they existed at all, they were not organized on a county or municipal basis, but were dependent upon the efforts of private citizens.

The reader will now have some idea of the various authorities and persons responsible for the administration of the County of Middlesex in the year 1888.

FIRST ATTEMPTS AT REFORM

The question of a reform in county government had been considered for many years previously, and particularly with regard to the metropolitan area. The local government of London proper—that is, of the area which now forms the Administrative County of London—was considerably different from other areas. In the first place, there was the City Corporation, which then, as now, was responsible for the local government of the square mile forming the ancient City of London. There were also a number of other bodies called "vestries". These preceded what are now the metropolitan borough councils, and they carried out similar duties, although on a rather smaller scale. There was also another body, known as the "Metropolitan Board of Works", which, established in 1855, to some small extent corresponded with the present London County Council, at any rate as regards the area under its control. This body was not directly elected—that is to say, its members were not elected by the ratepayers—but were nominated by the vestries to which we have just referred. Of course it had nothing like the wide powers possessed by the present London County Council, or indeed any other

county council. The Board after some years acquired a rather unsatisfactory reputation, which perhaps was partly due to the absence of direct representatives of the ratepayers.

HOW COUNTY COUNCILS CAME TO BE ESTABLISHED

We will now consider how county councils came to be established, how they were constituted, for what parts of the county, and what duties were originally given to them by Parliament.

You are all aware of one of the great principles of the English constitution— that is to say, those who pay taxes are entitled to be represented on the governing bodies. This, of course, applies to Parliament, but is capable of application to local government administration, and that is probably one of the principal reasons why about the year 1870 consideration began to be given to the establishment of a new system of county government. The suggestion first put forward proposed a system of local government for the parish and the county; for the parish there would have been a parish board elected by the ratepayers; for the county there was contemplated a county finance board, half the members being justices of the peace, and the other half being elected by the chairmen of the various parish boards. This proposal did not meet with any cordial welcome, and was dropped. Subsequently Parliament created the Local Government Board, to which were transferred the duties of the former Poor Law Board and certain other departments, including the local government division of the Home Office. We have already referred to the establishment of sanitary authorities.

As you may know, the justices are appointed by the Crown, and to all intents and purposes they hold office for life. In so far, therefore, as the justices were administrators, they could not be said to be direct representatives of those who pay the rates (we have already mentioned this disadvantage in regard to the Metropolitan Board of Works).

Those who were considering the reform of county government next contemplated a reformation of the City Corporation, to control all London. There were many difficulties in the way, one of which was the fact that the City was intensely jealous of its rights and privileges. Another was due to the control of the police which, in the metropolitan area outside the City, is under the Home Secretary, though the City Corporation controls its own police force. One section of opinion was anxious to give London full control of its police, whilst the other wished to retain control at any rate of the Metropolitan Police Force (other than the City) under the Home Office, so nothing ensued out of this proposal.

THE LOCAL GOVERNMENT ACT, 1888

IN 1888 what became the Local Government Act of that year was considered by Parliament. It provided for the establishment of county councils, with constitutions somewhat on the lines of a council of a borough. There were, however, some slight differences. Every borough has its own mayor and a council composed of aldermen and councillors. You may not, however, be aware that whilst the councillors are elected by what are now called the " local government electors ", who are mainly the ratepayers, the aldermen are elected by the councillors, whilst the mayor is elected by the councillors and aldermen, or certain of them. The councillors hold office for three years, but the aldermen remain for six and both can be re-elected.

County councils were similarly constituted of aldermen and councillors, the councillors being directly elected by the local government electors (for which purpose each county was divided into electoral divisions), the aldermen being elected by the councillors, the proportion being one alderman for every three councillors. The aldermen and councillors of a county council hold office for six years and for three years respectively, just as in the case of a borough. There is, however, no mayor, the aldermen and councillors being required to elect a chairman, who need not necessarily be one of themselves. The chairman holds office for one year, and can be re-elected. A vice-chairman has also to be appointed, to act during the absence or incapacity of the chairman. The vice-chairman is, however, a member of the county council.

How the Number of Counties was decided.

We should now see how many county councils were created by the Act of 1888. As this Act applies to England and Wales, one would at first conclude that, as there are fifty-two counties, there must be fifty-two county councils, but this is not so. Several counties were given more than one county council. One can appreciate why Yorkshire, with its large area and its division into three Ridings, should be given three county councils, but why there should be three for Lincolnshire and two for Sussex and Suffolk is not so clear, particularly as other counties equally large, such as Lancashire, have only one.

No doubt this was due in some cases to historic boundaries and in others to the fact that the county councils were in a sense the successors to the administrative business of the justices and, as the justices of certain counties had divided themselves into regional groups for judicial and administrative purposes, the establishment of county councils followed these lines.

For that part of London administered by the Metropolitan Board of Works, the London County Council was set up in place of the Board, and here the County of Middlesex suffered a very hard fate, as we shall see. (The Board of Works

THE COUNCIL CHAMBER   MIDDLESEX GUILDHALL

had had no jurisdiction in matters concerning the administration of justice.)

How the new County of London Affected Middlesex

The Metropolitan area of the London County Council included a large part of the geographical County of Middlesex, a large part, although not so great in proportion, of the County of Surrey, and some small portions of one or two adjacent counties. These were, for administrative purposes, taken out of their geographical counties, and constituted the area of the London County Council, so that the ancient geographical County of Middlesex was thereby very considerably diminished.

For the government of the remainder of the County, the Middlesex County Council was established and in the process of time the County of Middlesex has acquired a population little, if any, less than that which the old geographical County had in 1888.

For some limited purposes, however, the old geographical county area continued to function. The High Courts of Justice, whose headquarters are at the Law Courts in the Strand, still regard Middlesex as being the old area for many purposes, and until the last few years the provisions of the Middlesex Registry Acts (which required that various documents affecting land should be registered at the Middlesex Deeds Registry) applied to deeds affecting land within the old geographical limits.

The fact that the Middlesex Guildhall is not in the area now administered by the Middlesex County Council is a relic of the days before the creation of the London County Council when the Middlesex justices functioned in the City of Westminster. Although the general rule is that the Quarter Sessions for every county shall be held within that county, the Act of 1888 recognized the association of the Middlesex Guildhall with Westminster, and enabled the Quarter Sessions to be held in future at any place in the County of London, such place being deemed, for technical purposes, to be " within the County ".

It is somewhat curious to know that at the time of the passing of the 1888 Act, the justices presiding at the Sessions for the County of Middlesex were paid. The Act abolished this, at any rate as regards the Quarter Sessions for the new administrative county, but in 1934 the Middlesex County Council obtained an Act of Parliament under which a paid chairman and deputy chairman of the Court of Quarter Sessions could and, in fact, have been appointed.

THE ADMINISTRATION OF JUSTICE

Justices of the Peace are appointed by the Crown, usually upon the recommendation of the County Advisory Committee

INTERIOR OF FIRST COURT

MIDDLESEX GUILDHALL

presided over by the Lord Lieutenant. Their names are entered upon the " Commission of the Peace "—an old parchment roll kept in the custody of the Clerk of the Peace. Generally speaking, there is one commission of the peace for each county, but many of the boroughs (outside Middlesex) have separate commissions and the borough justices have slightly different powers from the county justices.

The justices in every county were, even in early times, divided into groups for different districts, and they dealt with minor offences committed in their area. These groups are called " petty sessional divisions ". The more serious offences were not triable at petty sessions, but by the justices as a whole sitting in what is called a " Court of Quarter Sessions "—because as a rule such sessions are held quarterly. In Middlesex, as in certain other counties, the number of cases has become so great that " Quarter Sessions " are insufficient, and the courts therefore sit practically every intermediate month, such sittings being known as " Intermediate Sessions ".

There are certain more serious offences which cannot be dealt with either at petty or quarter sessions. Some of these are set out hereunder and such cases are referred to the higher Courts :—treason, murder, capital (and certain other) felonies, offences against the King's title, etc., the Government, etc., blasphemy, forgery, bigamy, libel, certain types of bribery, offences under the Official Secrets Acts, and a number of other major offences.

The justices who sat in petty sessional divisions appointed their clerk for each division, whilst the justices sitting in quarter sessions appointed a clerk to act generally for the whole county, who was given the title of " Clerk of the Peace ". The 1888 Act provided that the clerk of the peace for each county (with the exception of the new County of London) should be the clerk of the county council, and this was the position for upwards of forty years, and you will hear later of how and when this was changed.

Control of the Police

In the Metropolitan area (outside the City of London) where, as we have said, the police force was under the control of the Home Secretary, no change was

VOTE RECORDER IN COUNCIL CHAMBER

made under the 1888 Act. In other counties outside the Metropolitan Police District (which includes, in addition to the whole of the Counties of London and Middlesex, parts of Surrey and several adjacent counties) the control of the police was transferred to bodies called " standing joint committees ", composed of representatives appointed, one half by the justices at Quarter Sessions, and the other half by the county council. Even in Middlesex, although the police remained under the control of the Home Office, a " standing joint committee " was appointed with functions other than those relating to the police.

Functions of the Standing Joint Committee

These functions can be briefly referred to. It will be realized that in 1888 most counties had shire halls, guildhalls or other buildings, in which the Courts of Quarter Sessions were held and where the officers engaged in connection with county administration were accommodated. It would have been impracticable to provide that one building of this nature should be under the control of two distinct bodies—that is, the justices for judicial matters and the county council for administrative work—and in many counties it would have been unnecessary for the county council to have been required to utilize separate premises.

The standing joint committees were accordingly given charge of all matters relating to accommodation for the quarter sessions and all property to be utilized jointly (although where additional new offices are required for administrative purposes only, then the county council alone has charge of these). This is the case in the County of Middlesex, where the Guildhall is under the control of the Standing Joint Committee, but the council offices in Great George Street and Middlesex House and the local offices in various parts of the County are entirely under the control of the County Council.

Similarly the standing joint committees had the control of the officers who served both the quarter sessions and the county council. It has already been mentioned that the clerks of the peace became clerks of the county council, and it followed that the deputy clerks of the peace became deputy clerks of the county council. The standing joint committee appointed and controlled these officers until 1931; the change which then took place is referred to later.

The standing joint committees also consider the provision of petty sessional court houses and in Middlesex this committee has, since April 1938, been responsible for appointing the clerks to the justices and their assistants.

FUNCTIONS TRANSFERRED TO COUNTY COUNCILS BY THE 1888 ACT

The principal administrative business of the justices expressly transferred to county councils by the Act of 1888 comprised the following:—

(1) Matters relating to the levying of rates for county purposes.

(2) The borrowing of money. In this connection you will appreciate that where a county council or any local authority incurs expenditure of a capital nature, such as the purchase of land or the erection of buildings, it is not desirable that the cost should immediately be paid out of the rates, but that future ratepayers who will have the benefit of the expenditure should also contribute. It is the practice, therefore, with expenditure of this nature, that a loan should be raised, which is repayable with interest by instalments over a period of years, which varies according to the particular class of expenditure. In some cases, notably loans for the acquisition of land, the period allowed for repayment is 60 years, so that the cost is spread over a long time.

(3) The control of the accounts of the county and of the county treasurer.

(4) The *ownership* of shire halls, county halls, courts and premises used for the administration of justice and county buildings generally was transferred to the county councils, but this did not affect the *control* of the standing joint committees.

(5) The powers of granting licences for places intended to be used for music and dancing and the licensing of racecourses. Music and dancing licences are now regulated by a Local Act, which will be mentioned later.

(6) The licensing of premises for the public performance of stage plays.

(7) Matters relating to the provision and maintenance of asylums for pauper lunatics. These buildings have for some years been known as mental hospitals, but recently the word " mental " has been omitted from the title wherever possible so that, for example, Springfield Mental Hospital is now known as " Springfield Hospital ".

(8) Establishment and maintenance of reformatory and industrial schools provided for children and other young

MIDDLESEX HOUSE (NEW OFFICES, VAUXHALL BRIDGE ROAD)   *Entrance Hall*

people who have committed offences, where the offences are either of a minor character or the circumstances are such that whilst some punishment is necessary, it is not desirable that the offenders should be sent to prison. The powers of a county council in this respect have also been altered in recent years.

(9) The maintenance of main roads and of county bridges and their approaches.

(10) Matters affecting the county surveyor, the county treasurer and all other county officers whose salaries are paid from the county rate (except the clerk of the peace and his deputy and the clerks to justices at petty sessions).

(11) Matters relating to coroners and their districts.

(12) The division of the county into polling districts for the purposes of

Parliamentary elections, and the appointment of polling places. This does not include the division of the county into Parliamentary constituencies, which is effected only by Parliament itself.

(13) The execution of various Acts of Parliament relating to precautions against diseases of animals, protection of wild birds, supervision of weights and measures and of gas meters. Some of these duties were, however, entrusted to the larger authorities in the county.

(14) Carrying out the provisions of the Acts relating to explosives.

Other Functions Transferred to County Councils

The Act of 1888 gave the Council additional duties to those formerly transacted by the justices, of which the following are the most important. Responsibility for the maintenance of all main roads in the county (but here again the larger local authorities were entitled to carry out works of maintenance and repair and to execute improvements, such as road widening, county councils bearing the cost of maintenance and contributing towards the cost of improvement). These powers were considerably altered and extended some forty years later.

A main road may be described as a road which serves as a through connection between various parts of the country and is used mainly for this purpose, and not for ordinary town or village traffic; that is why the cost of maintenance was made a county charge. Local roads continued for many years after 1888 to be the responsibility of the local highway authorities, and are still so outside rural districts.

The county councils were also given a number of powers connected with the performance of their duties. They were empowered to buy land for these purposes, and with the consent of the Local Government Board (now the Ministry of Health) to sell land no longer required.

They were empowered to oppose Bills in Parliament, but, curiously enough, it was not until 1903 that a county council was authorized to promote a Bill.

The county councils were empowered to make bye-laws for the good rule and government of the county, but such bye-laws required confirmation by the Local Government Board (now the Ministry of Health), and could not extend to any part of the county which was comprised in a municipal borough.

County councils were also authorized to appoint medical officers of health and such other officers as were considered necessary. In later years the appointment of a county medical officer became compulsory.

In some cases, however, the powers and duties of certain smaller authorities were transferred from the borough councils or the borough justices to the county councils. These provisions are rather complicated, and it will be sufficient to say that few extended to Middlesex, in which no boroughs had separate courts of quarter sessions or separate commissions of the peace.

Other functions which county councils were required to exercise under the 1888 Act related to the alteration of the boundaries of the smaller local government areas in the county and which were not municipal boroughs, and the division of these into wards or districts. They could also convert a rural district into an urban district, and vice versa. The power of converting rural districts into urban districts has been so extensively exercised in Middlesex that since 1934 rural districts have ceased to exist.

We have now shown how county councils were established, and have given a general idea of the duties with which they were first entrusted.

ADDITIONAL POWERS GRANTED BY PARLIAMENT AFTER 1888

THE first Statute to be noticed (though afterwards replaced by provisions of the Education Act of 1921) is the Technical Instruction Act of 1889 which enabled local authorities to supply technical or manual instruction, within certain limits; the next is the Lunacy Act of 1890. This, however, was what is known as a " Consolidating Act "— that is to say, it revised and consolidated in one Act the provisions of various earlier Acts dealing with this subject, with no material addition to the existing powers.

In 1891 the Highways and Bridges Act was passed, which somewhat extended the powers of the county councils in regard to the construction and improvement of roads and bridges.

In 1892 Parliament turned its attention

CHAIRMAN'S ROSTRUM   COUNCIL CHAMBER

to the provision of small-holdings, which can best be described as " small farms ". The Act of that year enabled county councils to acquire land for the purpose of providing small-holdings for those

SMALLHOLDER'S COTTAGE, MOOR LANE, STAINES

people who desired to buy and cultivate them. It will be appreciated that it is easier and more economical for a county council to buy a large area of land, and then sell it in small portions to the small-holders, than it would have been if each small-holder had to negotiate with the landowner for his particular holding. The Act also required the county councils to set up small-holdings committees, and enabled the county councils to finance tenants desirous of purchasing their holdings.

County councils were also invested, by the Military Lands Acts, with powers to acquire land for the benefit of the " Volunteer Corps ", now the Territorial Army.

The Shops Act of the same year restricted the hours during which persons under the age of 18 might be employed in shops and county councils were authorized to appoint inspectors to ensure that the restrictions were observed.

In the following year county councils were authorized to institute proceedings against persons who sold soil fertilizers or cattle food which did not conform with the provisions of the Fertilizers and Feeding-Stuff Acts. These provisions were chiefly to prevent false information being given to the purchaser or the sale of articles containing worthless or harmful substances.

By another Statute of 1893, county councils were given certain duties in connection with the provision of isolation hospitals—that is to say, hospitals for persons suffering from infectious diseases. For this purpose, a county council could constitute a hospital district composed of one or more local areas. These powers were extended in 1901.

THE LOCAL GOVERNMENT ACT OF 1894

A Statute of importance is the Local Government Act of 1894, which, after providing for the constitution of councils of urban and rural districts, also established parish councils and parish meetings. County councils were given certain powers of supervision over parish councils, and certain duties in regard to the other authorities, notably in relation to their composition and the division of their districts into wards. In certain circumstances some of the powers of a district council could be transferred to the county council. The Act also extended the powers of the county council in regard to alteration of areas of district councils. There are no longer any parish councils in Middlesex. These provisions were altered by the Local Government Act of 1929.

THE MUSIC AND DANCING LICENCES (MIDDLESEX) ACT, 1894

In 1894, what is known as a Local Act was passed—that is to say, one which did not affect the country as a whole, but merely the County of Middlesex. By the Act, the County Council was authorized to control places used for public dancing or music or similar public entertainment, and with this object to register the premises so used and to grant licences to the proprietors.

This Statute superseded in Middlesex the provisions of a very much older one—

namely, the Disorderly Houses Act of 1751, which provided for the issue of licences by Quarter Sessions before any premises in the Cities of London or Westminster or within twenty miles thereof were kept for public dancing or other like entertainments. You will remember that the powers of Quarter Sessions to grant these licences were transferred to the County Council by the 1888 Act.

In the same year Acts of Parliament were passed which gave the County Council wider powers relating to the protection of wild birds and the prevention of diseases of animals.

Powers to Construct Light Railways, &c.

In 1896, the Council was empowered to regulate the use by locomotives of county bridges, and in the same year it was empowered to apply to the Railway Commissioners for an Order authorizing the construction of a light railway. For practical purposes there is no distinction between a light railway and a tramway, except that at that time tramways consisted almost entirely of horse-drawn vehicles. With the introduction of electric traction this distinction very soon disappeared. The County Council obtained a number of Light-Railway Orders after the passing of the Act, but it did not work the railways, leasing them to the Metropolitan Electric Tramways, which Company had constructed a tramway system with which the light railways were linked up.

With the establishment of the London Passenger Transport Board in 1930, all the Council's light railways, as well as the Company's tramways, were transferred to the Board. As you know, the light railways and tramways have now to a considerable extent been replaced by trolley buses.

The Locomotives Act of 1898 gave the County Council power to control the use of locomotives and heavily laden vehicles on highways.

MIDDLESEX COUNTY COUNCIL ACT, 1898

In this year the County Council obtained a Local Act which extended its

powers for preventing the pollution of streams. The Act also enabled the County Council to lend money to the local authorities in the County, to contribute towards the cost incurred by them in acquiring open spaces and to enter into agreements concerning main roads and highways.

The Education Act, 1899, should here be mentioned, as it provided for the establishment of the "Board of Education".

SMALL DWELLINGS ACQUISITION ACT OF 1899

This is the last Statute of the nineteenth century affecting county councils which calls for mention, and enabled county councils and other local authorities to lend money to persons desirous of buying houses for their occupation, if the value did not exceed £400. A county council was only enabled to operate the Act in those parts of the county in which the local council had not adopted it. The Act, so far as the County Council was concerned, remained a dead letter for a quarter of a century.

It will be seen that the close of the century had already shown that Parliament was ready and willing to give county councils still further powers, and in the twentieth century, as will be seen, these were increased beyond all anticipation.

THE EDUCATION ACT OF 1902

The fact that the twentieth century commenced in a rather unhappy manner with the Boer War and the death of Queen Victoria, did not restrain Parliament from adding to the duties of county councils. In fact, an Act of very great importance was passed—namely, the Education Act of 1902.

We have already mentioned that under the Local Government Act of 1888 duties in regard to education were not transferred to or conferred upon county councils, and we have also mentioned that at that time the local administration of elementary education was carried out by school

GARDEN SEAT
(HORSE BUS TYPE
OF 1890)

HORSE-DRAWN
TRAMWAY
OR LIGHT RAILWAY
1896

boards. These bodies, it will be re-membered, were responsible for what were then designated " board schools ", but which are now known as " council " or " provided schools ". These board schools, being maintained entirely out of public funds, were not concerned with denominational religious instruction.

There were a number of other schools provided by various religious authorities in which religious instruction of their respective denominations was given. These schools, although aided to some extent by the Government, received no assistance from the local authorities.

The Act abolished in the first place all

the school boards and transferred their powers and duties in regard to elementary education to the councils of counties and county boroughs. In the case, however, of county areas with any borough having a population of over 10,000 according to the census of 1901, or any urban district council with a population, according to the same census, of 20,000, the council of that borough or urban district became the authority for elementary education in that particular area, *to the exclusion of the county council.*

It will, however, be noticed that the population was reckoned according to the census of 1901, but if the borough or urban district had not the prescribed population on that date, the fact that it subsequently reached this figure did not entitle it to assume the powers of the county council. This will explain why, when at present almost every borough or urban district in Middlesex has a population exceeding the prescribed figures, the County Council continues to be responsible for elementary education in many of them. The only occasion upon which a borough or urban district could deprive a county council of its powers was where there was an extension of the borough or district boundaries, and it was ascertained that the population of the enlarged area was, according to the 1901 census, not less than the prescribed figure.

It may be mentioned that since 1931 the creation of new authorities for elementary education is restricted, so that the County Council can only lose its position in regard to elementary education when a borough or an urban district which was then an authority for elementary education extends its area by taking in a portion of the county area.

The Education Act, however, accomplished very much more than the abolition of school boards and the transfer of their powers. In regard to elementary education, the county council or the local council, as the case might be, became financially responsible for the administration of many schools which had been carried on by the authorities of various denominations.

As regards these schools which were then designated "non-provided schools", whilst the education authority became responsible for the cost of providing ordinary secular education, and the school was thrown open to any child irrespective of the religion which its parents professed, the trustees or persons who had originally established the school remained responsible for the upkeep of the buildings, and they retained the right to appoint the teachers, subject to certain control by the education authority to secure that the teachers were competent to give secular instruction. The education authority and the local council (where not the education authority) were given the right to appoint representatives on the body of managers.

The Education Act did not, however, only deal with elementary education, but contained new and very wide powers in regard to higher education. These powers were conferred upon county councils, but the councils of county boroughs and the local councils, although they might have in their areas the population before referred to, were not given these powers, so that the County Council in this respect is the education authority for the whole of the County, although it may be mentioned that the council of any non-county borough or urban district was empowered to raise a rate of 1*d.* in the pound and apply the same to appropriate purposes connected with higher education.

The powers in regard to higher education not only enabled the council concerned to build secondary and technical schools, but also placed them in a position to give financial assistance to other schools which provided education of this type. Higher education authorities were further permitted to establish colleges for the training of teachers. Every education authority, even if it had powers relating to elementary education alone, was required to set up an education committee, and for that purpose a scheme

INNER STRONGROOM IN THE GUILDHALL, where County Records are kept

had to be approved by the Board of Education, and the education authority was required to refer all matters to the education committee for consideration and report.

THE MIDWIVES ACT OF 1902

This Statute might be regarded as the first step in connection with the establishment of maternity and child welfare services, and gave county councils and the councils of county boroughs powers in regard to the supervision of midwives practising in their areas.

Promotion of Bills

The next Act to which we need refer is the County Councils (Bills in Parliament) Act of 1903, which gave general powers to county councils to promote Bills in Parliament. It will be remembered that previously county councils could only oppose Bills.

The Open Spaces Act of 1906 consolidated and extended the powers of county councils to provide and maintain open spaces, public parks, and pleasure-grounds, and to contribute towards such expenses incurred by local authorities. This last-mentioned power had, however, been possessed by the Middlesex County Council under the Local Act of 1898.

COUNTY COUNCIL OF MIDDLESEX (General Powers) ACT, 1906

Reference should also be made to the Local Act obtained by the Council in 1906, which, amongst other things, conferred extensive powers upon the Council in regard to the improvement of streams most of which have now been transferred to the catchment boards set up for the River Thames and the River Lee under the Land Drainage Act of 1930. The Act also enabled the Council to prescribe frontage lines—that is to say, lines in advance of which buildings might not be erected on the more important roads, and empowered the County Council to acquire the land in advance of the frontage line in order to effect any future road widening. The Council was also empowered to require the proprietors of employment agencies to be registered, and was given appropriate powers of control and supervision. The local authorities in the County were authorized to regulate the manufacture and sale of ice-cream in the interest of public health. The Council was also empowered to purchase the old market at Brentford Town Hall. This was acquired shortly after the passing of the Act, but the market rights were only recently abolished.

LEGISLATION FROM 1907–1909

In 1907 the Notification of Births Act was passed. This was originally what is called an " Adoptive Act "—that is to say, its provisions took effect only where the authority for the distrct concerned adopted it, and county councils were included amongst the local authorities entitled to adopt the Act. The Act required notification of the birth of every child to be sent to the medical officer of health for the area concerned. The Act did not, however, long continue to be of an adoptive nature, as in 1915 its provisions became applicable to the whole country.

In the following year the Small-Holdings and Allotments Act of 1908 considerably extended the powers which had been conferred upon county councils by the earlier Small-Holdings Act of providing small-holdings and, in particular, county councils were enabled to purchase land to lease or sell for small-holdings.

Another Statute of the same year entitled representatives of newspapers and members of the public to attend all meetings of county councils and other local authorities, including meetings of the education committees when those committees were dealing with matters which did not require to be submitted to the council for approval. As there are matters from time to time arising which, in the interests of the ratepayers, cannot well be discussed in public, the Act provided that the press and public might be excluded from meetings when the majority of the members of the council (or other bodies to which the Act applied) were of opinion that such exclusion was desirable in the public interest.

The " Children's Charter "

In 1908 the Childrens Act, which was then frequently referred to as the " Children's Charter ", was passed by Parliament. This Act covered a variety of subjects. In the first place, it dealt with what is called " infant life protection ", and its most important provisions were for notice to be given to the local authority by persons who undertook the care of young children for reward. (This did not, of course, apply to the proprietors of boarding-schools and similar establishments.)

The local authority was given the necessary powers for seeing that the premises in which such children were accommodated were kept in proper condition, and that

JUNIOR AND INFANT SCHOOL, VICARS GREEN, ALPERTON   Main Entrance

the person in whose charge they were took proper care of them. At the time of the passing of the Act, the guardians appointed under the Poor Law Act were made the local authority, but when the boards of guardians were abolished in 1930, these powers were transferred to the councils which were authorities for maternity and child welfare. The Act contained new provisions for establishment of what were then called " reformatory " or " industrial schools ", to which children and young persons who had committed offences, generally of a minor nature, could be sent, but these provisions have been largely extended by an Act of 1933.

Reference should also be made to the Old Age Pensions Act, 1908, under which persons who had attained the age of 70 and had little or no means were entitled to pensions from the State. Claims were dealt with by local pensions committees and the county councils appoint committees in those county districts with a population of less than 20,000, of which there are now very few.

Cinema Legislation

By the year 1909 cinematograph films were being exhibited to such a degree as to make laws necessary for the regulation of the buildings in which these exhibitions took place, although the cinemas then existing were probably only a tithe of those which are now found all over the country. This Act precluded the exhibition of cinematograph films of an inflammable nature unless a licence had first been obtained from the council of the county or county borough in which the building was situate, and the councils were empowered to attach conditions to the licences. These conditions were mainly directed to the prevention of fire. It was a common practice then to insert a condition in a cinematograph licence precluding the premises from being open on Sundays.

FACSIMILE OF CHARTER GRANTED BY CHARLES II FOR MARKET RIGHTS AT BRENTFORD. THE ORIGINAL IS NOW PRESERVED AT THE GUILDHALL

THE OLD MARKET PLACE, BRENTFORD—1848

A few years ago the Courts decided that the Cinematograph Act did not authorize the granting of a licence which enabled the premises to be opened on Sundays. In consequence of this decision, Parliament passed an amending Act, under which each district was enabled to decide for itself whether or not Sunday opening of cinemas should be generally permitted, and if the district favoured such opening, the Home Secretary was empowered to make an Order conferring upon the county council power to grant a general Sunday-opening licence. In a district where such an Order has not been obtained permission to open on Sundays can only be granted on rare occasions.

The First Town-Planning Act

In 1909, the first Town-Planning Act was passed, but county councils (other than London) were not made authorities for this purpose, and it was not for another twenty years that other county councils were enabled to participate in town-planning matters. The Act also dealt with provisions in regard to the housing of the working classes with which county councils other than London had no great concern, and included amongst its miscellaneous provisions the following:

Every county council was obliged to appoint a county medical officer of health, who was required to carry out such duties as might be assigned to him by the Local Government Board (now the Ministry of Health), together with such other functions as the county council might decide. Each county council was obliged to establish a public health and housing committee, to which all matters relating to public health and housing of the working classes were referred. In regard to public health, the county councils had, even then, certain responsi-

CHERTSEY ROAD   *Removal of old houses*

bilities, but in regard to housing, their functions were practically limited to acting in default of certain local authorities.

It might be noted here that in consequence of the great increase in the duties of the Middlesex County Council in regard both to public health and housing, it obtained special statutory power in 1930 enabling separate committees to be appointed for each of these two functions.

DEVELOPMENT AND ROAD IMPROVEMENTS ACT, 1909

The same year saw the passing of the Development and Road Improvements Act of 1909. This Act constituted a body known as the Development Commissioners, which was enabled to make advances for certain public purposes out of Government funds. The Commission still functions, but its activities are not very great. The Act also contained some very useful provisions in regard to road improvements. With that object, a Road Board was established, which was empowered to construct new roads and also to make advances to county councils and other highway authorities for the construction of new roads and the improvement of existing roads. The powers of the Road Board were transferred to the Minister of Transport in 1919, *but it is largely in consequence of this Act that the County Council was given the financial assistance necessary to enable the vast network of arterial roads to be constructed in this County.*

THE NATIONAL INSURANCE ACT, 1909

Another Act of the same year was the National Insurance Act, under which a system of insurance against ill-health was made compulsory for a large number of the lower-paid workers. Except as an employer of labour, the only effect of the

RE-HOUSING, CHERTSEY ROAD   ERNCROFT ESTATE

Act upon the County Council was in regard to the appointment of a County Insurance Committee. Only a small proportion of the members of this committee is appointed by the County Council, which has otherwise no concern with its functions.

Kingston Bridge

In 1911 the Middlesex and Surrey County Councils were empowered to take over Kingston Bridge from the Trustees of the Kingston Municipal Charities and to carry out works of widening and improvement to the bridge.

THE SHOPS ACT, 1912

Under the Shops Act of 1912, which was largely a Consolidating Act, further provision was made for securing half-holidays for shop assistants and for the closing of shops on the weekly half-holiday. The County Council is, how-ever, only responsible for the administration of this Act in urban districts with a population of 20,000 or less.

Legislation Affecting Mental Deficiency and Tuberculosis

It will be remembered that the County Council was already responsible for the care of lunatics, by virtue of the Local Government Act of 1888 and the Lunacy Act of 1890. The distinction between a lunatic and a mental defective is not always easy to follow, but one of the principal objects of the 1913 Act was to secure that persons who at an early age proved to be much below the ordinary mental standard should be properly trained and cared for. The Act of 1913 required the County Council to set up a mental deficiency committee, to deal with its functions under the Act, except in relation to children who, although below normal, were nevertheless not so seriously defective as to be incapable of receiving education. These excepted children were left to the education authority to deal with until they attained the age of sixteen. The Council was empowered to provide institutions for mental defectives and to deal with those mentally defective persons to whom its attention was directed by their parents or guardians, or where otherwise found necessary.

In the same year the County Council was given authority to arrange for the treatment of persons suffering from tuberculosis.

WAR-TIME LEGISLATION

In 1914 the County Council obtained an important Local Act. This Statute authorized the construction of the Great West Road, which was the first of the series of arterial roads in Middlesex. Owing to the Great War breaking out in August of that year, the construction of the road remained in abeyance during the war years. The outbreak of war naturally curtailed the output of legislation affecting local authorities, but nevertheless some additions were made to their powers and duties between 1914 and 1918.

By the Notification of Births Act, 1915, the provisions of the 1907 Act already mentioned were generally applied.

Reference may also be made to the Milk and Dairies Consolidation Act, 1915, which, as appears from its title, was largely a consolidating measure. The duties of the County Council under this Act were generally left to be defined by an Order of the Minister of Health. They principally relate to the supervision of dairies and the supply of milk suitable for human consumption. Special care is taken to prevent the sale of milk from cows suffering from tuberculosis.

Other Statutes which affected local authorities were mainly of a temporary character, to deal with emergencies arising in consequence of the War.

In the year 1918 several important Statutes were passed, the first being the Maternity and Child Welfare Act, which required local authorities to make provision for the welfare of expectant mothers and of children under the age of five years. The Authorities for the purposes of this Act were those concerned with the administration of the Notification of Births Acts, which we have already mentioned. It will be gathered from this that the County Council is only the authority for maternity and child-welfare purposes in a limited area of the County.

The Midwives Act of the same year effected considerable amendments to the Midwives Act of 1902, which we have already noted.

LEGISLATION AFFECTING THE FRANCHISE

The Representation of the People Act, 1918, although it did not directly confer duties upon the County Council, should be mentioned. It has already been explained that county councillors as well as councillors of boroughs and of urban districts are elected periodically. The persons who have the right to vote at these elections are termed "local government electors".

Prior to 1918 the franchise—that is to say, the right to vote at Parliamentary and local government elections—was regulated by different Statutes. The franchise was simplified by the 1918 Act, which in its turn was amended in 1928, so that at the present time the principal qualification for the right to vote at a local government election is residence for three months immediately preceding the qualifying date, which is the 1st June in every year.

In 1928 women were given rights of voting.

IMPORTANT LEGISLATION DURING 1919

With the termination of the War the activities of Parliament considerably increased, particularly with regard to local government affairs. This was to a large extent due to the necessity, in the first place, of making good various deficiencies in the social services, notably in the provision of housing accommodation. which

THEOBALDS PARK   ENTRANCE DRIVE

had remained at a standstill during the War years, and secondly, to provide for the change of conditions as compared with the pre-war period.

In 1919 the office of Minister of Health was established by Parliament, and the powers of the Local Government Board, which was then abolished, were transferred to him with certain other duties. In the same year a Minister of Transport was appointed, who was given various functions previously exercised by the Road Board and by the Board of Trade.

Also in the same year considerable amendments were made to the Housing and Town Planning Act of 1909. These were particularly designed to expedite the building of working-class houses, and county councils were enabled to participate by lending money to public utility societies and housing trusts, which bodies were formed with the object of providing house accommodation. The Act brought county councils in touch with town-planning, by entitling them to be furnished with particulars of the proposals of the local authorities, and they were given the right to be heard at any public inquiry.

The Act also extended the powers of county councils under the Small Dwellings Act of 1899, by enabling advances to be made in respect of properties of a market value not exceeding £800, as compared with £400 under the 1899 Act. This change was, of course, due to the very considerable increase in prices as a result of the War.

This did not exhaust the output of legislation for 1919. The Public Libraries Act of that year enabled county councils to provide libraries in those parts of a county for which the local authority had not previously adopted the 1892 Act. *It is due to this Act that the County Council has been able to provide a library system in various portions of the County.*

By the Land Settlement Facilities Act of that year, the object of which was to facilitate the settlement of demobilized soldiers on small-holdings, the powers of the County Council (given to it in 1908) to provide small-holdings were considerably increased. The Act provided for Government grants to be made towards the losses which county councils and other authorities would sustain. Before the year closed yet another Act was passed to promote the provision of working-class houses.

LEGISLATION DURING 1920–1924

In the following year the most important Statute was the Roads Act of 1920, which made the County Council responsible for the issue of licences to enable mechanically propelled vehicles to be used on the public roads and for the collection of the necessary duties. The County Council also became responsible for the registration of the motor vehicles and the allocation of the index marks.

The Blind Persons Act of 1920 required county councils to arrange the promotion of the welfare of the blind and, in particular, to give financial assistance to those who could not, by reason of their disability, earn a living.

Another Statute to which reference should be made is the Unemployment (Relief Works) Act, 1920. This Act was passed with a view to providing work for the relief of unemployment, and it enabled county councils to acquire land compulsorily, either by an Order confirmed by the Minister of Transport or, in urgent cases, with the Minister's written authority, for road construction and improvement, thus

COUNTY LIBRARY, RUISLIP   Restored 16th-century barn

108

GUNNERSBURY PARK, BRENTFORD

avoiding delay in making special application to Parliament for the necessary powers. It was in pursuance of these powers that the greater portion of the arterial roads in Middlesex was constructed by the County Council.

In 1921 the most important Statute was the Education Act which consolidated previous provisions and included power to provide meals for children attending elementary schools and medical inspection for school-children. There was also the Public Health (Tuberculosis) Act, which enabled the County Council to make arrangements for the after-care of persons who had suffered from tuberculosis.

THE MIDDLESEX COUNTY COUNCIL ACT, 1921

This important Local Act, in addition to extending the Council's powers for the protection of streams, and enabling the establishment of a Fire Insurance Fund, established the superannuation scheme for the officers and other employees of the Council.

In 1922 a Superannuation Act was passed, but it was of an adoptive nature, and local authorities had discretion as to whether or not they would avail themselves of these powers. Middlesex, having already a Local Act, did not adopt the general Act. In the same year the powers of the Council in regard to measures for the prevention of fire at cinemas were extended.

In 1923 the only Statute of importance was the Housing Act, which increased the Council's powers of making advances under the Small Dwellings Acquisition Acts, and also enabled it to make advances in respect of newly erected houses of higher value.

In the following year the only Statute of importance affecting the Council was the London Traffic Act, under which an advisory committee was formed for the Metropolitan area, and its functions were principally to advise the Minister of Transport on various matters affecting London traffic. The Middlesex County

Council was entitled to representation on that Committee.

The Housing (Financial Provisions) Act of 1924 enabled the Council to lend money to persons building or purchasing new houses up to a value of £1,500.

IMPORTANT LEGISLATION DURING 1925

In 1925 Parliamentary activities considerably increased the duties of the County Council. The Local Land Charges Act of that year required the County Council to set up a register of local land charges affecting land within the County—that is to say, particulars of restrictions and other matters enforceable by the County Council in relation to particular land, which was to be identified by reference to a map, had to be entered in the register. In the absence of such entry, the restrictions ceased to be enforceable against the purchasers of the land affected. Provision was made enabling prospective purchasers to search the register and for the issue of official search certificates.

Parliament also extended the powers of the Council in regard to the regulation of advertisements.

The Roads Improvement Act of the same year enabled the County Council to plant trees and lay out grass margins on highways, to prevent the obstruction of view at street corners, and contained a general power for the prescription of building lines.

The Public Health Act of 1925 empowered the County Council to prescribe improvement lines along main roads, these being very much the same as frontage lines. The Act also enabled the Council to provide grounds for cricket, football and other games and to let them to clubs.

THE RATING AND VALUATION ACT, 1925

A very important Act of this year was the Rating and Valuation Act. Rates are charges levied to defray the expenses incurred by county councils and local councils and in regard to other services.

Up to that time there were, generally speaking, two classes of rate: the general rate, which was levied by the local council, and the poor rate, which was levied by the guardians appointed under the Poor Law Acts. The expenses of county councils were included in the poor rate. Each rate was levied on the occupiers of all property in the area, according to the annual value of the property. This annual value was determined by a committee of the guardians called the "Assessment Committee".

It has already been explained that there

PINKHAM MANSIONS, GREAT CHERTSEY ROAD,
Re-housing

was a number of unions in nearly every county, and as there was generally a similar number of assessment committees, it was found that the standard of assessment was not uniform throughout the County. It accordingly followed that where a rate was levied for County purposes, if the standard of assessment in one part of the County was low as compared with the other part, the ratepayers in the former would bear a smaller share of the expenditure than those in the latter.

The Rating and Valuation Act entirely reformed the procedure. It provided for the constitution of assessment committees in accordance with a scheme prepared by the County Council, and entirely remodelled the procedure in regard to assessments. The County Council was required to establish a County Valuation Committee for the purpose of securing that as far as possible the standard of assessment throughout a County should be uniform. The local council was made the rating authority for its area. The Act also provided that there should be a general rate levied by each rating authority for the purpose of defraying the whole of the general expenditure within the particular area, so that the poor rate was no longer separately levied. Provision was made for an additional rate, called a " special rate ", to be levied on parts of an area where services were established, but which did not extend to the whole district.

THE MIDDLESEX COUNTY COUNCIL ACT, 1925

It has already been mentioned that the County Council was given power in 1896 to construct light railways, which had been leased to the Metropolitan Electric Tramways. This lease was about to expire, and the Act enabled the Council to grant a new lease and to construct additional light railways (although of but small length) in Acton and Finchley. It also enabled the County Council to prescribe what are known as " frontage lines " (that is to say, fence lines) and " building lines " (that is to say, the line to which the main walls of houses and other buildings may be erected) on the more important roads, with a view to facilitating future widening. The Council was empowered, in certain circumstances, to purchase the land lying between the frontage or building line and the road, in order to carry out the road improvement. The various Housing Acts were also consolidated in this year.

LEGISLATION DURING 1926–1928

The Midwives Act of 1926 extended the Council's duties in regard to the supervision of midwives, whilst the Small-Holdings and Allotments Act increased its powers in regard to the provision and letting of small-holdings. The Housing (Rural Workers) Act of the same year enabled the Council to give financial assistance in the provision of housing accommodation for rural workers, but as the County had become so largely urbanized, the powers of the Act have been little used.

The Nursing Homes and Registration Act of 1927 conferred powers upon the County Council to see that nursing homes provided proper accommodation and were properly conducted. The County Council was not, however, the authority under this Act for the whole of the County.

In order to assist trade, the Rating and Valuation (Apportionments) Act of 1928 provided for the relief from rates of properties in which various industries were carried on. The Act is largely of a technical character, so it can only be briefly noted. The Act effected the entire relief from rates of agricultural land and the relief, to an extent of three-quarters, of properties used for industrial purposes, and of railways and lands occupied by transport undertakings.

MIDDLESEX AND SURREY (Thames Bridges, &c.) ACT, 1928

The Middlesex and Surrey County Councils obtained an Act of Parliament authorizing the two Councils to construct two new bridges over the River Thames with the necessary approach roads, and to rebuild the Hampton Court Bridge. The two new bridges are known as the Twickenham and Chiswick Bridges, and carry part of the Chertsey arterial road. The old Richmond Bridge was also transferred to the two Councils.

The Act contained some amendments of the Council's Superannuation Act of 1921. The Council was also enabled, in connection with the construction of new roads, to acquire additional land for recoupment purposes—that is to say, the Council could buy more land than was required for the construction of the road, and when the work was finished, the surplus lands having a road frontage would be considerably enhanced in value so that the Council could sell these at a profit and so reduce the actual cost of the road.

THE LOCAL GOVERNMENT ACT OF 1929

1928 brought the first signs of far-reaching changes in local government, to be brought into full effect in the following year by the Local Government Act of 1929, changes greater perhaps than any contained in any Statute since the establishment of county councils in 1888. The Act dealt with a variety of matters, and a short explanation of the circumstances leading up to the more important changes may be useful.

For many years there had been a considerable increase in the population of the country, and also, notably since the War, a certain amount of migration from one area to another. Furthermore, there had been many changes in the ordinary habits of the population. Motor-cars, which were the property of only the more wealthy classes some thirty years ago, had become the property of people in almost every walk of life. There was an almost equally large increase in the use of motor transport for commercial purposes. The existing roads were not able to cope with this great increase in the traffic and the increased use and the heavier weight of the vehicles naturally resulted in greater wear and tear, thus necessitating greater expenditure on maintenance.

It was found that the changes during the last thirty years in various ways had resulted in unduly heavy burdens on the financial resources of the local authorities in certain areas, particularly rural districts. The fact that a particular district was situate between two important centres resulted in the roads in that district bearing

CHISWICK BRIDGE   GREAT CHERTSEY ROAD

TWICKENHAM BRIDGE   GREAT CHERTSEY ROAD

a very heavy volume of through traffic. It was also found that " dormitory " towns —that is to say, places in which a very large percentage of the population was engaged in occupations in towns some miles away—had to provide public services for a greater number of people than their more fortunate neighbours, which threw a greater strain upon the local authorities of the " dormitory " towns. As a result of this, it became apparent that it was desirable to spread the cost in regard to certain services over a greater area.

Another factor was the extension of the area charged with the relief of the poor.

In regard to the main highways, the Ministry of Transport had some time since instituted a system of road classification—that is to say, the roads carrying most through traffic were classified as " main traffic arteries ", and grants were made out of the Road Fund to the highway authorities responsible for their repair and improvement.

CHANGES IN ADMINISTRATION OF POOR LAW

For several years the method of Poor Law administration had been under consideration, and after the War it was decided that Boards of Guardians should be abolished and all their duties relating to the relief of the poor should be transferred to the councils of the counties or county boroughs, and the remaining functions of the guardians were to be similarly transferred, with one or two exceptions.

The Middlesex County Council therefore succeeded to these powers and duties of the guardians. In order that individual guardians so displaced might still be in a position to render public service, the Act required county councils to set up a scheme for modified local administration by means of guardians committees, on which members of the county councils were appointed in a comparatively small proportion, the remaining places being filled by persons nominated by the county council and the local councils in the particular area. These guardians committees have only very limited powers, the county councils having full financial control.

The 1929 Act extended the Public Health Act of 1875 to enable the county council to establish hospitals for the reception and treatment of sick persons and to appropriate any Poor Law establishments for this purpose. Similarly the Council was empowered to provide certain forms of assistance other than poor relief. Steps in this direction have already been made. In 1936 all the Poor Law hospitals were appropriated as public health hospitals, and assistance to blind persons and their dependants is no longer given under the Poor Law.

Highways and Town Planning

The Act provided that the County Council should be financially responsible for the maintenance and repair of all the classified roads in the County. A proportion of these roads were what is called " claimed " by the local authorities— that is, certain local councils had the right to carry out the maintenance and repair of these roads in place of the County Council. In such cases, the County Council was placed under an obligation to make appropriate contributions to the cost of road improvement, as well as to repay the cost of maintenance.

The County Council was also empowered to participate in town-planning schemes, and the Act enabled it to be made the authority responsible for the execution of any provisions in a Scheme by agreement with the local authority.

Amalgamation of Small Areas

It had been clear for some time that for administrative reasons it was not desirable that there should be a large number of small local authorities in any county. The County Council was therefore required to review the position in Middlesex and for that purpose to consider the combination of adjacent local authorities, as well as the alterations of local boundaries where an amalgamation was not thought desirable. Provision was made for further reviews, although on a more limited scale, at the end of each subsequent period of ten years. As a result of this review, the remaining rural districts in the County have disappeared, and the number of local councils has been reduced. The rapid increase in the population of the County rendered this task less extensive than might otherwise have been the case.

Miscellaneous Provisions

Amongst other miscellaneous provisions may be mentioned the powers given to county councils to secure through the local authorities the provision of adequate hospital accommodation for infectious diseases, and for securing that medical officers of health, wherever practicable, are to be restricted from private practice, in order that they may devote their whole time to public-health matters.

The Act also provided that the Minister of Health could make the local authority for elementary education the authority for maternity and child-welfare services, and to entrust to the maternity and child-welfare authorities the powers in regard to the supervision of midwives.

We have already mentioned the change in rating effected by the Act of the previous year. The Local Government Act of 1929 contained the necessary provisions to bring this change into full operation, and also provided that grants should be received from the Government towards the losses sustained by the local authorities by reason of the exemption of agricultural lands from rating and of the partial exemption of industrial and certain other properties.

Amongst the functions transferred from the guardians to the county councils by this Act should be mentioned those in regard to the registration of births, deaths and marriages, to vaccination and to infant-life protection. In regard to registration, the County Council is required to prepare a scheme for the future administration of this function. In several instances the last named functions were transferred to the local councils. The transfer of all these powers became effective on the 1st April, 1930, and, as may be imagined, the Act contained a large number of provisions incident to the change-over. It will be recollected that the transfer of the guardians' powers, in particular, involved not only the transfer of the guardians' property, but also of the large number of officers in their employment.

It might be mentioned, although it does not affect Middlesex, that rural district councils ceased to be highway authorities, and the Act laid the cost of the maintenance of roads in rural districts on the county councils in which those areas were situate.

THE BRIDGES ACT, 1929

The Bridges Act of 1929 provided for the reconstruction of what are commonly called " weak " bridges—that is to say, bridges carrying public roads over railways, canals, rivers, etc.—for the maintenance of which bridges the owner of the railway, canal, etc., was responsible. Most of these bridges, notably those over railways and canals, were constructed very many years ago, when the railway or canal concerned was made. The owners of the bridges, however, were only responsible for maintaining them in a state sufficient to take the traffic which might then have been expected. Many of such bridges were quite inadequate for present-day traffic requirements. The county councils and other highway author-

ities were therefore empowered to agree with the owner of the bridge for its transfer, with a view to appropriate improvements being effected, the owners being obliged to make an appropriate payment in respect of the burdens from which they were relieved. In case of disagreement the Minister of Transport was empowered to make an Order for the reconstruction or improvement of the bridge where necessary.

In this year the County Council also became responsible for the treatment of persons suffering from small-pox.

ACTS OF 1930

In 1930 the Lunacy and Mental Treatment Act enabled the County Council to treat persons suffering from mental illness without the necessity of their being certified as " lunatics ", and in particular such persons could become voluntary patients in the Council's mental hospitals.

The Poor Law Act of 1930 should also be mentioned, by reason of the transfer to county councils of Poor-Law functions, and it re-enacted the whole of the Poor-Law provisions in amended form.

The Land Drainage Act of 1930 provided for the institution of catchment boards for the areas of the principal rivers. Schemes have been made under this Act as a result of which the powers of the County Council in regard to streams in the northern and western portions of the County have been transferred to the Lee and Thames Catchment Boards respectively.

The Road Traffic Act of 1930 increased the County Council's powers of control of vehicles of heavy weight and of licences to drive motor vehicles.

THE MIDDLESEX COUNTY COUNCIL ACT, 1930

The County Council obtained another Local Act in this year. This provided, amongst other things, for the transfer to the Council of the Duke of Northumberland's River which traverses the west and south-west parts of the County, and enabled the Council to construct a bridge carrying the Grand Union Canal *over* the North Circular Road. The Act also conferred powers upon the local authorities in the County to regulate street trading, giving the Council extended powers in regard to employment agencies, and making certain amendments in the Council's Superannuation Act.

The Public Works Facilities Act, though a temporary Statute, is interesting, as in order to provide work for the unemployed it made it temporarily possible for local authorities to obtain power to carry out major works without promoting Bills in Parliament, provided that a high percentage of unemployed were engaged on these works.

Effect of the Financial Crisis in 1931

In the following year the financial crisis curtailed local government activities, apart from urgent works or those which coincided with the economy proposals of the Government. Other Acts which materially affected the County Council included the Local Government (Clerks) Act, 1931, under which county councils were empowered to appoint their own Clerks (which power, it will be remembered, was, under the 1888 Act, exercisable by the Standing Joint Committee, the Clerk of the Peace being also Clerk of the County Council). The Act of 1931 rendered it possible for the clerkship of the council to be held by an individual who was not Clerk of the Peace. The right to appoint the Clerk of the Peace was given to the Court of Quarter Sessions.

An Act was also passed to deal with a decision of the Courts that the opening of cinemas on Sundays was held to be illegal. This Act was of a temporary nature, and enabled local authorities which had previously allowed cinemas to open on Sundays to continue to grant licences for that purpose.

The Education Act, 1931, precluded the creation of new local authorities for elementary education. The Small-Holdings and Allotments Act was also slightly amended.

THE MIDDLESEX COUNTY COUNCIL (Sewerage) ACT, 1931

It is also necessary to refer to this very important Local Act of 1931, under which the County Council was constituted the authority for the main drainage of the western portion of the County, and proceeded with the construction of the sewage works at Mogden.

This was one of the last schemes which ranked for special Government grant from the Unemployment Grants Committee, and the County Council secured a Government grant of 75 per cent. of the cost of construction of the works on condition that 75 per cent. of the labour employed was recruited from the unemployed through the local labour exchanges.

LEGISLATION OF 1932

The financial situation did not prevent the passing of several Acts in 1932. Those which affected the County Council included the Children and Young Persons Act, which, in addition to amending the law in regard to juvenile offenders, conferred additional powers upon county councils and other authorities in regard to the employment of children, the regulation of street trading by young persons, and infant-life protection. The Act also substituted approved and certified schools for the reformatory and industrial schools to which juveniles who had been guilty of minor offences were sent.

The Town and Country Planning Act of that year made considerable amendments to the law of town-planning, but these did not materially affect the County Council, as the powers remained with the local authorities.

The temporary Act of the preceding year in regard to Sunday opening of cinemas and other places of entertainment was replaced in 1932 by the Sunday Entertainments Act. This Act enabled county councils and other authorities which had previously allowed cinemas to open regularly on Sundays to continue to grant licences for that purpose. Where,

DOLPHIN BRIDGE, UXBRIDGE, 1929   *A weak bridge now widened*

however, as was the case in Middlesex, Sunday opening had not been generally permitted, the council of a borough or urban district was able to obtain an Order from the Home Secretary under which such licences could be granted. Many of the boroughs and urban districts in Middlesex having obtained such Orders, the County Council then granted the necessary licences. The Act also provides for the allocation to charities of profits from Sunday opening.

THE LONDON PASSENGER TRANSPORT ACT, 1933

The principal Statute which affected local government in Middlesex was the London Passenger Transport Act, 1933, under which the Transport Board was established and took over the light railways belonging to the County Council.

The various Acts relating to children and young persons were consolidated, but no further change was made in the law.

In 1930 the Minister of Health had set up a committee to consider the consolidation of the various Statutes relating to local government and to the public health. This committee made its report in 1932, as a result of which the Local Government Act of 1933 was passed.

THE LOCAL GOVERNMENT ACT, 1933

This Act repealed much of the Act of 1888 relating to the constitution of county councils and to their administrative procedure, and similar provisions in other statutes dealing with borough and urban and rural district councils, so that as far as possible uniformity was established. The Act did not, however, add to or reduce the county councils' functions and duties.

The Shops Act of 1934 controlled the hours of employment of young persons in shops and certain places of business and contained provisions for the health and comfort of workers in shops and factories.

Another Act dealt with betting and lotteries, a rather complicated subject, and empowered the County Council to grant licences for betting on certain " sporting " premises. The Act declared all lotteries to be illegal, except specified small or private lotteries which are part of certain entertainments or where the sale of tickets is limited.

THE MIDDLESEX COUNTY COUNCIL ACT, 1934

This Local Act, in addition to extending the powers of the County Council in regard to highways and open spaces and consolidating the Middlesex superannuation Acts, contained provisions enabling the local authorities to control the use of movable dwellings and camping-grounds and to license massage establishments. The County Council was empowered to control boxing entertainments much in the same way as music and dancing, and to a limited extent it was enabled to prevent " ribbon development ". (This term is explained more fully under the Act of 1935.) The Act also relieved the County Council of the necessity to appoint guardians' committees and subsequently the County Council was authorized to appoint officers to deal with applications for relief.

It might be mentioned that the same Act made provision for the payment of salaries to the chairman and deputy chairman of quarter sessions. These gentlemen, who up to then had been appointed by the justices, had acted in an honorary capacity, but, as might be expected, the increasing population of the County brought about an increase in the number of offenders, so that great demands were being made on the time of the justices. A salaried chairman and deputy chairman are now appointed by the Lord Chancellor.

Effect of Unemployment Act

The Unemployment Act of 1934 was also of considerable importance, although it did not come into force until some time later. Its principal effect, so far as the County Council was concerned, was to transfer the responsibility for the maintenance of able-bodied unemployed persons from the County Council to the Unemployment Assistance Board.

RESTRICTION OF RIBBON DEVELOPMENT ACT, 1935

Under this Act the County Council is able to control the erection of houses along or adjacent to the county roads, and new means of access to such roads. This control can, under certain conditions, be extended to other roads, and may be applied to lands forming the site of new roads.

The Housing Act of 1935 curtailed the Council's powers of assisting persons desirous of purchasing their houses under the Small Dwellings Acquisition Acts or the earlier Housing Act, by limiting its powers to cases where the value of the house did not exceed £800.

Legislation Affecting Education

In 1936 a number of important Statutes were passed. Under the Education Act provision was made for the age of compulsory school attendance to be increased from fourteen to fifteen, and the Act enabled county councils and other local authorities to give financial assistance to the managers of non-provided schools, to provide education for the additional children.

Miscellaneous Legislation

The Midwives Act of the same year created a municipal midwifery service,

A CONGESTED ROAD

the County Council being required to arrange for salaried midwives to be available in certain parts of the County for which it was the authority.

It might also be mentioned that the Middlesex Deeds Registry, which had been established for over 200 years, was closed as a result of an Act of Parliament passed in 1936, and what is known as " registration of title " in connection with sales of land became compulsory in the County of Middlesex as from the 1st January, 1937.

Various amendments to the Shops Act were also made by Parliament, notably in regard to Sunday closing. The Housing Acts were consolidated and re-enacted. The provisions of the Weights and Measures Act were extended to the measuring, sale and conveyance of sand and ballast, and the Acts relating to old-age pensions were consolidated.

The Trunk Roads Act transferred from the County Council to the Minister of Transport the responsibility for the most important traffic arteries. The County Council, however, still acts as agent of the Minister in regard to the maintenance of the roads.

The Departmental Committee which we have mentioned before, made a second report in regard to the consolidation of portions of the Public Health Acts, as a result of which the Public Health Act of 1936 was passed. This was almost entirely a consolidating measure, and accordingly it made no appreciable difference in the duties of the County Council.

THE LONDON AND MIDDLESEX (Improvements, &c.) ACT, 1936

This Act authorized the construction of an extension of the Great West Road from Chiswick into London to link up with Cromwell Road in Kensington.

The Act also gave to the Standing Joint Committee the power to appoint and control the clerks to the justices and their staff.

The Physical Training and Recreation Act, 1937, conferred much greater powers on the County Council in regard to the provision of facilities for sports, recreation and physical training, and also in connection with the provision of, and assistance towards, community centres.

The Local Government Superannuation Act, 1937, required local authorities to provide for the superannuation of all administrative, professional or clerical employees.

The Air Raid Precautions Act, 1937, required the County Council, in consultation with the local councils, to prepare and submit to the Home Secretary a scheme indicating the distribution of the necessary duties for guarding against loss of life and avoidable damage by air-raids in the event of war. Under this Act, during the crisis of 1938, gas masks were supplied, trenches were dug in parks and open spaces, and other precautionary measures were taken.

The Blind Persons Act, 1938, extended the previous powers of the Council, particularly in regard to grants of financial assistance to blind persons and members of their households.

The Street Playgrounds Act enabled the County Council and other local authorities to prohibit traffic on certain classes of roads which could, with advantage, be used as playgrounds for children.

Some amendments, mainly relating to procedure before juvenile courts, were made to the Children and Young Persons Act of 1933.

The Departmental Committee on Local Government, referred to on two previous occasions, made its third report, and an Act was passed consolidating the previous laws relating to the sale of food and drugs.

THE MIDDLESEX COUNTY COUNCIL ACTS OF 1938

In this year the Council obtained two Local Acts. The Middlesex County Council (General Powers Act), 1938, gave the Council further powers in regard to the control of highways, and controlling the development of lands adjoining important roads. The powers of the Council for acquiring land to be reserved as open spaces or playing fields were extended, and further control was given over the development of land suitable for this purpose, and open spaces, towards the cost of which the Council contributed, were protected from use for other purposes. By this Act the Council will obtain complete control of the mental hospitals, taking the place of the Visiting Committee.

As there were some important differences between the Council's superannuation provisions of 1934 and those applied by the Local Government Superannuation Act of 1937, the General Powers Act of 1938 modified these differences as far as possible.

The powers of the Council to control boxing entertainments were extended to wrestling entertainments, and another provision made it illegal for persons to sell articles to children entering or leaving a school or a playground or to offer such articles by way of exchange.

The Middlesex County Council (Sewerage) Act of 1938 makes the Council responsible for the main drainage of the eastern portion of the County in addition to the western area included in the Sewerage Act of 1931. Some portions of the County, notably Acton and Willesden, still continue to have their sewage treated by other authorities, but on the other hand this new scheme for East Middlesex includes the treatment of sewage for certain districts in Essex and Hertfordshire. These immense works will, of course, take some years to complete, but the work has been in progress for some time.

It will be seen from the foregoing that the duties which the County Council has to perform are both many and varied and it is probable that Parliament will add still further to these duties in the course of the next few years.

PART THREE

COUNTY SERVICES

1. FINANCE

LITTLE can be done without money. The many activities of a county council call for very large expenditure. As an illustration, in the last financial year the Middlesex County Council spent on the rate accounts nearly £8,000,000 and on all accounts over £13,000,000. The diagrams on page 124 show where the money for the rate services came from and how it was spent. If to the County Council's expenditure is added that of the borough councils and urban district councils within the county borders, the resultant expenditure exceeds that of the governments of many independent States. The ratepayers, who chiefly find the money for these authorities, may well be anxious to ensure that their interests are adequately protected. The volume and magnitude of the financial transactions also necessitate a sound financial organisation to look after the collection and payment of money.

The Finance Department is in intimate contact with every branch of the Council's activities, and modern business methods are essential to the smooth running of the finances of the County services, consequently its development has been comparable with that of the largest commercial undertakings.

THE FINANCE COMMITTEE

County councils are required by Statute to appoint finance committees and the recommendation of the finance committee is required to enable payments to be made. This is necessary to prevent the Council committing itself to expenditure which might be beyond its means. As a protection in ensuring that every proposal involving expenditure is carefully examined, it is also laid down by Statute that no liability exceeding £50 may be incurred on the County Council's behalf until the Finance Committee has submitted an estimate of the proposed expenditure to the Council. In this way attention is directed towards all material expenditure on new policy or commitments. No county council can plead ignorance of the estimated cost of any proposal which it has approved.

In addition to its duties of examining and submitting estimates, the Finance Committee also examines and approves all accounts for payment which are submitted to it by each spending committee. It has also the important duty of making all arrangements for financing expenditure, including the raising of any necessary loans.

The chief financial officer is the County Accountant. In addition to his responsibility for the conduct of the Finance Department, one of his principal duties is to prepare, in conjunction with the other chief departmental officers, an estimate of the expenditure of each committee for the ensuing year.

It is the duty of the County Accountant to draw attention to any expenditure incurred which has not been sanctioned by the County Council, to see that the charges are proper and to warn the Finance Committee if there is any likelihood that any Committee's estimated expenditure for the year will be exceeded.

Apart from the purely clerical tasks calling for technical knowledge, the chief financial officer has administrative duties, including the organization and control of the staff of his department, and advisory duties to other executives and to committees of the Council, the importance of which cannot be exaggerated, having regard to the important part which expenditure plays in arriving at every decision of the Council.

THE ANNUAL ESTIMATES

The task of preparing the estimates commences in the autumn, and the financial year commences on 1st April and ends on 31st March. Thus, the estimates for the year 1st April 1939 to 31st March 1940 were commenced in October 1938. A comparison of the figures prepared is made with those for the current year, a revised estimate for which is made at the same time, and with the expenditure for the preceding year, the actual figures for which are by then available. The attention of each Committee is drawn to increases and decreases of expenditure and income on all principal heads of account, and probable new commitments are also considered and estimates included. Each committee is naturally anxious to pursue its programme of work, but it must at the same time be advised upon the financial effect on the county rates of each major proposal.

After the committees have approved their estimates, a sub-committee of the Finance Committee commences a detailed examination, usually with the assistance of the chairman and chief officer of each committee. This work commences in January. Alterations may, by mutual agreement, be made in the estimates, but usually agreement between the spending committees and the Finance Committee is possible before the final stages are entered upon.

At the end of January, all the figures are assembled in readiness for a meeting of the Finance Committee, at which the rates for the ensuing year will be considered upon the recommendation of the sub-committee. The Finance Committee's proposals are submitted to the County Council at its meeting in February, and it then approves or amends the recommendations. The County precept, which is dealt with below, is issued after this meeting. The occasion is one on which the chairman of the Finance Committee makes a speech outlining the proposals, and calling attention to outstanding financial matters and to particular events which have caused changes to be made since the previous year. Copies of the County Council's budget are available for inspection at all libraries in the County, together with copies of the memorandum by the chairman of the Finance Committee. These documents will enable any readers who desire to amplify their knowledge of the County finances to obtain very complete information.

Internal Audits

The collection and disbursement of money is the chief duty of the department, together with the necessary recording in such a way that accurate statements may be prepared showing the cost of each or all of the Council's activities. It is, however, necessary to keep in constant touch with all officers responsible for the payment and collection of money or money's worth (such as stocks and stores), and for this purpose many members of the staff are employed on internal audit. This name " internal audit " distinguishes the check from the " external audit " made by the Government auditors. At first sight these two duties, accounting and audit, do not appear to create many difficulties, but there are so many branches of the work and so many differing features in each branch that local government finance is by no means a simple subject.

The whole of a local authority's powers and duties is governed by Acts of Parliament. Unless expenditure is authorized by statute, it is illegal. Therefore knowledge of the extent of the Council's powers is necessary. Then in some directions, notably education, the Government shares the cost. Accordingly, the accounts must be modelled to produce the information required by the appropriate Government Department.

WHERE THE MONEY COMES FROM

County councils have three sources of revenue:—

(a) the receipts from charges of various kinds which they are allowed by law to levy;
(b) government grants;
(c) rates.

The first, charges for services, are numerous, and include contributions of patients and relatives for hospital treatment, for treatment of mental patients, and of children at dental and other clinics. A substantial revenue comes from fees for secondary schools and technical institutes, and rentals of properties and small holdings also swell the total. Local taxation licences purchased in post offices within the County for dogs, guns and armorial bearings are paid over to the County Council.

Government grants are of two kinds: those on a percentage of cost and " block grants ". Amongst the former are the Ministry of Transport contributions towards upkeep of roads, 60 per cent. of the cost of Class I roads and 50 per cent. of the cost of Class II roads. The Ministry of Agriculture assists with the cost of " small holdings ". The Board of Education pays for 50 per cent. of the cost of higher education. In the case of elementary education, there is a grant formula as a result of which the County Council receives about 40 per cent. of the cost from the Board of Education.

The block grant is a sum exceeding £40,000,000 per annum apportioned amongst the county councils and county boroughs, according to their needs as decided by a formula taking into consideration—population, rateable value per head of population, number of children under 5 years of age, unemployment, and number of persons per mile of road. Out of the county apportionment, a grant based on the population is first distributed directly to the borough, urban and rural district councils within each county, and the balance is paid to the county council. Middlesex, being a comparatively prosperous area, does not benefit greatly and, the population being so great, the grant paid to the district councils in the County entirely absorbs the County apportionment. In fact, the County Council *has to pay the Treasury the product of a penny rate* to assist in the payment of this grant.

Rates

The balance of the County Council's requirements is obtained by rates which are raised, not by a direct levy upon the ratepayers, but by a precept on each borough and district council, as rating authority, within the County. This precept requires each authority to pay to the County Council a rate of so many pence in the £ by instalments spread over the financial year. The rating authorities have to supply an estimate of the product of a 1d. rate to the County Council to enable the latter to calculate the rate required. The authorities include the County Council's precept, together with their own requirements in the demand made on the ratepayers. If you look at a rate-demand note, you will find on the back of it details which show how much is required for the principal services.

For the bulk of its services the County precept is levied over the whole County, but for some services, where certain boroughs or urban districts are responsible for the administration, what is known as a " special County rate " is levied on the authorities in the remaining areas in which the County Council administers the service. For example, Ealing Borough is entirely responsible for elementary education within its area, and it would obviously be unjust for the ratepayers of that borough to be called upon

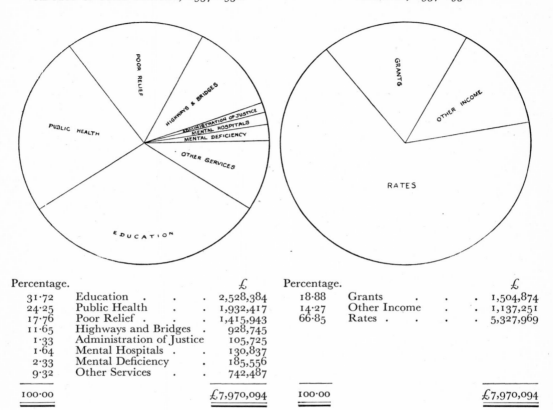

GROSS EXPENDITURE OF THE COUNCIL IN RESPECT OF RATE SERVICES, 1937–1938.

INCOME OF THE COUNCIL IN RESPECT OF RATE SERVICES, 1937–1938.

Percentage.		£
31·72	Education . . .	2,528,384
24·25	Public Health . .	1,932,417
17·76	Poor Relief . .	1,415,943
11·65	Highways and Bridges .	928,745
1·33	Administration of Justice	105,725
1·64	Mental Hospitals . .	130,837
2·33	Mental Deficiency .	185,556
9·32	Other Services . .	742,487
100·00		£7,970,094

Percentage.		£
18·88	Grants . . .	1,504,874
14·27	Other Income . .	1,137,251
66·85	Rates . . .	5,327,969
100·00		£7,970,094

to pay as well the County charge for elementary education in those areas where the County Council is responsible. Special County rates are levied for—

Elementary Education.
Registration of Electors.
Maternity and Child Welfare.
Midwives Act.
Public Libraries.
West Middlesex Drainage Scheme.
East Middlesex Drainage Scheme.

} Services which are administered by the County Council in parts of the administrative County

The everyday expenditure on the upkeep of hospitals, schools and roads, salaries and wages and on the many other services is known as revenue expenditure, as distinct from capital expenditure.

Briefly, the building of a new school or any other project resulting in an acquisition of lasting value, with which the local authority's service is carried on, is capital expenditure. In most cases it would be too heavy to charge on the rates in the same way as revenue expenditure, and borrowings are therefore made by stock issues or mortgages, although there is nothing to prevent the County Council from charging to revenue this type of expenditure, and, in fact, every year the product of a 2d. rate is used to finance innumerable small capital works. Loans must be repaid according to the terms of issue.

In the revenue account of a local authority will be found charges for interest on the loans, and also charges for annual repayments of principal or, alternatively, provision for repayment in the form of sinking-fund contributions. Whilst a limited company raising its capital by means of shares has no obligation to repay to its subscribers, every penny of money raised by a local authority must be repaid in a fixed time. The provision made in the revenue account is based roughly on the life of the asset, but, except in rare cases, the maximum period is 60 years.

Thus, loans for purchasing land for the school sites will be repaid in 60 years, for the buildings in 50 years and for the initial furnishing equipment in 15 years. These periods are generally fixed by the Ministry of Health, which issues a sanction for every loan (except where the sanction is given by a Local Act of Parliament obtained by the County Council). The Ministry thus exercises considerable control over the borrowing powers of local authorities, and can refuse sanction.

The good management of loans is an important phase of the work of the Finance Committee and its chief officer, in connection with which knowledge of the money market and public finance is necessary.

2. EDUCATION

IN order clearly to understand the position and conditions of education before this service was administered by the County Council through its Education Committee, it is necessary to give a very brief historical outline leading up to that period.

THE EDUCATION ACT OF 1870

The Education Act of 1870 made the provision of elementary education necessary for all those for whom efficient and suitable provision did not already exist, and although reference is made to this in connection with the local government legislation, it may be helpful to refer to the position here in rather more detail.

Where schools in sufficient number and size were not already provided, or were not at once provided by voluntary agencies, the deficiency had to be met by a "school board" elected for that purpose. The boards had to build their own schools, and were entitled to receive Government grants in the same way as voluntary schools.

The boards were empowered to meet their charges by issuing a demand on the rating authorities, and were also given power to enforce attendance.

Voluntary schools remained an integral part of primary education, and board schools were only erected in districts where voluntary effort was insufficient.

This Act of 1870 resulted in the steady provision of schools, partly by the school boards and partly by the voluntary managers, and by 1900 there were 2545 such boards in existence.

Education in Middlesex

The Middlesex County Council passed its first resolution dealing with technical education in January 1891 and in 1895 it purchased the first of its polytechnics.

SUBSEQUENT LEGISLATION

In the year 1899 Parliament passed an Act establishing the Board of Education, charged with the supervision of matters relating to education in England and Wales, and in 1902 the Education Act (referred to in detail on p. 97) was passed, abolishing the school boards and placing the responsibility for education upon councils elected for the general purposes of local government. This made it possible for non-county boroughs with a population of 10,000 or over at the 1901 Census, and urban districts with a population of 20,000 at the same date, to become authorities for elementary education only. The Act also empowered the local education authorities for higher education to provide and maintain secondary schools.

In January 1901 the Middlesex County Council provided its first county secondary school by opening a co-educational school at Tottenham Polytechnic.

In 1904 the Board of Education issued secondary school regulations defining the scope and grade of such schools, and standards were set for the building of new schools and the improvement of existing ones.

Two further Acts of Parliament were subsequently passed: the Act of 1918, which required local education authorities to provide for the progressive development and comprehensive organization of education in their areas, and the Education Act of 1921, which consolidated existing Acts concerning education.

DEVELOPMENT OF EDUCATION SERVICES

The Education Committee of the Middlesex County Council was constituted on 5th March, 1903, under a scheme made under section 17 of the Education Act, 1902, and has therefore been in existence for about thirty-six years. The following statistics are interesting as showing the development of the education services:

Elementary Schools

	Number of school departments (provided and non-provided).	Number of pupils on roll.
1904 . .	158	32,972
1938 . .	251	83,042

In comparing the totals for 1904 and 1938, it should be remembered: (1) that a large number of elementary schools situated in the former urban districts of Brentford, Greenford and Hanwell, and the parishes of Northolt and Edgware, which were maintained by the County Council in 1904, were not so maintained in 1938, having been transferred to the control of the appropriate education authorities in the County as a result of administrative changes, and (2) that a number of the older schools have been closed, since the buildings were no longer regarded as suitable for further use.

Secondary Schools

	Number of secondary schools provided or aided by the County Council.	Number of pupils in attendance.
1904 .	9	1,263
1938 .	51	25,089

Technical Education

	Number of technical and art schools.	Approximate total number of students at these technical and art schools and at evening class centres.
1902 . .	6	9,941
1938 . .	13	39,210

Increase in Population

At the 1931 Census, which covered the period 1921–1931, the County of Middlesex showed the highest rate of increase of population of any of the administrative counties of England and Wales. Since 1931 the increase has continued at an even greater rate. In consequence of the influx of population, large tracts of land formerly used for agricultural purposes have been "built up" with houses, small towns like Harrow and Uxbridge have grown into urban communities of considerable size, quiet villages have to all intents and purposes lost their identity and become merged into one huge township, extending with almost unbroken continuity from Enfield in the north-east to Uxbridge in the west and Staines in the south-west.

One of the first social needs of a new community is schools for its children, and

TWICKENHAM TECHNICAL INSTITUTE AND ART SCHOOL   *Front Elevation*

it has been one of the statutory duties of the County Council to supply this need. The County Council is the local education authority for higher education throughout the administrative county, and for elementary education in fourteen out of the twenty-six county districts into which the County is divided for the purposes of local government. The County Council accordingly has the responsibility of providing and maintaining secondary, technical, commercial and art schools throughout the County, and of making arrangements for the elementary education of the children in an area which contains more than one-third of the population of the whole County.

Elementary Education

On the 31st March, 1928, the number of children in the County Council's elementary schools was 37,384. Ten years later this number had grown to 81,000, an increase of 44,400 and an average increase of 4500 a year. Within a decade the County Council has been called upon to provide a complete new system of elementary schools for a child population which is equal to that of towns of the size of Leicester or Stoke-on-Trent, and at the same time to maintain and improve a very large number of existing elementary schools.

This has involved the purchase and reconditioning of a large acreage of land for use as sites for the new schools and as playing-fields for the scholars, the planning, erection, furnishing, equipping and staffing of a large number of schools, clinics and other buildings required for the various social services which now form part of the public system of education.

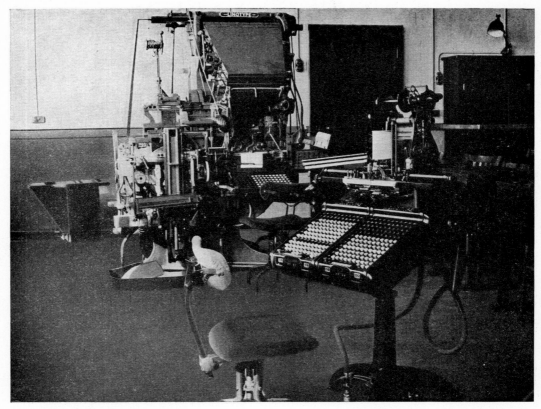

MONOTYPE AND LINOTYPE ROOM   TWICKENHAM TECHNICAL INSTITUTE

All these tasks have been performed under considerable pressure, due to the simultaneous demand for other services and to the rapidity with which the housing developments have been proceeding. Housing estates have been completed and occupied at a faster rate than the County Council could build its permanent schools, and, to tide over the emergency, the Council has been obliged to erect wooden buildings or to rent church halls and similar accommodation for use as temporary schools, until the new schools have been erected.

Higher Education

Simultaneously with these activities in the sphere of elementary education, the County Council has undertaken a heavy programme of school-building for the purpose of extending and improving the system of higher education. Many existing secondary schools have been improved and enlarged, and a number of new secondary schools have been built in different parts of the County. Within the last nine years there has been an increase of over 4000 in the number of pupils attending secondary schools maintained and aided by the County Council.

The industrial development of Middlesex has kept pace with the increase in the population. Before the Great War, Middlesex was mainly a " dormitory " county (that is to say the resident population were, to a great extent, employed in neighbouring counties), the only industries of wide distribution were agriculture and

A METALWORK CLASS   *TWICKENHAM TECHNICAL INSTITUTE*

horticulture. To-day, Middlesex is an important centre of manufacturing industry and commerce, and under these conditions the public system of technical education has acquired an added importance.

The County Council's programme of school-building contemplates the provision of well-equipped technical colleges in all the important industrial centres in the County. These have already been provided in Acton, Chiswick, Ealing, Enfield, Harrow, Southall, Tottenham, Twickenham and Willesden. Extensions are now in course of erection at Acton, Chiswick, Willesden and Tottenham; new institutes are being built at Enfield and Hendon, and other institutes are to be built in Enfield, Greenford, Harrow, Kingsbury, Southgate, Staines and Uxbridge.

Capital Expenditure

The County Council's capital expenditure on sites, buildings and equipment during some of the periods under review gives an indication of the progress made in the provision of education buildings.

During five years ending 31st March, 1914

Elementary schools	£139,198
Secondary schools	195,736
Technical schools	20,653
Total	£355,587

During five years ending 31st March, 1937

Elementary schools	£978,954
Secondary schools	510,864
Technical schools	257,168
Total	£1,746,986

There is a constant need for more buildings and education facilities, and these are being provided by the County Council as speedily as possible.

I

A DRESSMAKING CLASS   TWICKENHAM TECHNICAL INSTITUTE

DRAWING FROM THE ANTIQUE   TWICKENHAM TECHNICAL INSTITUTE

TYPES OF SCHOOL BUILDINGS

An examination of the plans of schools and institutes of different periods shows the progress made and the following examples are given:

Elementary Schools—

Shepperton Council School was erected in 1906 to accommodate 430 scholars, in-

full extent, as it forms a means of access from one room to another, and also to the cloakrooms, lavatories and playground.

No staff-rooms were provided or rooms for manual training or cookery. The latter accommodation was provided in special buildings, called Centres.

Bacon Lane Council School is a Senior

THE GREEN SCHOOL, ISLEWORTH

Secondary School for Girls

cluding 160 infants, and is a typical example of school buildings provided at that time.

The classrooms, which were designed to accommodate 50 or 60 children each, are planned around a central assembly hall; but the hall is both a place of assembly and a corridor to the various classrooms grouped around it, and it receives light from the roof light overhead, and from these adjoining classrooms.

The main entrances also lead directly to the assembly hall by means of short corridors, adjoining which are the cloak-rooms.

This type of plan, whilst inexpensive in execution, has serious disadvantages; classrooms are not kept quiet, and it is difficult to utilize the assembly hall to its

School shortly to be erected with accom-modation for 560 boys and 560 girls.

In addition to the classrooms, special rooms are provided for geography, wood-work, metalwork, cookery, laundry, housecraft, science, crafts and art.

Both the boys and girls are provided with a library and gymnasium, the latter having changing-rooms with adjoining shower-baths.

Adequate staff accommodation is pro-vided, and all sanitary offices can be approached under cover, although separ-ated from the school buildings proper.

An assembly hall is provided for each sex, each hall is provided with a large stage, and the two halls can be combined into one large one on special occasions.

The planning is so arranged as to allow

EVELYN'S SCHOOL, YIEWSLEY　　　　　　　　　　　　　*Senior Boys*

every room the most suitable aspect for its particular purpose and its most convenient position in the building; such rooms as manual training, gymnasium and assembly halls being so arranged as to prevent, as far as possible, the sound of the classes, etc., from penetrating to the quieter rooms.

Secondary Schools—

The Green School, Isleworth, was erected in 1905 as a secondary school for girls, with accommodation for 100 scholars.

Here again the classrooms were grouped around a central assembly hall. Two staff-rooms were provided. The classrooms are planned to accommodate 25 scholars each, and a science-room also is reached from the hall.

The Green School, as now existing, was brought up to date in 1932, with accommodation for 330 scholars.

The original classrooms and science room are still retained, the original cloakrooms and lavatories have been remodelled and further accommodation has

STANBURN COUNCIL SCHOOL, LITTLE STANMORE　　　　　　　　*Junior Mixed*

THE GREEN SCHOOL, ISLEWORTH
Assembly Hall

been provided at the rear of the old school, approached by means of a corridor from the old assembly hall.

In addition to six additional classrooms for 30 scholars each, one of which can be used as a stage in conjunction with the assembly hall, there are rooms for botany, cookery, art, library, adequate staff rooms and greatly increased lavatory and cloak-room accommodation.

All rooms are approached from corridors around a quadrangle and the various rooms are placed with proper aspect for their uses, that is to say, the art and cookery rooms have a north-west aspect and classrooms face to the south-east or south-west.

Technical Institutes and Polytechnics

The Tottenham Polytechnic was acquired in 1896, and enlarged in 1910 by a two-storied wing on the south boundary of the site. The north side was occupied by Magistrates' Courts.

The Polytechnic as remodelled involved the demolition of the older parts of the building, together with the Magistrates' Courts, leaving only that portion of the building erected in 1908, consisting of assembly hall, six classrooms, two laboratories and a cookery-room. These rooms are retained for their present purposes, excepting two classrooms on the ground floor, which have been converted into an electrical installation workshop.

The building as remodelled provides accommodation for 200 boys in a junior technical school of building, 150 boys and girls in a junior school of commerce and part-time day and evening classes for 1500 students in engineering, building, commerce, domestic science and art courses.

PINNER COUNTY SCHOOL   Assembly Hall

The preceding paragraphs give some idea of the size, extent and detailed planning and arrangement of the various types of buildings about 30 years ago and at the present time.

General

The foregoing are examples of a secondary school and a technical institute which have been enlarged.

In cases, however, where the architect is not restricted by existing buildings or restricted site, entirely new schools have been erected as, for example, the Pinner County School and the Twickenham Technical Institute and Art School.

Pinner County School is designed to accommodate 508 boys and girls, and was formally opened in November 1937. The accommodation includes an assembly (and dining) hall, 14 classrooms, 4 laboratories, domestic science, art, manual train-ing and lecture rooms and a library, in addition to the usual general staff and cloakroom accommodation, etc.

Twickenham Technical Institute and Art School was opened in April 1938. It provides accommodation for students, and includes a junior technical school of engineering for boys, evening instruction in engineering, carpentry, joinery, wood-working machinery, plumbing, electrical installation, engineering workshop practice and welding. The school of art at Chiswick Polytechnic was transferred to these buildings, and includes a course for employees of the printing trade, drawing and design, life-drawing, antique silver-smithing, jewellery, fashion drawing, interior decoration, commercial design and advertising, cabinet making, painting and decorating, dressmaking, etc., leather-work, fabric painting, modelling and window and counter display.

TWICKENHAM TECHNICAL INSTITUTE AND ART SCHOOL   *Engineering Workshop*

The building is modern in character and planned round three quadrangles. This gives freedom of circulation and the maximum of light and air to all rooms. The workshops, laboratories and studios are equipped with the most modern machines and apparatus.

Apart from the changes in planning, the architectural treatment of school buildings has altered considerably during recent years.

In contrast to these extensive and costly modern buildings, so splendidly equipped, it is interesting to note that the County Council has for some years with the approval of the Board of Education maintained a small elementary school, consisting of a single class, for children of bargees

TWICKENHAM TECHNICAL INSTITUTE AND ART SCHOOL   *Lithography Room : School of Art*

PINNER COUNTY SCHOOL   *Secondary school for boys and girls*

working on the Grand Union Canal. The " school " is, in fact, a barge, provided by the Grand Union Canal Carrying Company, and moored in the Canal at West Drayton.

COST OF SCHOOL BUILDINGS

The financial crisis in 1931 made economy in design most necessary, and the approval of the Board of Education to a reduction of one foot in the height of teaching rooms assisted in this direction.

Such a reduction in height, however, made it necessary to extend the length of window-spaces, tending to make the whole of the outer walls of classrooms glazed areas with narrow supporting pillars in reinforced concrete.

A new type of design was evolved, which is of a modernist character consisting of a reinforced concrete skeleton structure with floors, roofs and staircases in a similar material, filled in externally with a minimum amount of brick cavity walling.

The general result, apart from a reduction in cost, was greatly improved lighting and ventilation, and greater protection from the risk of fire.

In most cases the old pitched roofs in timber, tile or slate have been discarded, and replaced by flat concrete roofs finished with asphalte and terminating with projecting eaves or parapets.

It is generally agreed that the present type of building is ideal for its purpose, although some people regret the passing of the previous styles, which were of a more domestic character.

The cost of elementary schools in the period between 1906 and 1910 varied from £11 to £14 per place, Shepperton Council School, with accommodation for 430 scholars, costing approximately £4746.

Bacon Lane Senior Council School, which is referred to in detail on p. 131, will cost about £78,210, or £69 per place.

The Green School, Isleworth, referred to on p. 132, cost about £4000, or £40 per place. The cost of the additions recently erected at this school was about £23,000, or £100 per place.

Pinner County School, referred to on p. 134, cost approximately £48,619.

It is not possible to calculate this cost in respect of polytechnics or technical institutes; but the contract price for the alterations and additions now being carried out at *Tottenham Polytechnic* is about £65,312, and that for the *Twickenham Technical Institute* was about £93,018.

CONDITIONS OF ADMISSION TO COUNTY SECONDARY SCHOOLS

Pupils are admitted to secondary schools usually when between 11 and 12 years of age. Each year the Education Committee conducts a general entrance examination for all children of this age whose parents desire their admission to secondary schools, and who usually are recommended as suitable candidates for a secondary school course by the heads of the schools which they are attending. The factors which are taken into account in determining the suitability of candidates for a secondary school course are:—

(1) The marks gained by them as a result of the written tests at the examination.
(2) The marks gained in any other test they may have been required to undergo.
(3) Their school record.

An intelligence test is also given as an additional check on the results, and has the effect of calling attention to candidates whose marks in the written examination would have disqualified them, but who, on further investigation, sometimes are considered worthy of admission to a secondary school.

Places in secondary schools are offered to candidates who qualify as a result of these tests, and steps are then taken to determine the amount of the fees payable by the parents. The standard fee in Middlesex is £15 15s. per annum, inclusive of games fee, books, stationery and apparatus. All Middlesex pupils admitted to secondary schools are regarded as special pupils, i.e., holders of special places, and are eligible to apply for admission with total or partial remission of fees. When, after investigation, it is found that the financial circumstances of the parents do not warrant a remission or reduction of fees, full fees are payable. The parents' "capacity to pay" is determined in the light of a scale which takes all reasonable factors into account, including expenditure of an unusual character. During the last three years the scale has been reviewed with the approval of the Board of Education, and, as a result, a larger number of pupils has been receiving financial assistance.

In 1933, 14,826 pupils in secondary

LADY MARGARET SCHOOL, SOUTHALL   *Junior Mixed and Infants*

schools were receiving assistance by way of total or partial remission of fees; in October 1938, the number had increased to a total of 20,404.

At the general entrance examination held in the Spring, 1938, the number of candidates who took the examination was 14,401 and 5038 of these reached the qualifying standard. Of these, 4572 were admitted to a secondary school in September 1938. The large majority of these went to Middlesex secondary schools, but approximately 334 were sent to out-county schools, and the County Council is paying the additional out-county fee in respect of them. Whether the qualified candidates went to Middlesex or non-

(*Continued on page* 140)

The following table shows the cost of assistance granted by way of maintenance allowances and remission of fees at schools and institutions under the regulations for higher education :—

Nature of Assistance.	1934–1935 Actual.	1937–1938 Actual.	1938–1939 Estimated.
	£	£	£
Loss of Income by way of total or partial remission of Tuition Fees—			
Maintained Secondary Schools	137,679	180,292	189,265
Maintained Senior Technical, Junior Technical, Art and Commercial Schools and Evening Centres	7,291	13,500	15,524
Amounts payable to Governors of Maintained Schools in respect of total remission of Games Fees—			
Secondary Schools	6,046	7,780	8,340
Junior Technical and Commercial Schools	553	650	750
Amounts payable to parents or school authorities in respect of in-County fees (or part thereof) of Middlesex Pupils at out-County Schools—			
Secondary	6,003	17,153	20,140
Technical	298	516	530
Amounts payable to Governors of Non-Maintained Secondary Schools in respect of total or partial remission of fees of Middlesex pupils—			
Middlesex Endowed Schools	17,097	20,905	22,935
Middlesex Aided Schools	11,816	17,595	18,709
Amounts payable for tuition fees and maintenance allowances as detailed under heading " Aid to Students "—			
Tuition Fees—Secondary Schools	7,270	11,182	13,035
Maintenance Allowances—			
Universities, etc.	9,607	14,733	16,980
Secondary Schools	34,147	48,216	64,483
Technical Schools	7,981	14,926	17,265
Schools for Blind, Deaf, etc.	4,672	6,174	6,503
Summary.	250,460	353,622	394,459
Secondary Education	220,058	303,123	336,907
Technical Education	16,123	29,592	34,069
University Education	9,607	14,733	16,980
Schools for Blind, Deaf, etc.	4,672	6,174	6,503
	250,460	353,622	394,459

In addition the County Council assists approved students by granting loans free of interest. The total amount in the hands of students at the 31st March, 1934, was £29,340, and the estimated amount at 31st March, 1939, is £32,584.

AID TO STUDENTS

Summary of Awards granted by the Committee for the years 1934–1938

Nature of Award.	1934.	1935.	1936.	1937.	1938.
Special Places at Secondary Schools—Total remission of fees	2,627	2,755	2,697	2,521	3,264
Special Places at Secondary Schools—Partial remission of fees	1,029	1,088	1,089	1,087	833
Intermediate Awards at Secondary Schools .	212	423	510	484	610
Junior Awards at Secondary Schools . .	1,251	1,479	1,564	1,788	*
Senior County Awards . . .	74	91	93	89	116
Blind, etc., Students	25	28	38	33	51
Senior Technical Awards	25	33	50	65	90
Intermediate Technical and Commercial Awards *	—	—	—	66	72
Junior Technical Awards . . .	530	529	523	530	590
Junior Commercial Awards . . .	218	196	244	252	276
Art Awards	110	99	100	120	122
Sea Training Awards	2	2	2	1	—

* Junior Awards as such were discontinued after 1937. The number of awards current at October 1938, granted under Scale 2, shows an approximate increase of 30 per cent. on the 1937 Junior Award figure.

Total number of Awards current on the 1st *October in each of the years* 1934–1938

Nature of Award.	1934.	1935.	1936.	1937.	1938.
At Secondary Schools	16,084	17,594	18,672	19,314	20,404
At Universities	225	223	245	263	292
At Blind and Deaf Institutes . . .	60	62	70	76	111
Senior Technical Awards . . .	42	53	84	105	146
Intermediate Technical and Commercial Awards *	—	—	—	109	116
Junior Technical Awards . . .	1,025	1,239	1,200	1,207	1,326
Junior Commercial Awards . . .	374	411	460	503	574
Art Awards	260	299	300	307	314
Sea Training Awards	4	3	3	2	—

* This allocation was first made in 1937. The awards are tenable only at Middlesex Institutes. They were formerly included in Senior Technical Awards.

ADMISSIONS TO SECONDARY SCHOOLS

Autumn Term.	Total number of Admissions.	No. of Pupils Paying Full Fees.	No. of Pupils Paying Part Fees.	No. of Pupils Holding Free Places.	Percentage of		
					Pupils Paying Full Fees.	Pupils Paying Part Fees.	Pupils Holding Free Places.
1934 . .	4,532	1,230	916	2,386	27·1	20·2	52·6
1935 . .	4,419	1,003	937	2,479	22·7	21·2	56·1
1936 . .	4,423	1,041	928	2,454	23·5	21·0	55·5
1937 . .	4,385	969	993	2,423	22·1	22·6	55·3
1938 . .	4,456	776	690	2,990	17·4	15·5	67·1

Middlesex secondary schools, consideration was given to their need for assistance in regard to the tuition fees payable and to their expenses for travelling and school dinners. The majority of those who qualified but did not proceed to a secondary school were not desirous of following up the offer of a secondary school place made by the Education Committee.

COUNTY LIBRARIES

The County Library Service was inaugurated in 1922. As the authority under the Public Libraries Act, 1919, the County Council is responsible for the library service in the whole of its elementary education area, with the exception of the Boroughs of Southall and Twickenham, the Councils of which had become library authorities under earlier legislation.

The County Library system now operates through the following centres:—

Branch Libraries	9
Adult Library Centres . . .	65
Institute Centres	17
Total	91

The book stocks at these centres are changed at frequent and regular intervals, thereby ensuring a varied selection of books. Every effort is made to satisfy the requirements of individual borrowers, and during last year 13,175 volumes were supplied by headquarters in response to special requests. An endeavour is also made to stimulate the reading of books, and to guide the reader in his choice of reading matter. Exhibitions of books at the libraries, the production of a comprehensive series of subject catalogues and the publication of a library magazine entitled *Books for All* have had the desired effect: the percentage of the issue of non-fiction during 1937–1938 was 20·5, as compared with 17·5 the previous year.

That the service has been appreciated by the public may be assumed from the steady annual increase in the total stock, borrowers registered, and the books borrowed, as shown at top of next column.

	Stock.	Borrowers Registered.	Books Issued.
1933–1934	188,950	84,894	1,655,614
1934–1935	190,206	90,351	1,947,525
1935–1936	209,942	104,266	2,270,504
1936–1937	239,717	115,688	2,091,379
1937–1938	267,940	119,046	2,339,164

To meet the public demand, the Council has embarked upon a programme of library development which when completed will provide a full-time library service in every district for which the County Council is the library authority. Full-time branch libraries have now been established at Ruislip (2), Hayes, Yiewsley, Hillingdon, Southgate, Kenton, Friern Barnet and Uxbridge. In the near future, further libraries will be opened in Harrow and Potters Bar.

Some 210 school departments are now supplied with books on a basis in proportion to school population, ensuring that all children between the ages of 7 and 15 have an adequate supply of books, and that each school has in its possession books of permanent value. Visits of children of school-leaving age from senior elementary schools are maintained at branch libraries, and the library staff arrange talks and story hours for the children attending the libraries. The County Library also administers the distribution of gramophone records and lantern slides for use in schools.

For some years an experimental hospital library service has been carried out at the Hillingdon County Hospital. The experiment has achieved so much success that the County Council has approved the inauguration of a library service at its public health and public assistance establishments. Centres have also been established at several of the Council's mental hospitals.

It will be appreciated that the County Library Service has made considerable progress during the past years, and there is no doubt that the completion of its building programme will produce even better results in the future.

3. PUBLIC HEALTH

A VERY important branch of the work undertaken by the County Council is concerned with the health of the people of Middlesex. Some of the services are intended to prevent the occurrence of disease, whilst others provide medical and nursing care for those who have become ill. This work is undertaken by the Public Health Department.

MATERNITY AND CHILD WELFARE

The welfare of a nation depends very largely indeed upon the health of its children, so let us first consider what the County Council has done and is doing to make the children of Middlesex as healthy as it is possible for them to be. At the beginning of the present century, of every 1000 children who were born in Middlesex, 131 died before they were one year old. In 1937 this figure had been reduced to 46. The deaths within the first year of life, therefore, have been reduced by approximately two-thirds, and this represents a saving of child-life in Middlesex alone of something like 2500 children every year.

There are a number of ways in which this great improvement has been brought about, but one of the most important is undoubtedly the maternity and child-welfare service which for many years has been carried out by the County Council and by the borough and district councils in Middlesex. Welfare centres have been set up in convenient places throughout the County, where young mothers get the benefit of skilled advice from doctors on the best ways of feeding, clothing and generally caring for their babies. Milk and other foods are supplied free of charge to those who are not able to afford to buy them. Childish ailments receive suitable advice and treatment at an early stage, before they are likely to have done any serious harm, and as the child grows up, any necessary treatment for its eyes and teeth is given.

Meanwhile, the mother's health is also being attended to. In connection with the maternity and child-welfare service the County Council employs a staff of trained nurses who are called "health visitors", and who visit young children in their homes, and give mothers valuable advice on the way to maintain their children's health. These nurses also keep a friendly and watchful eye upon those unfortunate children who, having lost their parents, are cared for in foster homes.

THE SCHOOL MEDICAL SERVICES

Every child attending an elementary school is seen by the school doctor at least four times during its school life—that is to say, at the age of five or six, when it first goes to school, at the age of seven, at the age of ten, and finally just before leaving school. At the time of inspection the doctor wishes to assure himself that every boy or girl he sees is healthy and strong, but if he finds any defect needing treatment, he advises the mother as to how the trouble should best be attended to.

The County Council itself arranges for a good deal of medical treatment for sick children under its care. Small ailments, such as cuts, scratches, chilblains, skin troubles, etc., receive attention at the school clinics. Defective sight is attended to here, and glasses are supplied. Arrangements are made for children who need their tonsils and adenoids removed to go into hospital, and particular attention is given to the treatment of conditions which are likely to lead to crippling deformities. Blind, deaf, epileptic and physically or mentally defective children also receive treatment, supervision and special education.

HAREFIELD SANATORIUM   VIEW FROM THE AIR

The care of the teeth of young people is a very important matter. A school dentist visits every elementary school once a year, and endeavours to see every boy or girl in attendance. The dentist not only advises where treatment is necessary, but is willing to carry it out at the school clinic. During 1937 a total of nearly 24,000 children received dental treatment at the County Council's clinics.

Milk is a particularly valuable food for young people, and very careful experiments have shown that healthy children who, in addition to their ordinary meals, drink a daily allowance of milk, grow taller and heavier, and are less likely to catch colds and other illnesses, than children who do not drink milk. In all the Council's schools ar-

rangements exist for milk to be supplied to children, and those whom the doctor thinks should have it but whose parents are not in a position to pay for it, can receive it free of charge.

It may also be mentioned that officers of the County Council periodically visit farms where " tuberculin-tested " milk and " accredited " milk are produced (these are the highest grades of raw milk on the market), in order to see that the supply is clean and wholesome.

ARRANGEMENTS FOR VACCINATION

In vaccination, medical science has discovered an agency which, when properly applied, is a complete protection against small-pox, and this terrible disease, which at one time ravaged whole continents, has been brought under control almost entirely by this discovery. Arrangements for giving the public the benefit of vaccination are in the hands of the County Council, which appoints many doctors as public vaccinators to give this service free of charge to the people of Middlesex. It is a little unfortunate that vaccination is not more generally accepted by the people as a means of protection, but, notwithstanding this, no cases of small-pox have occurred in Middlesex for the last two or three years. The County Council also arranges to provide isolation hospital accommodation for treating cases of small-pox which may occur in the County.

THE TREATMENT OF TUBERCULOSIS

So far, the account which has been given of the work of the Public Health Department has dealt mainly with the prevention of disease, but there remain to be considered those functions of the County Council which deal more with the treatment of established diseases than with problems of prevention. It is not always possible to draw a hard-and-fast line between prevention and treatment, because the treatment of some apparently trifling condition may be the means of preventing some more serious development.

For a number of years the County Council has been concerned with the prevention and treatment of tuberculosis. This disease was known during the last century as the " white scourge ", because of the great toll it took of the lives of the people, mostly young men and women. Thanks to the advance of medical knowledge, improvements in housing and other factors, this disease has been brought under control. Tuberculosis clinics have been set up in centres of population,

HILLINGDON COUNTY HOSPITAL   WARD BLOCK, etc.

NORTH MIDDLESEX COUNTY HOSPITAL (NORTH FRONT)   *Approved design for new building*

NORTH MIDDLESEX COUNTY HOSPITAL (SOUTH FRONT)   *Approved design for new building*

HILLINGDON COUNTY HOSPITAL   *Approved design for new building*

where specially qualified doctors examine free of charge any persons in whom there is the slightest reason to suspect that tuberculosis may be present.

The object of the clinics is first to recognize the presence of tuberculosis (if it exists) at the earliest possible moment, as the earlier

for 150 male and 150 female patients respectively; a single-storey block for 178 children, incorporating a school, and a detached single-storey block for eighteen observation cases; a separate block containing dining-room, kitchens, etc., on the ground floor, with a large

REDHILL COUNTY HOSPITAL   EDGWARE

the case is recognized and brought under treatment, the better the prospect of cure. The second purpose of tuberculosis clinics is to keep under observation all cases of tuberculosis which have been discovered, and to make suitable arrangements for them to receive whatever form of treatment is considered best for them.

The County Council has established two sanatoria—that is to say, open-air hospitals for the treatment of tuberculosis —one at Harefield and one at South Mimms, both in the County of Middlesex. The Harefield Sanatorium, which has recently been entirely rebuilt, and was opened in October, 1937, by His Royal Highness the Duke of Gloucester, is considered to be the finest and most up-to-date sanatorium in this country. It is in one of the most bracing and healthy parts of Middlesex.

The accommodation for patients includes a large three-storied building with central administrative section flanked by two three-storey wings, of three superimposed wards of 50 beds each, providing beds

recreation-room equipped with a cinematograph projector, etc., on the first floor; a well-equipped laundry block and accommodation for other ancillary services, appropriate to an institution of this nature and size.

The Clare Hall Sanatorium, South Mimms, is situate in the extreme north of the County and provides accommodation for 186 patients suffering from pulmonary tuberculosis.

Both Harefield and Clare Hall Sanatoria have, in affiliation with the County Council's general hospitals, been approved by the General Nursing Council as training-schools for nurses, and a sister-tutor has been appointed at each sanatorium for the purpose of giving the necessary special instruction in tuberculosis nursing.

In addition to this permanent provision for the institutional treatment of cases of pulmonary disease, further beds are obtained as required in other sanatoria and hospitals in various parts of the country.

K

THE GENERAL HOSPITAL SERVICE

The most recent addition to the County Council's work, and in some respects the most important, is the general hospital service of the County. Before the year 1930 such hospitals in the County as were supported out of the rates belonged to boards of guardians of the poor. These bodies, as you have read in Part II, were abolished in 1930, and the five general hospitals in Middlesex which had been maintained by the guardians became the property of the County Council.

Since that time the County Council has been very active in bringing these great institutions thoroughly up to date, equipping them with the finest and most modern apparatus and instruments, and appointing to each one a team of highly qualified and skilful physicians and surgeons. The Council's hospitals in Middlesex as a whole compare favourably with the best hospitals in this country, and are able to undertake the treatment of every kind of disease, accident or injury. The names of the hospitals and the approximate number of beds in each are as follows :—

Central Middlesex County Hospital, Acton Lane, Willesden, N.W. 10 . . .	900
Hillingdon County Hospital, Hillingdon, Uxbridge, Middlesex	250
North Middlesex County Hospital, Silver Street, Edmonton, N. 18 . . .	1,400
Redhill County Hospital, Edgware, Middlesex	550
West Middlesex County Hospital, Isleworth	1,450

In addition to these great hospitals, the County Council has convalescent homes at Harefield, Woburn Sands and Milford-on-Sea, and has recently acquired two others which shortly will be in occupation—one at Netley, overlooking Southampton Water, and one at Mundesley-on-Sea in Norfolk.

Since 1930, the Council has been actively engaged in endeavouring to provide sufficient accommodation for the ever-growing population of the County, and at the same time ensuring that the services rendered on behalf of the sick attain the highest possible degree of efficiency.

Chase Farm Schools at Enfield which were formerly used by the Poor Law guardians as Poor Law schools, have been extended and modernized to accommodate 541 of the inmates of the old Edmonton House, and this institution was recently opened by the Minister of Health. The children who were at the Schools have been accommodated in small scattered homes and the old Edmonton House site is being utilized for the large new buildings of the North Middlesex County Hospital.

The vast new extensions of the Redhill County Hospital at Edgware have recently been completed and the new buildings were opened in October 1938 by the Lord Lieutenant of the County.

It may also be noted that the County Council provides doctors and nursing care for poor people who are ill in their own homes. Some sixty doctors practising in the County are employed by the County Council for this purpose, and considerable sums of money are paid every year to the various district nursing associations in the County for the help they give to poor people in need of nursing at home.

4. PUBLIC ASSISTANCE

THE Public Assistance Department, although it is nearly the latest to be added to the Council's activities deals, in fact, with one of the oldest forms of local government extant.

Up to the days of Queen Elizabeth, people who were destitute could, as previously stated, only get assistance either from private charity or from the Church. The Reformation, by depriving

CHASE FARM : *An old people's home*   *ENFIELD*

the religious communities of the bulk of their resources, left the poor entirely dependent on private charity in times of need. Queen Elizabeth and her Ministers found it necessary to pass an Act of Parliament whereby poor persons not able to work should be relieved by the parish. Their children were to be apprenticed, and unemployed persons had to be set to work. It is a great tribute to the Elizabethans that the fundamentals of this law are still in operation to-day.

In the early part of the nineteenth century, when McAdam (a Middlesex man) and other famous roadmakers so improved the roads that people were enabled to travel about more easily and extensively, parishes were united into Unions for the relief of the poor. These Unions were generally grouped round a market town. In the twentieth century the invention of the petrol engine, and the consequent use of the motor omnibus and the motor-car, again improved travelling facilities. The Poor Law Unions disappeared, and the work of the boards of guardians was handed over to the county councils and the county borough councils. This was but one effect on local government of improved means of transport.

ADMINISTRATIVE MACHINERY OF TO-DAY

The care of the destitute poor in Middlesex is now a duty of the County Council. In England every person who is destitute has the right to receive public assistance; no one need starve. This great work is carried out by the Public Health Committee. The whole County is divided into relief districts, with a relieving officer for each district. Large institutions are provided for those persons who, for any reason, cannot be assisted in their own homes. Orphans and other children whose parents cannot maintain them are maintained in small houses, each house in charge of a foster-mother. Many thousands of families, principally old people and widows with children, are maintained in their own homes at the expense of the County Council.

At the head of this organization is the Director of Public Assistance, who is responsible to the County Council for the proper relief of all destitute persons within the County.

THE ADMINISTRATIVE MACHINERY AT WORK

Imagine that some old age pensioner finds it extremely difficult to manage on his pension of 10s. per week. He consults, it may be, his local vicar or minister or neighbour, and he is told to make application to the relieving officer. At one time these relieving officers were regarded with dread, and in Dickens' " Oliver Twist " you will read of such officials under the name of " the parish beadle ". Times have changed, and the relieving officer is no longer dreaded by the poor, but is regarded as their friend. The applicant for relief finds out the address of the local relief office, goes there and furnishes the officer with a statement of his circumstances, and is asked to return perhaps later in the day or on the following morning to see the adjudicating officer. This officer interviews him in private, and decides what assistance should be given to him by the County Council in addition to his old age pension. The applicant can then return to his home happy in the knowledge that he will be able to end his days in much more comfort than his old age pension would have permitted.

A widow who has just lost her husband and has several young children to look after may also seek the aid of the relieving officer. A husband has fallen sick and his wages have stopped; his wife asks for help and receives it. Assistance is not only given in money, but in many other forms. A child is delicate and is sent to the seaside to regain its health. A mother

has to go into hospital and there is no one to look after her children; the Council takes the little ones into one of its children's homes and cares for them until the mother returns. Some unfortunate cripple has fallen on evil days and wants help to obtain a renewal of his artificial limb, and the help is forthcoming. *There are to-day in Middlesex some 12,000 households which are entirely maintained by the County Council.*

Despite all these facilities to enable people to keep their homes together, there are nevertheless many people who, by reason of age or physical or mental infirmity, are not able to live at home and have to be taken care of in institutions. The County Council has several institutions, ranging in size from a home for 28 older women to a large establishment capable of taking 600 people. One such home—White Webbs—is an old mansion situate in lovely grounds near Enfield. About 70 old men live here. They have a bowling-green in the grounds and the municipal golf course adjoins the mansion, giving them an attractive outlook.

The largest establishment, Chase Farm (which has been referred to earlier), also in North Middlesex, takes about 600 residents of both sexes, nearly all of whom are old people. It is perched on the high ridge of land which runs northward from the Alexandra Palace into Hertfordshire, and has lovely views over the surrounding country. The old people have bowling-greens, lawns and a small private park in which to take the air. Delightful little shelters and comfortable seats are placed about the grounds.

The residents at all these places are free to go and come as they wish, and the care taken of these old people is in striking contrast to the pictures of the old workhouse of 100 years ago as depicted in " Oliver Twist ".

THE CARE OF CHILDREN

An attractive side of the work of the department is the care of children who, having lost their fathers and mothers,

CHASE FARM, ENFIELD   *A Recreation Room and Dining Hall*

have no one to look after them. Or possibly the parents have become so poor that they are unable to keep their children, and in some instances the parents are taken ill and have to be admitted to a hospital, leaving no one to look after their families. All these children are taken care of by the County Council.

The Council has about 60 ordinary-sized houses, each in charge of a foster mother. From 8 to 12 children live in each of these homes and attend the ordinary day school. They are dressed like other children, and have the same opportunities of earning scholarships and passing into secondary and technical schools.

One girl was successful in winning scholarships right through to the University. Another girl was sufficiently clever to be trained as a teacher. A boy who was very fond of animals was enabled to train as a veterinary surgeon. Of course by no means all the children are

able to win scholarships, but those who can do so improve their careers accordingly.

When the children have finished their school-days, they are placed in situations. Some boys pass into the Royal Navy or the Mercantile Marine through training-ships, such as the " Exmouth " and the " Conway ". Others are apprenticed to trades. The girls become nursemaids, cooks, housemaids, and quite a number have been trained as children's nurses, and later on have entered a hospital and become fully trained nurses.

Whilst in the homes the boys are encouraged to join the Boy Scout movement and the girls to enter the Girl Guides. They are taught household tasks, and every effort is made to make them happy and comfortable.

Once a year they are taken to the seaside for a fortnight, an outing which is looked forward to throughout the year.

It must not be thought that the children in the Council's homes are all drawn from the poorest classes. There are many children of professional men, such as doctors, dentists, accountants, or trades- men and of other people who at one time were well to do, but either through the loss of their parents or some financial disaster the children have come into the care of the County Council.

CASUAL WARDS

Another feature of the Department is the supervision of the Council's Casual Wards. At these institutions vagrants, or destitute wayfarers, as they are called, can obtain a night's lodging on their way through the County.

The history of vagrancy is an interesting

ISLEWORTH CASUAL WARDS—wood-chopping sheds

one, and goes back to the Middle Ages, when so many of the barons killed each other during the Wars of the Roses, leaving behind them hordes of retainers, lordless and destitute. For many years these sturdy beggars roaming the countryside were a constant source of trouble to the people. Various harsh measures to com- bat the trouble were resorted to but without success. During the nineteenth century " casual wards " were established throughout the country at convenient distances apart, where homeless men on tramp could obtain food and shelter.

There are now only two such casual wards in Middlesex, one at Edmonton and the other at Isleworth, and both

are modern. Men making their way from the west country to the east coast tramp the Great West Road and apply for admission to the Isleworth Casual Ward. Similarly, men coming down from the north along the Great North Road, or from the north-west along the old Watling Street, stop at Edmonton.

It may interest you to know what happens to a tramp when he enters a casual ward. First of all he registers his name at the office, and then goes into a day-room. Here he is provided with hot tea, and bread and margarine. After a while he is called into the bathing-room, where he has a shower-bath with clean warm water. He is given a night-shirt, dressing-gown and slippers, and taken to the dormitory where he is to sleep, or he may have the choice of a single cubicle to himself. A bedstead with mattress, pillow and blankets is provided.

Next morning all the men are aroused about 6 a.m. and have breakfast served to them about 7.30 a.m. After breakfast each man is assigned to a particular task of work, which he has to perform in return for his food and shelter. Some chop firewood, some clean up the wards, and others with a taste for gardening are assigned work in the gardens. When the work is done the men are at liberty to repair their own clothing and boots, or wash their gar- ments in the laundry.

After another night's rest, the men take their discharge after breakfast and pro- ceed to the next casual ward on their route. To obviate the need for begging en route, each man is provided with a packet of bread and cheese.

A vagrant who regularly resorts to the casual wards need not be dirty or ragged, and in fact you would not recognize many of these men as regular tramps if you saw them on the road. There are others, however, who only go to a casual ward when they cannot get enough money to pay for a bed in a common lodging-house.

Why do men tramp the roads? Some do it in search of work, like those who go from one part of the country to another after seasonal work such as potato-lifting, strawberry-gathering and hop-picking. Large public works attract men in search of a job, though the old-time " navvy " has largely disappeared. Many men remain on the road and adopt a vagrant's life because they prefer it to the irksomeness of settled work and a routine existence.

Occasionally boys in search of adventure leave their homes and take to the highways. Great efforts are being made to-day to persuade these youths to take up training in hostels and get back to regular work. Every effort is made also to persuade elderly men to forsake the road and settle down in an institution.

With the facilities provided, there is really no need for the homeless to have to " beg " for a night's lodging in this country.

5. MENTAL TREATMENT AND MENTAL DEFICIENCY

AS you read in Part Two, the duties of the visiting committees of quarter sessions with regard to lunatic asylums were, by the Act of 1888, transferred to county councils, and the county councils appointed the visiting committees. These committees have wide powers of management and financial control, although the county councils remain responsible for the payment of the cost of maintenance of all the rate-aided patients at the various mental hospitals, and the consent of the county councils is necessary for any capital expenditure.

The Mental Treatment Act, 1920, provided for the treatment of voluntary patients in mental hospitals and these private fee-paying patients in the majority of cases pay a higher maintenance rate than that received for the rate-aided patients.

You also read of the action of the Middlesex County Council in 1938 in promoting a Bill in Parliament to enable the County Council to become the Visiting Committee, as from 1st April, 1939, and to appoint a standing committee to which many of its duties will be transferred to bring the procedure in line with the other committees of the County Council.

There are three County mental hospitals: the Springfield (Mental) Hospital at Tooting, and the Napsbury and Shenley (Mental) Hospitals near St. Albans—photographs of which are on this page and the two following pages.

Springfield (*Mental*) *Hospital* was opened in 1841 as a County Mental Hospital for Surrey, with provision for 360 beds for each sex. Eleven years later it had accommodation for 900 patients, the women's side by that time exceeding the

SPRINGFIELD (MENTAL) HOSPITAL   WANDSWORTH

NAPSBURY (MENTAL) HOSPITAL

men's by about 100 beds. Further extensions were made from time to time, and in 1879 a new recreation hall and new church were added, the latter being a particularly pleasing structure.

The hospital was transferred to the Middlesex County Council after the Local Government Act, 1888, and later many additions were completed, including the construction of a detached annexe for 260 low-grade mental defectives, 180 children and 80 adults, which was a notable provision giving expression to a growing feeling, in advance of the provisions of the Mental Deficiency Act of 1913, that separate accommodation and specialized methods of training were needed for these types of cases.

During the Great War this hospital served a noble purpose, as one of the chief army neurological hospitals.

There is a close co-operation between Springfield and the Westminster Hospital so far as treatment and teaching work are concerned, including the expansion of training facilities for nursing staffs, to the great advantage of both hospitals. There are now 2000 patients in the hospital, and the grounds cover an area of 145 acres, including 83 acres of farm land and 14 acres of garden.

Napsbury (Mental) Hospital was opened in June 1905. The County Council acquired the freehold of the Napsbury Manor Farm situate about 2 miles south of St. Albans, and having an area of 412 acres. The hospital was originally built to accommodate about 1200 patients, but has from time to time been extended, and there are over 1800 patients being treated there at present.

The southern aspect of the estate secures the maximum of sunlight and protection from the cold north and north-east winds, whilst the level plateau about half-way down the estate readily lends itself to the suitable distribution of the buildings, with the best aspect and protection from the wind and with extensive and beautiful views from the windows. The numerous plantations and trees in the estate have all been carefully preserved, and the buildings adjusted accordingly, obtaining a picturesque and natural setting for the buildings.

Shenley (Mental) Hospital was opened by the late King George V in May 1934. The first section of the scheme was planned to provide accommodation for 1047 patients and the entire administrative centre for the full programme of 2000 patients and approximately 500 staff. The hospital is planned on the " villa " system, with small nursing units ranging from 20 to 45 patients.

The administrative centre was built on an axial line running north and south, the hospital buildings and villas for male and for female patients being placed east and west of it respectively. The site is somewhat conical in shape, and the arrangement of the layout has been governed to a large extent by the contours, but the buildings have a main southerly aspect.

METHODS OF TREATMENT

The skilled care and attention bestowed upon the patients of all the County mental hospitals are believed to answer Macbeth's plea and

" . . . minister to a mind diseas'd ;
    Pluck from the memory a rooted sorrow ;
    Raze out the written troubles of the brain."

There are two methods of dealing with mental defectives: by institutional care or by community care.

Community care is divided into :—

    (*a*) guardianship, (*b*) licence of patients to community care, (*c*) supervision.

SHENLEY (MENTAL) HOSPITAL   VIEW FROM THE AIR

Extensive use is made of guardianship where this form of treatment is found to be suitable for patients.

The granting of licences allows patients to be given a trial in community life. Most of such patients live in their own homes and have some occupation either at home or in paid situations. They are visited by the Committee's officers, and arrangements are made with respect to maintenance, wages, pocket-money, employment, clothing and medical treatment.

With regard to supervision, the cases are those living in their own homes in the community, for whom this form of treatment affords sufficient protection. Under the 1913–27 Acts it is the duty of the local authority to provide training and occupation for cases under supervision, and they are visited by the Committee's officers who make periodical reports, so that in the event of a case becoming unsuitable for the "supervision" system, provision is made for admission to guardianship or to an institution. It is these cases, under supervision and guardianship, who attend the occupation centres provided by the Committee, or who are visited by the home teachers previously mentioned.

The Middlesex Colony at Shenley, built to accommodate over 1000 patients, was opened by the Minister of Health in 1933. Many industries are carried on here by the patients, including boot repairing, tailoring, brush-making, carpentering, rug-making, etc. The Colony is situated in grounds of about 420 acres, and stands about 250 feet above sea level, and is situated on the land allocated to it on the north side of the main Shenley Hospital estate. The buildings are surrounded by farm lands, and there are considerable areas of wooded land. The gardens around the buildings are being laid out and planted by the patients.

The reception hall, which was opened during Jubilee week in 1935, is the centre of all the general recreative activities of the Colony. A Scout Troop and Girl Guide Company are successfully carried on by the patients.

Bramley House Certified Institution at Enfield was purchased in 1930, after having been held on lease since 1914. During 1936 alterations and extensions were effected so as to admit an additional sixteen patients, making a total of sixty-six mentally high-grade girls.

The Institution is a very pleasant, homelike building and occupies an area of approximately seven acres. The patients excel in rug-making and sock-making, and socks are sold to the Middlesex Colony at Shenley.

Craufurd Home Certified Institution, Maidenhead, was opened in April 1929, and accommodated 116 patients, including grown women of medium to low mental grade and a number of cot and chair cases. The Home has recently been closed and the patients transferred to the Shenley Colony.

Occupation Centres and Home Teaching

The occupation centres and home-teaching scheme is intended for patients who do not require the more expensive institutional treatment. Patients who, for reasons of health, physical condition or distance, are not able to attend occupation centres are visited and instructed by home teachers.

The details of the scheme are managed by the Central Association for Mental Welfare—a very competent voluntary body—but the patients and the centres are under the financial and general control of the Mental Deficiency Committee, which is solely responsible for the treatment, teaching, etc., of the patients.

There are eight centres in the County, and six home teachers. The number of patients annually attending the centres varies, but the average number is 280–290. The average number visited by the home teachers is 187.

All forms of handwork, knitting, rug-making, raffiawork, cane chair-seating, basket-work, needlework, etc., are taught, and only very bad cases are excluded from a centre. They are also taught physical exercises and sense and speech training. At one of the centres there is a carpentering class which makes saleable articles.

6. ROADS AND BRIDGES

IT is probably not too much to assume that the work entailed in the maintenance and construction of the roads and bridges in the County forms the popular estimate of the whole of the duties of the County Engineer and Surveyor. Indeed, it was for this purpose alone that the office was created, and before outlining the present scope of the work of his Department, it may be interesting to follow the development of the highway and highway administration in England in general, and in Middlesex in particular.

The Earliest Roads in England

The earliest roads in England were tracks made by the Ancient Britons, and in Middlesex there is evidence of three of these, all of which commenced at the great ford across the Thames near Brentford. The first ran eastwards through the districts known to-day as Strand-on-the-Green, Chiswick, Fulham, and Chelsea to Charing Cross; the second led between Hanwell and Ealing over Horsendon and Sudbury Hills to Brockley Hill at Stanmore, where there was an encampment, and the third went by way of Hanwell and Hayes to the ford across the River Colne at Uxbridge. When the Romans colonized Britain, they constructed a network of military roads, solidly built of stone on good foundations, and three of these pass through the County: Ermine Street (the route of which is followed to-day by the Hertford Road as far as Edmonton), running from Bishopsgate through Tottenham and Waltham Cross to Lincoln; Watling Street, following the route now taken by the Edgware Road from Marble Arch to where it leaves the County to the North of Brockley Hill, and continuing through St. Albans to Wroxeter near Shrewsbury; and a third leading from London through Shepherd's Bush, Chiswick, Brentford, Hounslow, and Staines to Silchester, along the route now taken by

the Staines Road. Not until the nineteenth century were roads as sound as these again constructed, and during the intervening ages the principal means of communication, apart from the rivers, were mere tracks formed by constant usage, which were often not as good as those over which a farmer nowadays drives his carts through his fields.

Transport by Packhorse

Until towards the end of the sixteenth century the only means of transport was the packhorse. Travellers, who were principally soldiers, pilgrims or beggars, travelled on foot or horseback. Livestock of all descriptions, forming the food supply of the large towns, was driven in herds and killed on arrival. The other staple product, wool—a trade which grew enormously from the fourteenth century onwards—was carried on the packhorse. The way was often fraught with danger, and one of the first Acts of Parliament to deal with roads, passed in 1285, required all trees and shrubs within 200 feet of either side of the highway between market towns to be cut down, as a measure of protection against robbers. With the discovery of America, and the consequent sudden increase in wealth and trade, England found herself taken from the edge of the commercial world of the time, and placed at its centre. The traffic on the roads increased proportionately, and under the strain, particularly in wet weather, they became impassable to the new carriers' stage wagons and packhorses alike, and a serious check to the rising trade.

Responsibility of Parishes for Roads

Something had to be done; someone had to be made responsible for their upkeep, and in 1555 an Act of Parliament was passed establishing a principle which remained in operation for three hundred years. This Act decreed that each parish was responsible for the maintenance of the roads through it, and should supply the necessary labour and materials. At a special Highways Session, the justices of the peace annually appointed a Sur-

JAMES NICOL McADAM *3rd son of John Loudon McAdam From a portrait in the Middlesex Guildhall. General Surveyor of the Metropolis Turnpike roads.*

veyor to each parish, whose duties consisted of inspecting three times a year all roads, water-courses, and bridges, and reporting on their condition (under oath) to the justices. He also had to arrange for, and oversee, the six days' compulsory " statute labour " which each member of the community had to perform each year in the upkeep of the roads. The Act failed in its purpose. The Surveyor, who generally resented being saddled with an unpaid job, was usually quite unqualified —he might be the village butcher or

baker or anyone the justices might choose —and frequently was not above taking a bribe to shut his eyes to serious defects, or using his position to his own advantage. The system of " statute labour " also proved unsatisfactory; it was found almost impossible to make the poor perform their share of the work, and the wealthy could usually evade their responsibility with a cash payment. Parliament repeatedly tried to remedy the situation—an Act passed in 1654, for example, imposed a rate of sixpence in the pound on all parishes for the upkeep of their roads—but the system of commuting " statute labour " had become so general by 1773 that a general Highways Act was passed fixing the rates at which this could be done. This Act also enabled parishes to demand the appointment of a salaried surveyor to look after their roads, a facility which was used to full advantage in many instances.

An Act was passed in 1621 which restricted the size and type of traffic, and this kind of legislation was repeated with increasing detail and complication until the end of the eighteenth century.

Toll and Turnpike Roads

General conditions, however, remained deplorable, and during the seventeenth century, Parliament, with what was tantamount to a confession of failure in dealing with the matter, had allowed toll and turnpike roads to come into existence. The toll bridge was a familiar sight in the Middle Ages, but the turnpike system proper, by which barriers were placed across a road and tolls taken from all but pedestrians and a few privileged travellers, dates from 1663, when Parliament, on petition of a number of Justices, authorized the erection of toll barriers along the Great North Road. The recognition of the turnpike road by Parliament was a recognition of the principle that each person should contribute to the repair of the roads in proportion to the use he made of, or the convenience he derived from, them. The precedent was

TROUBLE ON THE ROAD, IN THE 17TH Century

quickly followed by application of the principle to other roads, which were placed under the control of bodies known as Turnpike Trusts. These Trusts were created by Acts of Parliament for a limited period, with option of renewal, and were empowered to collect tolls from travellers on the nominal condition of keeping the roads under their control in repair. The system spread very rapidly, so that by 1770 there were over 1100 Trusts, administering 23,000 miles of road, with 7800 toll-gates and employing 20,000 pikemen to collect the tolls. The system was unpopular to the point of causing riots, and although turnpike roads were generally better than others, they could be deplorable, particularly during the wet seasons of the year.

Influence of the Industrial Revolution

With the industrial revolution, towards the end of the eighteenth century, came the second great and sudden increase in the volume of traffic, and the need for serious and extensive reforms became acute. The first real move came from the Board of Agriculture, which was responsible for the first Parliamentary Committee to consider the administration of roads (1808–1830). This Committee proposed the appointment of paid county surveyors to work in conjunction with the Turnpike Trusts, and produced a plan for the consolidation of the turnpike system near London, the administration of which was particularly bad. This led to the consolidation of the principal Middlesex turnpikes in 1826.

McAdam and Telford

In the meantime, Sir John Sinclair, the President of the Board of Agriculture, brought to public notice John Loudon McAdam, who had invented the system of road surfacing which is known by his name to-day. Working as surveyor to a number of Turnpike Trusts, McAdam undertook the reform of many miles of turnpike roads. The Post Office was another Government body interested in this work, by reason of the increasing delays which the bad state of the roads was causing the Royal Mail coaches, and in 1810 the Postmaster-General appointed Thomas Telford to oversee the whole length of the London–Holyhead Road. This he did so effectively that other similar schemes were placed in his care. The results achieved by those two men inspired others to work along the same lines, and the reconstruction of roads was placed on a scientific basis.

The work, however, could not be carried out sufficiently quickly to meet the increasing traffic demands which the new industrial expansion placed on the highways. First the canals, and then the railways, took over the traffic, both goods and passenger, which had hitherto travelled by road. Turnpike Trusts became increasingly unpopular, and the loss of dues not only stopped the improvement schemes which they were beginning to carry out, but forced many of them into bankruptcy. Finally, force of circumstances compelled the Government to undertake the reform of road administration.

The General Highways Act, 1835

The first result was the passing of the General Highway Act, 1835, which made a meeting of the parish ratepayers the administrative body in highway management. Parishes with a population of more than 5000 (parishes could amalgamate for the purpose) were able to have a "highway board", and could nominate a salaried surveyor, empowered to levy a rate for the upkeep of the roads. The only qualifications for the post were the possession of an estate within the parish of an annual value of £10, or of a personal estate to the value of £100, or the occupation of hereditaments of an annual value of £20. The powers given by the Act, however, were not generally used, and the chief defect remained untouched; some 15,000 separate and mutually independent highway parishes remained, each controlling an absurdly small area. There was a slight improvement in 1848, when the Public Health Act of that year made the local "boards of health" the surveyors for roads in all the newly-created urban areas, and the Highway Act, 1862,

STREET ORDERLIES (19TH CENTURY)

"TRAFFIC TROUBLE IN '50"

DRAWN FROM A PAINTING BY LOUIS EUGENE LAMM, 1858

organized parishes into highway districts, formed by the justices, and administered by highway boards, which could appoint and pay officials. The position was further consolidated by the Local Government Act of the following year, which prevented parishes from adopting those provisions of the Public Health Act, 1848, which referred to the maintenance of roads, and thus made it impossible for so small an authority to undertake the administration of the roads.

The Creation of " Main Roads "

"Main Roads", as a new class of road, were created by the Highway and Locomotive Amendment Act, 1878. These roads included all roads which had ceased to be turnpike roads after 1870, and any other roads which were considered to be of sufficient importance by reason of their being the principal means of communication between towns, or thoroughfares leading to railway stations. One half of the cost of the maintenance of these main roads was placed upon the County, which was then administered by the justices of the peace, and the other half was borne by the local authorities.

By this Act, too, a county surveyor, who had hitherto only been responsible for county bridges and 300 feet of the highway on each side of such bridges, could be called upon to report to the justices on the condition of any of the highways under their jurisdiction about which complaints had been made, and the main outlines of the office as it is known to-day began to take form. He was appointed by the justices of the peace until county councils came into being with the passing of the Local Government Act, 1888, and the responsibility for the maintenance and repair of main roads passed into their hands. It is important to note that only main roads passed into the jurisdiction of the county councils. All other roads, with the exception of private thoroughfares, were the responsibility of the local councils.

Formation of the Road Board

The first attempt made by the Government to take executive control over the roads was the formation of the Road Board in 1909, with the passing of the Development and Road Improvement Funds Act. The Board was empowered to

CHERTSEY ROAD, FELTHAM   *A road of to-day*

make grants of money to local governing bodies for the purpose of improving existing roads and constructing new ones. The creation of this body marked the recognition by the Government of the advent of a new era of life on the roads. The Board continued in existence until 1919, when it was superseded by the Ministry of Transport, formed by Act of Parliament in that year, to deal with railways, tramways, waterways, roads, bridges, harbours, and docks. Under this Act, also, first and second-class roads were created, a percentage of the cost of maintenance and improvement of which, varying according to the class of road, was to be borne by the Ministry of Transport.

Financial Responsibility of the County

The Local Government Act, 1929, made the County financially re-
sponsible for all classified roads, some of which had not hitherto been considered by the Council as main roads, and there was therefore an increase in its activities in this respect. Further, a number of roads which had been controlled by the County as main roads had not been classified by the Ministry of Transport, and the Council still retained its authority over these. In actual practice, while the County Council bears the cost subject to grant, the work on a considerable number of its roads is executed by the local authorities under the supervision of the County Engineer.

Development in Administration

The latest development in road administration is the result of an Act of Parliament passed in 1936, by which the Government declared certain roads to be trunk roads. These are administered directly by, and at the expense of, the Ministry of Transport, although in most instances the execution of the actual work is delegated to the County authorities.

County Bridges

The term " County Bridge " is used in two senses : in a wider sense it includes all public bridges, but it is usually meant to imply a bridge lying within, and repairable by, a county, as distinct from such bridges as are the liability of a smaller administrative area or are under private ownership. The County was made the bridge authority by the Statute of Bridges, 1530, and until the county councils took over the responsibility on their formation in 1888, the justices in quarter sessions administered the provisions of this Statute, through a surveyor whom they appointed. An important Act relating to bridges was passed in

1929, which enabled highway authorities to enter into agreements with private owners of bridges—canal and railway companies, for example—with a view to taking over the responsibility for maintenance, improvement and reconstruction. This Act has assisted the County in its negotiations in connection with the work of bringing the bridges in Middlesex to a standard equal to modern traffic requirements.

To-day the County Engineer and Surveyor's Department is responsible for 373.27 miles of road and approximately 150 bridges in Middlesex and, in addition, it administers 41.67 miles of trunk road for the Ministry of Transport. The total cost of all these works, which include improvement, reconstruction and repair, amounts to approximately £1,360,000 per annum, which is an average of £3726 per day.

HONEYPOT LANE   *A road of yesterday*

HAMPTON COURT BRIDGE (18TH CENTURY)

THE PRESENT DAY

A generation ago, firstly the bicycle and, latterly, the motor vehicle, brought a return to the roads, which both goods and passenger traffic had abandoned for the railways. The new road-users found that while the highways in or around the towns were of a fairly high standard, nothing like the same conditions prevailed in open country. In fact it was not long before these roads proved quite inadequate to cope with the weight and intensity of the traffic created by the new and increasingly popular methods of transport. Surfaces crumbled, foundations gave way, and, later, roads designed to carry the small slow traffic of the coaching days proved inadequate in width and unsafe in design in the face of the large volume of fast traffic which soon appeared on them. Dust in summer and mud in winter had always been a source of nuisance on water-bound macadam roads where traffic was heavy, and this state of affairs was not only aggravated, but the road surfaces were literally pulled to pieces by the new pneumatic tyres.

Methods of Road Construction

The first attempt to cope with the difficulty consisted in painting the road surface with tar upon which grit was thrown and rolled in. Later the type of surfacing known as tarred macadam, composed of small tarred stones, was laid. Wood, asphalt, and granite sett surfaces had been in use for some time in the large cities, and as the need for impervious surfaces became more apparent, their use was greatly extended. Nowadays asphalt and bituminous compounds have become the most popular materials for surfacing important roads, although tarred macadam and concrete running surfaces are also extensively used. The foundations of the old macadam roads consisted of large, tightly-packed stones—the process was known as hand pitching—and

162

HAMPTON COURT BRIDGE   *Opened by H.R.H. the Prince of Wales, 1932*

while in some districts with good sub-soils these have been found to stand up to modern traffic conditions, foundations nowadays are usually constructed of concrete, reinforced with steel.

Scheme for Arterial Roads

By far the greatest problem, however, particularly around London, has been the provision and design of roads which would be adequate to cope with the amount of traffic using them. In 1912 the Local Government Board appointed a Departmental Committee to consider what improved means of road communication were necessary for the metropolis, and, as a result, proposals for constructing new roads, to be called " arterial " roads, were recommended, amongst which the following were planned to pass through Middlesex:

1. The CAMBRIDGE ROAD was designed to relieve the already serious congestion along the roads running in a northerly direction through the eastern part of the County. It was to commence in Tottenham, run northwards through Edmonton and Enfield, and terminate at Wormley in Hertfordshire.

2. The NORTH CIRCULAR ROAD was planned to relieve London as far as possible of that traffic wishing to cross, rather than enter it, and to intersect and connect every main road converging on London through Middlesex. It was to commence at the junction of the Great West Road and Chiswick High Road, run northwards and eastwards through Chiswick, Acton, Ealing, Wembley, Willesden, Hendon, Finchley, Friern Barnet, Hornsey, Southgate, and Edmonton, and pass into Essex at Ilford via Chingford and Woodford.

3. WESTERN AVENUE was intended as a bye-pass to the London–Oxford Road

NORTH CIRCULAR ROAD AT STONEBRIDGE PARK
Commencement of work

NORTH CIRCULAR ROAD AT FINCHLEY
The completed road

between Marble Arch and Uxbridge, and was planned to commence just west of the Edgware Road at Paddington, pass through North Hammersmith, and enter the County at Old Oak Common Lane, Acton, whence it ran almost due west through Acton, Park Royal, Perivale, Greenford, Northolt, and Harefield, to its termination near Denham in Buckinghamshire.

4. The GREAT WEST ROAD was designed as a bye-pass to Hammersmith Broadway and the High Streets of Chiswick, Brentford, and Hounslow, commencing at Cromwell Road West, Kensington, and terminating at the Bath Road, west of Hounslow.

5. The CHERTSEY ROAD was intended to relieve traffic to the south-west, and was planned to commence in the Chiswick High Road, and terminate in Middlesex at the River Thames at Shepperton.

Before any of these proposals could be put in hand, however, War had broken out, and the commencement of the works was postponed until 1920, when the County Council obtained the authority of the Ministry of Transport to the construction of various sections of these roads as a measure of relief against the heavy unemployment which followed the demobilization of the Forces. The Cambridge Road, the North Circular Road, and the section of the Great West Road from Hounslow to Chiswick are open to traffic and such has been the growth of motor-car traffic that schemes are now being prepared and executed for duplicating their carriage-ways and providing them with cycle tracks. Certain sections of the North Circular Road which run along roads already in existence have yet to be widened in order to bring them to the fully-planned width, and parliamentary powers have recently been obtained for

GYRATORY SCHEME
Cambridge Road and North Circular road at Edmonton

YEADING LANE   1931
After building of new road

YEADING LANE   1930

WESTERN AVENUE   Near Northolt

the continuation of the Great West Road to its termination in Kensington. Western Avenue has been completed as far as Harefield, and work on the final section, involving the construction of a viaduct some 1600 feet in length over the Colne Valley, is shortly to be commenced. The Chertsey Road, including the building of two new bridges over the Thames at Chiswick and Twickenham, has been completed as far as Feltham, and land is now being acquired to enable the construction of the final section in Middlesex. In 1923 the Ministry of Transport authorized two more new roads in the County; the Watford Bye-pass, which commences at Finchley Road in the Borough of Hampstead and leaves Middlesex near Aldenham Reservoir, and the Great North Way, or Barnet Bye-pass, which runs from the junction of Archway Road and North Hill, Highgate, to the County boundary about 2 miles north of Mimms Hall, South Mimms. The purpose of the former road is to relieve the congested Edgware Road, and that of the latter to relieve the Finchley and Great North Roads.

Safety Measures

Concurrently with the construction of these new roads, extensive schemes for the widening and improvement of most of the old roads, and many of the bridges, in the County, to make them equal to their present-day task, have been executed. These have involved the provision of dual carriage-ways for up and down traffic, separated by central islands or a grass verge; the provision of service or subsidiary roads parallel with the main carriageways to accommodate local and standing traffic where new development takes place; the construction, where space has permitted, of gyratory traffic layouts (or "roundabouts") at important road junctions or, where it has not, the installation of systems of automatic traffic signals; the provision of super elevation, or banking, on curves to lessen the danger from skidding; and, lastly, the provision of a multiplicity of traffic signs and road-markings to make the highway safe for motorist and pedestrian alike.

On numerous occasions the new roads have been criticized from the point of view of their barren ugliness as compared with the leafy lanes of yesterday. The County Council is making every effort to make its roads as beautiful as they are efficient. Grass verges are laid out at the sides, and Road and the Uxbridge Road; and the southern, which controls the remaining south-west portion of the County. Each of these areas is in charge of a divisional surveyor

KEW BRIDGE (18TH CENTURY)   Looking South

avenues of young trees and flowering-shrubs are planted along them—the County Council having its own nurseries, staffed by horticultural experts, for this purpose. It is regrettable, however, that after so much time, trouble, and money have been expended on these improvements, a certain section of the community should be so unappreciative as to involve the Council in additional expenditure each year in repairing thoughtless or wilful damage.

For the purpose of maintaining the county roads directly supervised by the Department, the County is divided into three divisions—the northern, comprising the north-eastern part of the County as far as the Edgware Road; the central, comprising the area between the Edgware

Reinstatement of Work Carried Out by Statutory Undertakers, etc.

Nowadays the citizen in urbanized areas expects to be supplied with all services, such as electricity, gas, water, and the disposal of sewage, and in order that these may be obtained as cheaply as possible, Parliament has given to statutory companies who supply these services, and local authorities, the power to lay their mains, cables or sewers under the public highway, placing upon them the responsibility of reinstating or restoring the surface disturbed. In actual practice these authorities only fill in their trenches with the excavated material, which they consolidate. The highway authorities then restore the surface at the expense of the statutory under-

Before reconstruction

LONG LANE BRIDGE, HILLINGDON

After reconstruction

takers, the cost having been previously agreed. This arrangement also relieves the companies of any subsequent liability for accidents which may be caused by settlement along the site of the trench at a later date.

It is fully realized by all authorities concerned that the frequent disturbance of roads by these operations causes a great deal of public annoyance, and although it is sometimes hard to believe, every effort is made to minimize this nuisance. The London Traffic Act, 1924, gives power to control a number of impor-

turn are circulated to all the statutory companies, who are thus able to know in advance when the works are to be executed. They are then able to proceed in advance of the road-works with any proposals which they may desire to carry out. As, under this Act, it is illegal to open any of these roads for laying mains within twelve months of their being re-sur-faced, except in cases of emergency, this may be as much an advantage to the statutory undertakers as to the highway authorities.

Some idea of the magnitude of this

Before reconstruction

BRIDGE OVER LONGFORD RIVER, HANWORTH

After reconstruction

tant roads in the Metropolitan Police Area, and is of the greatest assistance in this direction. Under this Act, each highway authority submits to the Ministry of Transport six-monthly programmes of work affecting these roads, and these in

work may be obtained from the fact that, on an average, the County Council receives something like £25,000 per annum for the work carried out on behalf of the various bodies which open the roads in this manner.

The Town Planning and Restriction of Ribbon Development Acts in relation to highways

Under these Acts, the County Engineer's Department is concerned, firstly, with the prevention of the erection of buildings on land which may be required for future road-widening purposes, and secondly, with ensuring that new developments fronting county roads shall include provision for the accommodation of vehicles serving them, so that main-road or through traffic will suffer only the minimum of inconvenience.

In its operations under the Town-Planning Acts, the County Council ensures that the local authorities' town-planning schemes make provision, wherever possible, for all contemplated road widenings, and that the control which the Act gives in respect of the number and position of new streets entering classified roads is suitably exercised.

The spoliation of the countryside by continuous development along road frontages in recent years caused Parliament to pass the Restriction of Ribbon Development Act, which gave control to the road authorities over development along frontages of roads, subject to compensa-

tion being paid where the developer was adversely affected. Development in Middlesex is not of the character which is met with outside the London Traffic Area, as large areas of back land, as well as main-road frontages, are developed at one time, and except in certain more rural districts, undeveloped frontages are rare.

The administration of this Act so far as Middlesex is concerned, therefore, is more generally confined to ensuring that building along main roads does not reduce the safety or efficiency of the existing or future carriageway. The conditions generally imposed by the County Council for this purpose ensure that a subsidiary roadway, known as a service road, shall be constructed along the frontage of shops or houses, outside the limits of any land required for future road widening. This is done as it is felt that the standing vehicles left by persons visiting the shops, or by tradesmen delivering goods to the houses, in effect reduce the useful width of the main-road carriage-way to the extent of one line of traffic. If there is any desirable natural feature, such as a line of trees, the service road is frequently set back

AQUEDUCT OVER NORTH CIRCULAR ROAD   *Taken from the Canal*

168

AQUEDUCT CARRYING THE CANAL OVER NORTH CIRCULAR ROAD, WILLESDEN   *Taken from Road*

behind this, in order that the amenities of the road may be preserved as far as possible.

Other Types of Development

Other types of development are dealt with in what is considered to be the most suitable and apt manner. Public-houses, and similar premises of public resort, for example, are required to provide car-parking space, and careful control is exercised to ensure that the entrances to and exits from these spaces are in such positions as to give the minimum of inconvenience to through traffic. The cinema is another type of building which is dealt with in a somewhat similar manner, and it is generally required that a short length of subsidiary road shall be constructed in front, so that cars dropping or picking up passengers at the main entrance may do so without causing obstruction to the main traffic stream.

It is considered that by the judicious use of the powers given under these two Acts, the County Council will be enabled to reduce the cost of future road-widening schemes, since the necessity for the acquisition and demolition of comparatively new buildings should not arise, and to ensure that new developments will not increase danger on the existing highway.

7. RIVERS, STREAMS AND DRAINAGE

THE rapid urbanization of the County at the end of the last century outstripped the provisions made by the local authorities for the disposal of their sewage, and consequently many of the rivers and streams became so seriously polluted as to cause great public concern. In 1898, therefore, the County Council applied to Parliament and obtained powers, firstly, to take proceedings against persons suspected of polluting rivers, and secondly, to enable cleansing and execution of such works as might be necessary to maintain an unobstructed flow of water. In taking this step, Middlesex became the first County authority to take over the control of its water-courses.

PUMP, BATH ROAD, STANWELL

Further powers have since been obtained, the most important of which enables the County Council to carry out improvements and to acquire land compulsorily for this purpose.

The County Council maintained all the important rivers in Middlesex until the passing of the Land Drainage Act, 1930, the purpose of which was to overcome conditions prevailing in certain parts of the country where the neglect of the water-courses had resulted in serious flooding and damage to agricultural land. It divided the country into drainage districts, coincident with the catchments areas of the rivers. The River Thames and the River Lee are the two main rivers into which the streams of Middlesex flow. The former, from its source to Teddington Lock, which is the highest point affected by the tide, is controlled by the Thames Conservancy Board, and the latter is under the jurisdiction of the Lee Conservancy Board. With the passing of the above Act, these bodies formed drainage districts for the catchment areas of their respective rivers and the main streams entering them. The County Council retained control of those streams in Middlesex which enter the Thames below Teddington Lock, as the Port of London Authority, who control this part of the Thames, are not interested in land drainage. In effect this means that the County retains control over the Rivers Brent and Crane and their tributaries, comprising a length of 68½ miles.

Artificial Rivers

There are two artificial rivers in the County—namely, the King's or Cardinal's River, constructed by Charles I to supply the ornamental waters of Hampton Court Palace and Grounds, and the Duke of Northumberland's River. The former was taken out of the River Colne at Harmondsworth, and passes through the parishes of Stanwell, Bedfont, Feltham, and Hampton to the Palace at Hampton Court. The latter was constructed in the reign of Henry VII at his own expense to serve the Abbess of Syon with water to drive a mill at Twickenham, and was later extended to the Convent's other mill at Isleworth, where its modern successor, Kidd's Mill, stands. The mills on the river have now ceased to function, and it therefore no longer serves the purpose for which it was originally intended. In view of the inconvenience of having a privately-owned river running across the County, over which roads, mains and cables could only pass at the will of a private owner or by obtain-

DUKE OF NORTHUMBERLAND'S RIVER, ENTERING THE RIVER CRANE AT BEDFONT

ing statutory powers, and in view of the desirability of the County Council having supervision of the flow of water in times of flood, the County Council came to the conclusion that the river should become publicly owned and controlled. Under the County Council's Act of 1930, therefore, the necessary authority was obtained to acquire the river, which is now the freehold property of the County Council.

Ensuring an Even Supply of Water

Prior to the building development which has taken place in the various catchment areas, rainfall reached the rivers by percolating through the subsoil, the time taken depending principally on the nature of the soil and the contour of the area. The maintenance of the streams was not a difficult task in those days; the flow of water into them was more uniform, and was spread over a longer period of time. Moreover, the low-lying pasture-land through which they passed became inundated in times of heavy rain, lessening the danger of flooding and forming a relief to the built-up areas, which were then confined to the higher land. The low-lying areas, however, are now being built upon and are incapable of giving relief as formerly. As development proceeds and impervious surfaces such as roofs, roads, and pavements increase, rainfall, unable to soak into the soil, is carried away by the road-drains, and reaches the streams in a very short time. The old course, which was capable of accommodating the natural stream, was thus converted into something in the nature of a surface-water sewer and, as it was sometimes inadequate

171

to perform its new duties, flooding occurred. The County Council therefore requested that an estimate be prepared of the ultimate requirements of each river when its catchment area was fully developed.

In view of the fact that each stream has its own peculiarities, and conditions

A MAIN SEWER UNDER CONSTRUCTION

in the catchment areas are subject to constant variation, it took some time to accumulate the necessary data for such a calculation. Rain-gauges which could record the amount and intensity of rainfall were installed in various parts of the County, and automatic flow-recorders registering the volume of water passing down them were placed in the streams. In this connection it is interesting to note that in conjunction with the improvements which are now being carried out on the River Crane at Twickenham, the very latest type of flow-recorders, based on a " flume-wave " principle, are being installed.

As a result of the information collected, much useful work has been done, and is still in progress, in straightening, diverting, and strengthening the banks of rivers. At the present time surveys of the remaining sections of the streams still under the Council's control are being made with a view to their enlarge-

ment, the construction of new bridges with more ample waterways, and the provision of movable weirs by means of which the water may be controlled during flood periods. The cost of these works is estimated at £400,000.

An outside staff constantly patrols the streams, clearing away weeds, repairing banks, removing debris, and performing any other works necessary to ensure an unobstructed flow of water. In built-up districts, however, particularly where the streams run by gardens at the rear of the houses, much time, labour, and money is expended in clearing away garden rubbish which is thoughtlessly thrown into them, in spite of the fact that the County Council has power to take proceedings against people found committing this nuisance.

THE WEST MIDDLESEX MAIN DRAINAGE SCHEME

Of all the public services enjoyed by civilized communities, none is more essential than the provision of an abundant supply of water. Under modern conditions, water is not merely required to enable man to live, but is used much more extensively to carry away all kinds of dirt and waste matter, not only from baths, sinks and lavatories in the houses of the people, but also from industrial

TWO SEWERS ENTERING LARGE MAIN SEWER

— MIDDLESEX COUNTY COUNCIL —

— MAP OF WEST MIDDLESEX DRAINAGE DISTRICT —

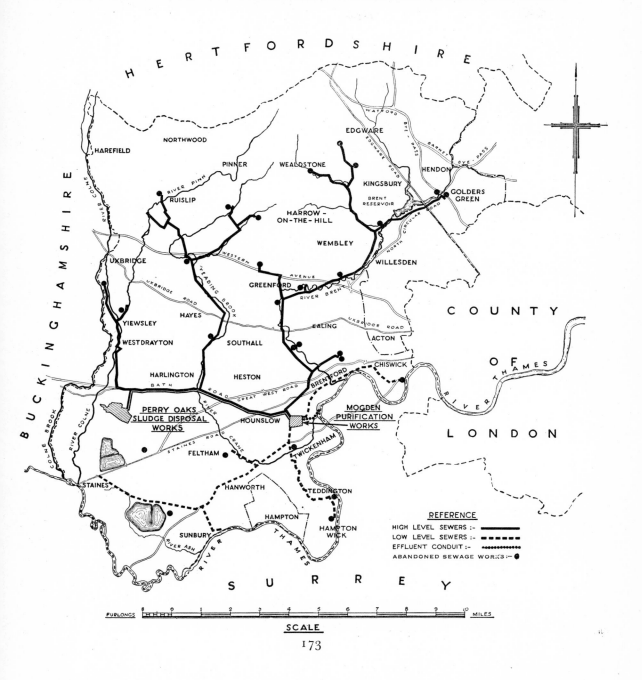

REFERENCE

HIGH LEVEL SEWERS :—
LOW LEVEL SEWERS :—
EFFLUENT CONDUIT :—
ABANDONED SEWAGE WORKS :—

SCALE

ISLEWORTH AIT, FROM THE AIR   *Showing six sewage outlets*

processes of every description. So universal has the use of water become that whereas a man needs only a few pints a day for drinking, he uses on an average no less than 40 gallons a day for other purposes.

When this used water leaves houses and factories, it is known as sewage, and is much too impure to be allowed to flow into the nearest stream or river, as it used to do in the past, without first being purified. For this purpose it is taken by drains from each building into sewers, along which it flows to the sewage purification works where it is treated by special processes. Sewers are generally laid beneath roads, but they may sometimes run across country, or even beneath houses. They are arranged in a similar manner to a river and its tributaries, commencing as small pipes of about 9 inches in diameter, and becoming steadily larger in size as they join up

with other sewers, until they may finally reach the size of the tube for an underground railway.

The Need for Co-operation

Until 1935 all the work of maintaining sewers and of purifying sewage in Middlesex was carried out by the local authority for each particular district. Not many years ago a large part of the County, particularly in the west, was predominantly rural in character. The comparatively small towns which then existed were separated by stretches of open country. Since the Great War the enormous amount of building development taking place everywhere in the area has been rapidly transforming the district into one vast town. As early as 1928 the population of the West Middlesex area had increased to such an extent that the local authorities were finding difficulty in extending their sewers and

174

MOGDEN, FROM THE AIR

in enlarging their sewage works to keep pace with the ever-increasing volume of sewage to be dealt with. It then became increasingly obvious that the difficulties of the area as a whole could not be overcome without some form of co-operation between the various districts, and the County Council undertook the task of considering the whole question.

As a result of this, it was finally agreed by the local authorities that the County Council should obtain powers, under a special Act of Parliament, to make provision for the main drainage and purification of sewage from an area embracing almost the whole of the western section of the County, known as the "West Middlesex sewerage district". This district, which has a total area of about 160 square miles—that is to say, an area about 35 per cent. greater than that of the County of London—includes seven boroughs and eight urban districts, which were formerly served by no less than twenty-eight separate local sewage works.

Scope of the Works

The new scheme, embodying the largest purification works in the world, caters for a population of 2,000,000, and was carried out between 1931 and 1935 at a cost of £5,500,000. It consisted of the construction of about 70 miles of main sewers, ranging from about 2 feet to 12 feet 9 inches in diameter, to link up the existing systems of local sewers with a new purification works at Mogden, Isleworth.

After the diversion of sewage into the new system early in 1936, all the twenty-eight old works, covering a total area of about 1000 acres in various parts of the County, were closed down.

The sewage from the whole of the district, from as far as Hendon and Mill Hill in the north, Uxbridge and Staines in the west, Sunbury and Twickenham in the south, and Ealing and Chiswick in the east, is drained by gravitation along the main sewers to the new purification works, some of it having travelled about 20 miles. Three-quarters of the total flow reaches the works in the high level sewers at about ground-level, but the remainder arrives by the low-level sewers at a considerable depth below the surface, and this has to be lifted about 50 feet by pumping before it passes forward with the high-level sewage for treatment.

Contrary to general conception, the amount of polluting matter in sewage is extremely small, being normally only about one part of solid matter to 2000 parts of water by weight. Yet the combined liquid as it arrives at the purification works is in a highly complicated state, and many decades have been occupied in evolving the processes at present in use for separating the impurities from the liquid and for transforming the separated sludge into a harmless condition. The removal of sand, grit, and heavy solid matter is a comparatively easy task, and is carried out by means of settlement in sedimentation tanks of various kinds. For the more difficult work of purification of fine suspended matter, and matter in solution, bacterial processes are used.

The Use of Bacteria

Bacteria are microscopic organisms, so tiny that it would take 25,000 of them placed side by side to make up 1 inch. A thimbleful of sewage can contain perhaps 10,000,000 of these small living cells, and given suitable conditions, they will bring about the most extraordinary changes in the physical and chemical properties of the materials to be dealt with. By their assistance the sewage is converted into a clear, sparkling liquid, which is then discharged into the River Thames at Isleworth Ait. The volume of sewage treated in this way in dry weather is about 45,000,000 gallons a day, but in wet weather the flow may reach a rate of over 300,000,000 gallons per day.

The impurities are removed from the sewage in a liquid form, known as sludge, of which 750,000 tons per annum have to be dealt with. Here again bacterial energy is used to transform the sludge into an absolutely inoffensive form, which can be dried without nuisance. During this process a gas is given off, consisting largely of methane, which is used for driving gas engines. *The entire power requirements of the purification works are provided from this sludge gas*, of which over 1,000,000 cubic feet per day are produced. Thus, in addition to purifying completely the whole of the sewage flow, it is interesting to reflect that at Mogden the sludge is made to remove itself from the sedimentation tanks, pump itself into the gas tanks, to heat itself to about 80° F., and again, at a later stage, to remove itself 7 miles to the Perry Oaks Works for final disposal. It is harnessed to lift the sewage at the main pumping-station, to operate sewage plant and pumps of all kinds, travelling cranes, and workshop machinery; it provides lighting and heating, charges batteries, cleans floors in buildings, operates synchronized clocks, and even carries visitors in lifts!

The present population served by the scheme is about 1,100,000, and this is increasing at the rate of about 50,000 per annum. In spite of the immense amount of work involved in constructing and operating a scheme of this kind, its total cost to the citizen of the district works out at a little over one penny per week per head, which can only be regarded as remarkably good value for the money expended.

8. ENTERTAINMENT LICENCES

Music and Dancing

MANY years ago Parliament appears to have reached the conclusion that the assembly of people for the purpose of public amusement required a measure of control, and as long ago as 1751, in the reign of George II, passed an Act known as the Disorderly Houses Act, prohibiting, amongst other things, the holding of public entertainments of music and dancing, except in premises licensed for the purpose by the justices. In 1875 the Public Entertainments Act slightly amended the 1751 Act, and by the Local Government Act, 1888, the powers given by these two Acts passed to the newly-formed county councils, so far as the area within 20 miles of London and Westminster cities was concerned. The County Council seems to have been dissatisfied with this limitation, and in 1894 promoted a special Act, known as the Music and Dancing Licences (Middlesex) Act, which gave it power to control public music and dancing entertainments over the whole of the County. This Act was amended by the Middlesex County Council (General Powers) Act, 1930, and the fee for a licence was increased from five shillings to ten shillings per annum. The Middlesex County Council Act, 1934, made provision for the control of boxing entertainments, and its Act of 1938 gave similar control of wrestling entertainments.

When the War broke out in 1914 there were 539 premises licensed for music and dancing, consisting of church halls, school halls, public halls, village halls, swimming-baths (in the winter time), club-rooms of public-houses and similar buildings. Since the War the number has steadily increased to a total of practically 1000, exclusive of cinematograph theatres which are referred to later.

Stage-Play Licences

In 1843, in Queen Victoria's reign, Parliament passed an Act prohibiting the holding of public stage-play entertainments except in premises licensed for the purpose. Most of the legitimate theatres where plays are performed are in the London area, and there are only a few in Middlesex, including two or three "music-halls"—that is, theatres where a type of entertainment known as "variety" is given, consisting of separate acts following in quick succession. A stage-play licence is granted for a period of one year from the 13th November, and the fee is £3.

The stage of a theatre must be separated from the rest of the building by a brick wall, and it must be possible to close the proscenium opening completely with a fireproof curtain. The stage roof must be high enough to permit of the curtain being raised in one piece, and the latter must be lowered in the presence of the audience to demonstrate that it is in working order.

Cinematograph Licences

It is necessary to realize that "moving" pictures on the screen are not in fact moving, but a series of stationary pictures changing at a speed of twenty-four per second. Whilst one picture is moving to give place to the next, a revolving shutter prevents light from coming through the lens of the projector. The speed, however, is such that the human eye cannot detect the dark periods, and so the effect of movement is imparted.

The "pictures" date from the early nineteenth century when the "Zoetrope" was invented. This machine produced pictures which apparently moved when a series of still animations, each slightly different from its neighbour, were viewed through a revolving slotted cylinder. It was Mr. William Friese-Green, however, who invented, in 1885, a camera to record movement by taking a succession of still pictures, and an apparatus on the lines of the old magic-lantern for showing them. The invention was improved by Mr. Robert Paul, who invented the

" Maltese Cross ", which is still used to give an intermittent movement to the film, allowing it to pause for a fraction of a second at the lens of the projector. Mr. Paul followed this up by the making of films, and in 1896 photographed the Derby. Films at this time used to be shown in converted shops, the projector being placed in the window and the picture thrown on to a screen stretched on the rear wall. The seating arrangements were primitive, and consisted of any odd chairs or boxes. The show started when the house was full and payment for admission had been collected, and was accompanied by music provided by a barrel-organ or piano.

At the close of the nineteenth century a disastrous fire occurring at a film exhibition held as the principal attraction of a charity bazaar in Paris proved a serious setback to films, and forced on the authorities the realization of the necessity for some measure of control over these exhibitions. During the performance a sudden flash lit up the projector, and the people seated near the apparatus rushed in panic for the nearest door. The fire, however, had caught the wooden hall and 130 persons were killed. The cause of the disaster was the ignition of the celluloid film—a danger which still exists, although many devices have been invented to reduce the risk.

The first effort to control this new form of entertainment was the prohibition of cinematograph exhibitions in premises licensed by the County Council for other amusements unless a special written permit was issued by the County Engineer after the apparatus had been inspected and found to have such safety devices as had then been thought out. In 1910 the Cinematograph Act, 1909, came into force, forbidding exhibitions of pictures by means of inflammable films except in premises licensed by a county council, and empowering the Secretary of State to make regulations for ensuring safety.

Immediately before this period, roller-skating had been a very popular pastime, and a large number of skating rinks were built in various parts of the County. As this amusement waned in popularity, the buildings were converted to cinematograph theatres, a few of which, considerably altered, remain to-day, and the converted shop began to give way to buildings designed for cinematograph exhibitions. The accommodation steadily increased, and nowadays cinemas accommodating 2000 persons are not uncommon. The largest theatre in the country was recently erected in Middlesex. It has seating accommodation for 4000 persons, and standing and waiting accommodation within the building for a further 2000. The small theatre, however, has not disappeared, and the smallest in the County, with accommodation for 330 persons, was completed a few months after the largest.

In 1929 the talking film, which had already been exhibited in a crude form at the British Empire Exhibition at Wembley and elsewhere as a novelty, came to this country, and soon firmly established itself. There were two systems. In the first, known as " sound-on-disc ", the sound was obtained from a gramophone record with an electric " pick-up ", its turn-table being run in synchronization with the projectors. This gave quite good results, but a break in the film or other minor accident led to a loss of synchronization. This system has now been superseded by a second method, known as " sound-on-film ", in which the sound-waves are photographed at the same time as the action, and synchronization is perfect.

The County Council now grants licences for about 140 cinemas, and by regulations and inspections it aims to make them safe and comfortable places of amusement. There must be a sufficient number of exits from every part of the house, which must be kept free from obstruction and constructed so as to open easily. The spacing of seating and the width and position of gangways must conform to fixed standards, and hydrants, fire-buckets, and extinguishers have to be provided in accessible positions. The

MOOR PARK GOLF LINKS   *GREEN BELT*

buildings must be constructed as far as possible of fire-resisting materials, and the projecting apparatus must be contained in a chamber of brick and concrete. The apertures through which the picture is projected have to be glazed and fitted with metal shutters on the inside, capable of release from the enclosure or the auditorium. After use, films must be rewound in a separate room, and kept in closed metal receptacles when not in use. The projector must have metal spool-boxes to contain the unexposed portions of the film, and be fitted with automatic and hand shutters to cut off the light and its attendant heat from the film in emergency.

Lavatory accommodation has to be provided for the audience, dressing-rooms for performers, and rest-rooms for the staff.

The electrical installation of the modern cinema is intricate and complicated, and is controlled by very stringent regulations. Heating and ventilation are important, and are now combined in a " Plenum " system. Fresh air is drawn in by means of fans, passed through a washer, which cleanses and humidifies it, and, after heating, forces it into the auditorium, whilst the vitiated air is expelled by extract fans.

All these regulations contain a mass of details, but this main summary should give some idea of the extent of the care taken by the County Council in its endeavours to ensure the comfort and safety of the general public.

Horse Racing

The Racecourses Licensing Act, 1879, forbids the holding of horse-racing meetings within an area of 10 miles of Charing Cross, without the Council's licence. There is only one such track in Middlesex, that at Alexandra Palace, which is partly in the Borough of Wood Green and partly in the Borough of Hornsey.

Greyhound Racing

By the Betting and Lotteries Act, 1934, the County Council has some control over greyhound racing tracks. Parliament limited the number of days upon which dog racing may be held to 104 in a year, and the County Council was directed to grant licences to tracks already in existence for a period of five years. In the case of new tracks, however, the County Council has some discretion, and may refuse a licence in certain circumstances. New licences are granted for a period of seven years.

General

Let us now consider briefly how the Council exercises the powers which Parliament has given it, and which, broadly speaking, are to grant licences to such persons as it may think fit, to use premises specified in the licence for the purpose of entertainment on such terms and conditions, and subject to such restrictions, as is by the licence prescribed, except under the Betting and Lotteries Act, already mentioned.

The person seeking a licence to hold public entertainments has the option of submitting the plans of the building which he proposes to erect or alter. This enables him to find out before he starts work whether they comply with the requirements necessary to fit the premises for such a licence. The plans are reported upon in detail by the County Engineer and, if approval is given, it is subject to any conditions he may think desirable. Notice of the application has to be placed on the site or building, and given to the police, and any ratepayer, upon satisfying the Clerk of the County Council that he has an interest, may lodge an objection and be heard by the Committee. Whether or not the plans have been deposited for approval, application for a licence has to be made in the same manner on completion of the building.

All licensed buildings are visited by the County Council's inspectors before the licence is renewed each year, and inspections are made from time to time during the progress of entertainments, particularly of cinematograph theatres, to ascertain that the regulations are being complied with. Offences are reported to the Committee, which may direct proceedings to be taken.

No films may be shown unless passed by the British Board of Film Censors, but film renters may appeal to the Committee against the Board's decision. The practice has been instituted of referring such appeals for joint inspection by the Committees of the County Councils of London, Middlesex, Surrey and Essex, which have the advantage of each other's views before deciding whether or not to endorse the Board's decision. This system also ensures considerable uniformity over a large area. Films are given a category—" Universal ", " Adult ", or " Horrific ". The first may be shown without restriction, but children under sixteen may not be admitted to an " A " film unless they are accompanied by their parent or guardian. Children when refused admission for this reason should not ask strangers to take them into the theatre. When an " H " category film is being exhibited no children may be admitted.

Under the Sunday Entertainments Act, 1932, the cinematograph theatres are allowed to open on Sundays in districts in which the local council decides accordingly, but a certain percentage of the takings has to be paid to the County Council, which divides the money amongst deserving local charitable undertakings. No member of the cinema staff may be employed on Sunday, unless he or she has had a day's rest in the preceding week.

It may be safely concluded, from the care taken as to exit provisions and the safeguards mentioned, that fire of such dimensions as to endanger the lives of an audience is hardly possible, and that the only way such a regrettable result is likely to be brought about is by the audience themselves becoming panic-stricken and preventing one another from using the means of egress provided for their safe escape. If we could all feel satisfied in our own minds that there is no danger of fire (not that minor fires may not occur in the fireproof chamber in which the apparatus is installed, because with inflammable film they may), then in an emergency we should be content to follow the directions of the management, and leave the building in perfect order and safety. A theatre holding 2000 persons can be emptied in under two minutes if everybody goes quietly to the nearest exit.

9. VALUATION

THE many public services, including education, health, police protection, roads and so forth, provided by county councils and the councils of boroughs, urban and rural districts—all have to be paid for.

The money necessary to supply these services is raised partly by means of a rate charged upon the occupiers of nearly every kind of existing land and buildings, and partly by a system of payments, termed grants, from the Government.

The amount which the occupier of a house or other property has to pay in rates is worked out according to the yearly rental worth of the property he occupies, and this is called the rateable value of that property. In order to find out how much each ratepayer has to contribute, the local authorities make an estimate of their liabilities at the beginning of the year and they know then how much money they will have to collect to pay for the cost of all the services in the coming year. From this amount they deduct the sums they calculate will be received as grants from the Government, and what is left is the amount to be met by the local ratepayers.

FIXING THE COUNTY RATE

You will have read in the chapter on the work of the Finance Department about estimating the normal cost of the local government services and in order to determine the sum payable by each individual ratepayer, the authority keeps a record of every property in the district showing its rateable value. The total rateable value of the district is, of course, the sum of all the rateable values of all the properties.

If the total rateable value were £240,000, a rate of 1d. for each £1 rateable value should produce £1000; subject, of course, to certain losses in collection. The amount found by multiplying the total rateable value by 1d. is termed the "product of a penny rate".

Now, suppose a local authority has to raise £120,000 from the ratepayers, we can find by a simple proportion sum what the rate for the year will have to be—i.e., if £1000 produces 1d. £120,000 produces 10s., so that the rate will be 10s., and each ratepayer will have to pay 10s. for each £1 rateable value of his assessment, and if his property is assessed at £20 rateable value, he will have to pay £10 altogether. This amount will be charged to his account in the authority's rate book, and the authority in due course serves a demand note upon the occupier which sets out all the particulars as to how the rate is made up.

Fixing and collecting the county rates is the work of the finance departments of the local councils, whilst the work of making assessments—that is, finding out the rateable value of each property—is carried out by the Valuation Department. It is about this Department that it is intended here to give you some particulars

THE LAKE, GRIMS DYKE   GREEN BELT

—how it does its work, and which properties are assessed and so forth.

Rating assessments really form the foundation stone of local government finance, as without these assessments it would be extremely difficult, if not impossible, to estimate each ratepayer's share of liability. As it is, a great responsibility rests upon all persons engaged in making these assessments, because the law says that each ratepayer must be justly and fairly assessed upon his property in relation to his fellow-men.

The occupier is the person assessed, and this was laid down by an Act of Parliament passed as long ago as 1601, and sometimes referred to as the Statute of Elizabeth. The sums collected were, in those days, used entirely to relieve the increased poverty caused by Henry VIII's action in suppressing the monasteries. Thus it will be seen that rating has a long history. Of course since that time many Acts have been passed altering the law, but still, even to-day, the effect of the Act of 1601 is felt, and parts of it are still in force, although the law is mainly enforced to-day by the Rating and Valuation Act, 1925.

The principal bodies with duties of preparing assessments are:—

1. Rating Authorities.
2. Assessment Committees.
3. County Valuation Committees.

RATING AUTHORITIES

The "rating authority" is the council of the local authority, and it is usual for its work to be delegated to a committee known as the valuation committee, whose task is to make assessments and record all particulars in the "valuation list" (which has to be prepared once every five years, although it may be altered and added to during the five-year period, on account of alterations in the value of the property). The valuation list, which is generally kept at the town hall or council offices, contains the address and a description of each property, together with the value placed upon it by the rating authority, and the names of the occupier and the owner.

When the time comes for a new valuation list to be prepared, what is termed a re-valuation takes place, and the value of each property is reviewed to find out whether the ratepayer is paying his correct proportion of rates; this does not mean that the rateable value is bound to be altered, as it may be found that he is paying his fair share, but should it be found that the rental value of his property has increased or decreased an amendment will be made in the valuation list.

ASSESSMENT COMMITTEES

Each county is divided into assessment areas, Middlesex being divided into five such areas, and a committee is appointed for each. If a ratepayer is dissatisfied with his assessment in the valuation list, he can appeal to this committee, and after hearing the ratepayer's grievance and the evidence of the rating authority, the committee decides whether or not the valuation in the valuation list is correct.

GRIMS DYKE   *GREEN BELT*

THE COUNTY VALUATION COMMITTEE

The council of every county has to appoint a valuation committee, which carries out very important work. In every county about three-quarters of all the rates collected have to be paid over by the local authorities to the county council, which is responsible for most of the public services. Therefore it is very necessary for the county council to know that each rating authority is making fair and just assessments, as otherwise some ratepayers would obtain an unfair advantage over others in different parts of the county. Hence, the county valuation committee is entrusted with the work of investigating the correctness of all valuation for rates in the county and of putting right such unfair treatment as they may find. They also have to assist rating authorities and assessment committees by calling conferences to discuss difficult problems and so forth.

VALUATION OF PROPERTY

The actual work of valuing property for the rating authorities and county valuation committees is done by specially trained officials, as the work is of a very intricate nature. If you pause for a moment to consider the many kinds of property in your own town or district, you will see how difficult this work really is.

Now, most kinds of property—that is, land and any buildings erected on land—are valued for assessment purposes, but not *every* kind, some being altogether excused from paying rates, whilst others are assessed on a proportion of their full value, this latter being known as de-rating. Then again, other properties receive special treatment because the occupiers do not obtain the same benefit from the services provided as do others.

In 1937 the total rateable value of properties in England and Wales was £298,530,000, and the amount of rates received by local authorities was £171,500,000. The average rate in the £ was 11s. 6d. and the average amount of

money received was equal to £4 4s. 5d. per head of the total population. The total annual rateable valuation of all the property in Middlesex amounts to about £20,000,000, and there are over half a million separate assessments.

TYPES OF PROPERTY ASSESSED

Now a word or two about the different kinds of property assessed for rating purposes. Dwelling-houses will occur to you as the most common type, and in fact these form the largest class of rateable property, both in number and value, although individually the value of houses is not as a rule very large. As with other property houses are assessed upon a just and reasonable estimate of the annual rental value, and as so many houses are occupied by tenants who pay rent, the rents paid provide a good guide in estimating the rateable values of this class of property. Houses are assessed in full.

Other properties of an everyday variety which are assessed for rates at their full values are shops, offices, showrooms and garages, hotels and public-houses, cinemas and theatres. The local authorities are often classed as occupiers of property— for instance, schools, town halls, libraries and swimming-baths are in their occupation—and because of their occupation they have to pay rates just as an ordinary ratepayer does.

Football and cricket grounds, racecourses and sports grounds of all kinds are assessable.

A more uncommon kind of property is that belonging to, and occupied by, tramway, gas, electricity and water companies, yet these, too, have to bear their fair share of rates. For example, tramway companies occupy depôts and offices for which they are assessed, and, in addition, the law says that they occupy the tramlines and overhead wires in the public streets, because no one else can use them and they are necessary for the tramway undertaking to be carried on; hence these items, too, have to be assessed. Rates, however, are not paid on the tramcars themselves, nor on electric trolley-buses, because they belong to the occupiers, and are not fixed property like buildings—in other words, they are similar to personal belongings, and are called chattels, and cannot be assessed, although many years ago they were liable for assessment.

In the case of gas-supply undertakings, you will know the appearance of the works where gas is extracted from coal and stored in gasometers. All the lands and buildings at the gas-works are rateable; the gasometers are naturally looked upon as buildings, and anything in the nature of a building or structure comes within the scope of assessment. The gas is supplied by means of pipes laid underground, and these are also rateable.

The reservoirs of a water company likewise have to be assessed; but if they are situate in an urban district, they are assessed at a lower rate, because, being land covered with water, many of the services provided out of rates would not prove of benefit in respect of the reservoirs, and it would be unjust to charge the occupier for something from which he could never receive any benefit.

DE-RATING

In order to assist in relieving the expenses of agriculture and industry, the Government some years ago decided to de-rate agricultural land and buildings, industrial and freight transport properties. As a result farm land and farm buildings are now exempt from rates, but the farmhouse wherein the farmer and his family live is still rated, though this is the only portion of the farm that is assessed.

Industrial premises—that is, factories of all kinds where manufacture is carried on—coal and other mines, quarries and brickfields, are assessed at one quarter of their full value. Should the property be used for a purpose which is not primarily or mainly a purpose of manufacturing—for instance, the purpose of a dwelling-house, retail shop, warehouse, garage or store-place—then the de-rating

relief cannot be given. In some cases, of course, premises are used partly for manufacture and partly for other purposes, such as those mentioned above, in which case, if the manufacturing side is the primary reason for the existence of the business, a proportionate amount of relief is granted.

Public utility undertakings, such as gas companies and the like, are not treated as industrial properties, and are not de-rated.

Docks, harbours, wharves and canals, and of course railways, are freight transport properties, and these are assessed upon one-fourth of their full value if the business they carry on is the transporting of merchandise not intended for the use of the occupiers of the property. Where passengers as well as merchandise are transported, the position is not altered, otherwise very few railways, for instance, would receive the benefit of de-rating; but the tube railways, which only carry passengers, are not able to be de-rated, for that reason. It must be noted that the relief which freight-carrying properties receive from rates has to be paid into a fund which is used to reduce the cost of transport charges upon certain kinds of heavy goods, such as iron and steel, so that industry benefits from this de-rating, and not the companies which provide the transport.

All the parts of a railway are rateable, including the running lines, stations, warehouses, engine-sheds, and in fact all the hundred-and-one items which make up the entire system. The undertaking as a whole is valued, and the value is split up and apportioned to each individual building or the lines in each parish, this work being carried out by a body known as the Railway Assessment Authority which was set up by special Act of Parliament in 1930.

Properties which are occupied for the purposes of the Crown are exempt from rates. These include not only the great Royal palaces and other offices of state, but also local police stations, post offices, telephone exchanges, premises used for the administration of justice and so forth. The Government, however, does make grants in the place of rates based upon a fair value for these premises, but these payments are entirely at the discretion of the Government, which cannot be compelled to pay if it decides not to do so.

Other properties which are exempt by Act of Parliament include churches, chapels, Sunday schools, schools provided by voluntary bodies, literary and scientific societies' premises, ambassadors' residences, certain light-houses and drill halls.

ACQUISITION OF LAND

In addition to the valuation side of the work, another section of the County Valuer's Department deals with negotiations for the acquisition and sale of lands in which the County Council is interested. In this capacity it has dealt with a very large area of land for the purposes of the " Green Belt ".

10. OPEN SPACES AND SPORTS GROUNDS

DURING the past few years a great advance has been made in the provision of open spaces and sports grounds in the County, and the County Council has voted considerable sums towards the purchase of lands either by other local authorities or by the County Council itself for such purposes.

The following statement gives particulars relating to proposals for new open spaces and sports grounds dealt with by the County Council during the past few years, including the more important additions to existing open spaces and sports grounds, but ignoring minor adjustments which have been agreed:—

Borough or Urban District or other area where situated.	Name or Description.	Year(s) of County Council's Resolution(s).	Area in Acres.
Acton	Springfield Gardens	1934	5·54
Brentford and Chiswick .	Chiswick House and Grounds, additional land	1935	1·5
County of Buckingham .	Ankerwycke Estate, Wraysbury	1936	110
,, ,, .	Huntsmoor Park, Iver	1937	6·31
County of Buckingham and Uxbridge U.D. . .	Denham Court	1935	306
Ealing	Perivale Park Golf Course	1934	90
,, ...	Land near St. Mary's Church, Northolt	1936	22·982
,, ...	Lime Tree Farm Estate, Northolt	1936	23
,, ...	Brent Valley Golf Course	1936	81
,, ...	Horsenden Hill Open Space, additional land, Brabsden Green	1937	1·25
,, ...	Land on Rectory Estate, Northolt	1936	64
,, ...	Land east of River Brent, Hanwell	1937	4·25
,, ...	The Ballot Box, Horsenden Hill	1937	1·25
Edmonton . . .	Bury Lodge	1934	4·5
,, . . .	Land at junction of Cambridge Road and Church Street	1935	·23
,, . . .	Jubilee Park	1935	37
,, . . .	Bush Hill Park, Land adjoining Cambridge Arterial Road	1937	8·85
Enfield	Enfield Chase	1936	2,005

Borough or Urban District or other area where situated.	Name or Description.	Year(s) of County Council's Resolution(s).	Area in Acres.
Enfield	Land on Ayland's Estate, Bullsmoor Lane	1936	10
,, ...	Trinity College Lands	1937	586·8
,, ...	Bush Hill Park Golf Course	1937	105
,, ...	Enfield Golf Course	1937	91·5
,, ...	Longford Farm, The Ridgeway	1937	5·65
Feltham	Footpath Meadow, Hanworth	1934	8·5
,, ...	Land adjoining River Crane	1936	11·696
,, ...	East Bedfont Open Space	1937	20·877
,, ...	River Crane Regional Open Space	1937	12
,, ...	East Bedfont Open Space (additional)	1937	58·593
,, ...	Faggs Road, East Bedfont	1937	13·09
Finchley	Victoria Recreation Ground, additional land	1934	·375
,, ...	Land south of " La Délivrance ", Regent's Park Road	1934	1·03
,, ...	Land at junction of Great North Way and North Circular Road	1937	2·62
,, ...	Windsor Open Space, Broughton Avenue	1937	1
,, ...	Land north side of Totteridge Lane	1937	·92
Harrow	Canons Park Open Space, additional land	1936	8·35
,, ...	Centenary Park, Stanmore	1934	24
,, ...	Kenton Recreation Ground, additional land	1934	4·613
,, ...	Bennetts Park, Pinner	1935	6·3
,, ...	Montesole Playing Fields, Pinner Green	1935	19
,, ...	Pinner Recreation Ground	1935	3·5
,, ...	Saddlers Mead, Hatch End	1936	10·3
,, ...	Part of Edgware Golf Course	1936	7
Hayes and Harlington .	Land in Brickfield Lane, Harlington	1936	1·25
,, ,, .	Yeading Brook Regional Open Space, additional land	1934–35	7·887
,, ,, .	Land at Pinkwell, Harlington	1937	9·11
,, ,, .	The Lake, Botwell	1937	3·45
,, ,, .	The Moats, Harlington	1937	10
,, ,, .	Yeading Brook Regional Open Space	1937	62
,, ,, .	Land near Yeading Lane	1937	·997
,, ,, .	Little Harlington Field	1937	10·578
,, ,, .	Berkeley Meadows	1937	3·208
Hertford, County of .	Moor Park, Rickmansworth	1937	350
Heston and Isleworth	Silver Hall, Isleworth	1937	3
,, ,, .	Various lands in Borough	1937	29·29
,, ,, .	Various lands in Borough	1937	54·015
,, ,, .	River Crane Regional Open Space	1937	65·146
Hornsey	Holy Innocents' School Site	1935	·427
,, ...	Land at Shepherd's Hill	1937	1 59
Potters Bar . . .	Furzefield Wood and adjoining land	1935	40
,, . . .	Wrotham Park, Old Fold Golf Course, Dyrham Park and adjoining lands	1937	1465
Ruislip-Northwood . .	Field End Road Open Space, Eastcote (additional land)	1935	4·792
,, ,, . .	Eastcote Recreation Ground	1934–35	10·5
,, ,, . .	King's End Golf Course, Ruislip, and adjoining land	1935–36	107·484
,, ,, . .	Eastcote House	1935	9·1
,, ,, . .	Mad Bess and Copse Wood Estates	1935	341·75
,, ,, . .	Land between Cuckoo Hill and Catlins Lane, Eastcote	1937	6

Borough or Urban District or other area where situated.	Name or Description.	Year(s) of County Council's Resolution(s).	Area in Acres.
Ruislip-Northwood	Land off Shenley Avenue, Ruislip	1936	3·22
,, ,,	Land east of Cheney Street, Eastcote	1936	5
,, ,,	Land south of High Road, Eastcote	1936	5·93
,, ,,	Haydon Hall, Eastcote	1936	14·7
,, ,,	Land on St. Catherine's Estate, Ruislip	1936	8·4
,, ,,	Land on Ruislip Gardens Estate	1937	6·512
,, ,,	Land adjoining Northolt Junction Estate	1937	39·7
,, ,,	Land at Herlwyn Avenue, Ruislip	1937	25
,, ,,	Land between Fore Street and Joel Street	1937	1·3
Southall	Dairy Meadow	1936	6·217
,,	Viaduct Field	1936	4·22
,,	Land in Dormers Wells Lane	1936	10
,,	Durdans Park	1936	29·2
,,	Jubilee Park	1936	11·13
,,	Land at Norwood Green	1936	2·62
Southgate	Hazelwood Lane Sports Ground	1934	12·3
,,	Tottenhall Road Sports Ground	1935–36	7·25
,,	Bramley Sports Ground	1935	19·836
,,	Clowes Sports Ground, Winchmore Hill	1935	22
,,	Streamside Walk, Winchmore Hill	1935	2·07
Staines	Shrublands, Woodthorpe Road, Ashford	1934	6·5
,,	Laleham House Estate	1934	69·5
,,	Laleham House Estate, additional land (Arcadia Café)	1937	1·38
,,	Land at Town Lane, Stanwell	1937	5·572
Sunbury-on-Thames	Land at Lower Hampton Road	1937	1·892
,,	Land in Feltham Hill Road, Ashford Common	1937	4·844
Teddington ⎱ Twickenham ⎰	Fulwell Golf Course	1935–36	210·788
,,	Strawberry Hill Golf Course	1936	31
Twickenham	Crane Park	1934	44
,,	Heathfield Pleasure Ground	1936	12·5
Uxbridge	Harefield Place Estate	1934	127·86
,,	Ickenham Recreation Ground	1935	2·106
,,	Yeading Brook Regional Open Space, additional land	1935	15·4
,,	Warren Farm, near South Harefield	1936	77·74
,,	Mount Pleasant Sports Ground, Harefield	1936	26·5
,,	Breakspears Estate, Harefield	1936	572·5
,,	Long Lane and Pole Hill Road, Hillingdon	1937	91·767
,,	Long Lane and Pole Hill Road, Hillingdon (additional)	1937	1·28
Wembley	Land at Perivale Lane, Alperton	1934	22·387
,,	Roe Green Park	1934	20·5
,,	Tokyngton Recreation Ground, additional land	1935	3·88
,,	Cardinal Vaughan Playing Field	1935	6·38
,,	Land adjoining Watford Road and Barn Hill Open Space	1936	365·4
,,	Roe Green Park, additional land	1936	5·5
,,	Imperial College of Science Sports Ground	1936	21·25
,,	Land adjacent to Barn Hill Open Space	1937	3
,,	Land adjoining Alperton Children's Playground	1937	·307
Willesden	Addition to Roundwood Park, Knowles Tower	1937	1·14
Yiewsley and West Drayton	Green Belt	1937	58·213

GENERAL POLICY

In view of the rapid building development taking place in the County, it has become increasingly necessary to hasten endeavours to secure sufficient land for the provision of public open spaces and sports grounds for the needs of the future population of the County.

In 1934 the County Council obtained parliamentary powers to acquire land in advance of immediate requirements, and in November of that year the General Purposes Committee considered the question of expediting the provision of open spaces. In 1933, only 6·5 per cent. of the County was covered by existing public open spaces and sports grounds, and from a survey made by the Greater London Regional Planning Committee, it appeared that land within the area of that committee was being absorbed for building at the rate of 1400 acres per annum.

The powers recently obtained from Parliament have rendered possible the more speedy acquisition of land with a view to preventing building development without disturbing its existing use, and the several local authorities in the County were informed that the County Council would be prepared to negotiate for the purchase (in advance of requirements) of lands considered suitable for the purposes of open spaces, and would render substantial financial assistance in the acquisition of approved areas and, upon an interim report of the Development Committee, the County Council approved in principle the acquisition of existing golf-courses and woodland areas in the County.

As a result of the above action, the councils of several county districts submitted a number of proposals which were enquired into by the Development Committee and by the Open Spaces Sub-Committee; a number of conferences with local authorities was held, and certain acquisitions approved. In consequence of the increased activity in this connection, both on the part of the County Council and of the councils of county districts, it

is now estimated that the open spaces and sports grounds, including those lands which it has been decided to purchase but which have not yet been dedicated, amount to over 10 per cent. of the area of the County.

An endeavour has been made to achieve a conspectus of the County's requirements in connection with regional open spaces and the " Green Belt ". Including those open spaces already sanctioned for purchase by the County Council, there has been borne in mind the extreme desirability of acquiring as regional open spaces about 10,000 acres, which would bring the total area—regional and local—to approximately 19,000 acres in all. This is the ideal aimed at because, with smaller purely local open spaces to which the County Council might be asked to contribute, the total acreage of open spaces would be brought up to about 20,000, which figure, while well exceeding 10 per cent. of the County's entire area—the minimum reservation almost uniformly agreed—has the additional merit of meeting the situation from an even more important angle.

Many experts are agreed that, in an urbanized county of the character of Middlesex, open spaces should be reserved in the proportion of seven acres to every 1000 persons. If a possible maximum population of three million in the County is assumed, it will be appreciated that, to cover the requirements of all recreational and health purposes, 21,000 acres of open spaces should be provided.

As to the cost, it was estimated in February 1936 that the total future financial commitment for the County Council, assuming that an average of 25 per cent. of the whole cost would be borne by the London County Council and 25 per cent. of the balance by the local authorities, would be in the neighbourhood of £1,500,000, and, so far as could then be intelligently anticipated, £1,000,000 of this sum would be required before the 31st March, 1937, while the balance of £500,000 would be spread

A MEET OF THE HUNT   ENFIELD CHASE

over a number of years and counter-balanced by the normal increase of rateable value of the County, thus involving no extra rate charge on the County finances.

It was felt that, unless the problem were tackled with foresight and courage and without delay in the comprehensive manner indicated, the result would be that over a period of years it would be necessary for the County Council to pay similar money for what would then be the equivalent of only half the area or, in other words, prices would be doubled.

It was anticipated that the proposed policy, if vigorously pursued, would result in a rapidly increasing rateable value, by reason of the fact that the remaining undeveloped areas would be covered more quickly and with a better type of property owing to competition for land. Further, the health of the people would be so much improved as automatically to effect a considerable saving in the future expenses of the public health services.

THE PROPOSED "GREEN BELT" ROUND LONDON

The proposals included the definite establishment of the " Green Belt "—so long regarded as a nebulous dream—which would in fact consist of a practically unbroken stretch of open country running from the extreme north-east of the County and finishing in the south-west on the borders of Buckinghamshire by the River Thames. They further included almost all the golf-courses worthy of being preserved and magnificent areas of agricultural and open country in the north and north-west of the County.

The policy briefly outlined above was approved in principle by the County Council at its meeting on the 27th February, 1936, and the Council then gave instructions to the General Purposes Committee to proceed as quickly as possible to submit recommendations with regard to suitable pieces of land.

Early in 1935 the London County Council had decided that it would contribute a sum not exceeding £2,000,000 over a period of three years towards the cost of the acquisition or, where legally possible, sterilization (that is, preservation for all time as an open space), by the councils of the counties of Buckingham, Essex, Hertford, Kent, Middlesex and Surrey, and of the County Boroughs of Croydon, East Ham and West Ham, of approved lands suitable for recreational purposes or forming part of a green belt around London.

The grants were to vary in amount according to the value to London of the lands proposed to be acquired or sterilized, but were not in any case to exceed 50 per cent. of the approved cost of acquisition or sterilization, and no part of the cost of laying-out or maintaining the lands would be included.

In Middlesex, a commencement on a scheme for a " green belt " had been made as far back as 1932, when the County Council agreed to contribute up to £226,000 towards the cost of the reservation of an area of about 753 acres, in the late Hendon Rural District. Accordingly, upon learning of the terms of the London County Council's resolution, the County Council readily expressed its appreciation of the offer and its willingness to co-operate in the matter.

ACQUISITION OF LAND SCHEDULED IN TOWN PLANNING SCHEMES

In order to encourage the proximity of new estates of small houses to permanently open land, the County Council

VIEW FROM ENFIELD RIDGEWAY, LOOKING EAST   GREEN BELT

WHITE WEBBS   ENFIELD

in February 1935 agreed in principle to contribute at least 25 per cent. of the cost of necessary expenditure incurred in securing as open space one-third of any land which would otherwise be scheduled under Town-Planning Schemes for residential development at twelve houses or more to the acre. Subsequently, in June 1936 this offer was, on the recommendation of the Development Committee, increased to 50 per cent.

REVENUE FROM OPEN SPACES AND SPORTS GROUNDS

In view of the very heavy charge upon local rates of the maintenance of open spaces and the desire of the County Council to encourage local authorities to increase the acreage of open spaces in their areas, the County Council has decided that local authorities shall not be required to pay back any of the income from municipal golf courses or from other games on public open spaces and has informed them that such income should be allocated towards the cost of maintenance of all open spaces in their particular districts.

In the case of sports grounds acquired under section 69 of the Public Health Act, 1925, and therefore eligible to be let to private clubs, the County Council still requires an appropriate proportion of the revenue received to be paid into the County fund but, in order to assist the local authorities, has decided that, in calculating the sums to be paid to the

RIVER PINN RESERVATION   *ICKENHAM*

County Council in any year, the local authorities may set off the nett losses on all such sports grounds against the nett profits on others.

ACQUISITION OF OPEN SPACES

For some time it has been the practice of the County Council, when contributing the larger part of expenditure incurred in the acquisition of land for open spaces, to require as a condition of its grant that it should itself become the freeholder of the property.

In June 1935 it was definitely decided that, in all future cases in which the County Council agreed to make a contribution of 50 per cent. or more of the cost involved, the freehold of the land should be conveyed to the County Council. In such cases the general practice is for the land to be leased to the borough or district council in whose area it is situated, on a 999 years' lease at a nominal rental. The procedure has the advantage of enabling the County Council to exercise greater control of the open spaces than would otherwise be the case and the County Council is in a stronger position in preventing any unauthorized dealing with the land.

MAINTENANCE OF REGIONAL OPEN SPACES

The recent widening in scope of the County Council's policy, particularly in connection with the reservation of large areas for inclusion in the proposed " Green Belt ", has necessitated certain arrangements being made for the management of estates on behalf of the County Council.

N   193

In several instances it has been found unnecessary or undesirable, for the time being, to lease lands to the local authorities concerned for use as public open spaces but desirable that the properties be temporarily retained in their agricultural condition, the existing tenant farmers being allowed to remain in possession of their holdings. No change has, however, been made in the County Council's policy of not, itself, managing actual parks and public open spaces.

OPEN-AIR SWIMMING-POOLS

During recent years there has been a great demand for facilities for open-air bathing and there has been an increasing tendency on the part of local authorities to avail themselves of their powers of providing open-air swimming-baths. A number of applications from borough and urban district councils has been considered for permission to provide such facilities on public open spaces towards the cost of the provision of which the County Council has contributed, and during the last few years the County Council has consented to the construction of open-air swimming-baths on public open spaces or sports grounds.

11. AGRICULTURE

DESPITE the enormous growth of population, the agricultural industry continues to be the greatest in the County, and very large capital sums are invested, not only in the freehold of farm lands, but also in buildings, glasshouses, heating plant, irrigation and other equipment essential to an intensively worked industry. The scientific skill and intensive methods which have been developed by many generations of farmers in Middlesex are common knowledge, and are widely referred to as examples of the most advanced husbandry.

The Agricultural Committee, as the official voice of the County in assisting in the solution of agricultural problems, always gives consideration to any matter affecting the welfare of the agricultural interests in the County, dealing with matters within the powers entrusted to it, or communicating with an appropriate authority which is in a position to render advice and assistance. The administrative powers and duties of the Committee may be briefly summarized as being covered by the following Acts:—

Ministry of Agriculture and Fisheries Act, 1919,
Corn Production Acts (Repeal) Act, 1921,
Agricultural Holdings Act, 1923,
Rent and Mortgage Interest Restrictions (Amendment) Act, 1933,
Small Holdings Acts, 1908–1926,
Fertilizers and Feeding Stuffs Act, 1926,
Diseases of Animals Acts, 1894–1935,
Destructive Insects and Pests Acts, 1877–1927.

AGRICULTURAL COMMITTEES (INJURIOUS WEEDS) ORDER, 1921

It is the duty of the Committee to take the necessary action, laid down in the Order, to prevent the growth and spreading of the injurious weeds scheduled by the Act.

AGRICULTURAL HOLDINGS ACT, 1923

This consolidating Act requires certain matters to be referred to county agricultural committees, including decisions as to whether or not an agricultural holding is being cultivated according to the

ENFIELD CHASE   GREEN BELT

" rules of good husbandry " and the " custom of the country " in the locality in which the holding is situated. In the event of such reference being made to the Committee in a case where the landlord has given notice to a tenant terminating the tenancy on the grounds of bad cultivation, if the landlord's contention is upheld, he is relieved from paying compensation for disturbance. The submission of these cases by landlords is relatively an expensive matter, and such cases are invariably strongly contested.

RENT AND MORTGAGE INTEREST RESTRICTIONS (AMENDMENT) ACT, 1933

Under Section 3 (1) (a) of this Act, the obligation of a landlord to provide alter-native housing accommodation is not required as a condition to an Order for possession or judgment, if the Court is satisfied from a certificate of the County Agricultural Committee that the dwelling-house is required for the occupation of a person engaged on work necessary for the proper working and cultivation of an agricultural holding. The fullest facilities are given to both landlords and tenants to appear before the Committee before a certificate is either granted or refused.

FERTILIZERS AND FEEDING-STUFFS ACT, 1926

A large number of samples, both formal and informal, of fertilizers and feeding-stuffs are taken every year, and the various merchants and vendors concerned, in the event of the samples proving unsatisfactory, are either warned by letter or proceedings are instituted against them.

SMALL HOLDINGS AND ALLOTMENTS

The County Council owns over 1500 acres of agricultural land, which is let out to over 150 small holders. An endeavour has been made to exact as high a standard of agricultural knowledge and business aptitude as can reasonably be enforced in the selection of tenants, and this has resulted in the securing of a very deserving and hard-working class of tenant.

ALLOTMENTS

The duty of providing allotments is imposed primarily on borough and urban district councils, and generally this is done by amicable arrangement between these bodies and the owners and occupiers of the land secured for allotments. Where compulsory powers are required, boroughs and urban district councils have the power to make the necessary orders. Undoubtedly owing to the great building development taking place in the County, there has been a great decline in the number of allotments, as landowners have, under the Small Holdings and Allotments Act, resumed possession of their property for building development but, on the other hand, there has been a very great increase in the number of gardens attached to houses which has been a welcome compensating feature.

DISEASES OF ANIMALS

Many Orders are made by the Ministry of Agriculture and Fisheries by which the County Council is required to take vigorous measures to deal with various diseases of animals, such as sheep scab and foot and mouth disease, and also with the movement of swine, and the Council is also bound by Order of the Minister to require the compulsory treatment of cattle for the prevention of warble fly. Co-operation between the inspectors under the Milk and Dairies Orders and the inspectors under the Diseases of Animals Acts has also resulted in tracing many animals affected with tuberculosis.

12. MISCELLANEOUS POWERS AND PUBLIC UTILITY SERVICES

Housing

The County Council has, in the last few years, made advances totalling over £5,900,000 by way of mortgage under the Housing Acts and Small Dwellings Acts to applicants desirous of financial help in the purchase of houses for their own occupation. These powers are referred to in Part Two.

Public Control and Local Taxation

The very numerous duties of the Public Control and Local Taxation Departments are dealt with in detail in Part Four.

Jury Lists, Registration of Electors, of Births, Deaths and Marriages, and of Local Land Charges

The Clerk of the County Council is responsible for the administration and supervision of the services dealing with the registration of births, deaths and marriages, as referred to in connection with the duties of the General Purposes Committee; and as Registration Officer for the County (excluding the Parliamentary boroughs) he is also responsible for the preparation each year of the list of electors and of persons liable to serve on juries. He also, as Local Registrar, is the responsible officer for keeping the register of local land charges, referred to in Part Two.

PUBLIC UTILITY SERVICES

The map inside the back cover shows the areas of administration of the London Passenger Transport Board, the Metropolitan Police and the Metropolitan Water Board.

The duties of the *London Passenger Transport Board* are defined in the London Passenger Transport Act, 1933 (to which reference was made in Part Two), by which the Board was constituted a " public authority " charged with the general responsibility for providing an adequate and properly co-ordinated system of passenger transport for the London Passenger Transport Area. This area extends to some 1986 square miles with a population which is now not far short of 10 millions, and covers the whole of the counties of London and Middlesex and parts of the counties of Bedfordshire, Buckinghamshire, Essex, Hertfordshire, Kent, Surrey and Sussex. In carrying out this primary duty the Board are enjoined, while avoiding the provision of unnecessary and wasteful competitive services, to take from time to time such steps as they consider necessary for extending and improving the facilities for passenger transport in their area so as to provide most efficiently and conveniently for its needs.

The Act provided for the transfer to or acquisition by the Board of all the local road and underground railway transport undertakings in their area, except for a few road undertakings providing services which overlapped the boundary of the area and certain underground railway undertakings partially or wholly owned by the main line railway companies. Co-ordination with the surburban services of the main-line railway companies was secured by the appointment of a standing joint committee consisting of representatives of the Board and of the main-line railways. This co-ordination was made effective through a pooling scheme creating a common financial interest and covering the receipts of the Board and of the main-line railways from passenger traffic local to the Board's area.

In the Greater London Area there are two police forces, the *Metropolitan Police* and the *City of London Police*. The Commissioner of Police for the Metropolis is appointed by the Crown, and acts under the authority of the Home Secretary. The cost of the Metropolitan Police is met to the extent of one-half by grants from His Majesty's Exchequer, and the remaining half by a police rate levied in the parishes within the Metropolitan Police District. The Commissioner of City Police is appointed by the Common Council subject to the approval of the Crown. The cost of the force is borne by the City Corporation, with a grant from His Majesty's Treasury.

The water supply of London and the surrounding districts is controlled by the *Metropolitan Water Board* and the area under the Board's control covers over 350 square miles and includes a population of approximately 7,000,000.

PART FOUR

CAREERS AND PROFESSIONS IN THE COUNTY SERVICE

THE first parts of this book will have shown you the vast development which has taken place in the work of local government up to the present time, and it will be obvious that the local government service continues to expand as Parliament places further duties upon it, but no mention has yet been made of the persons responsible for carrying out this great work.

You will have read in an earlier chapter of the constitution of the County Council, and how the members are duly elected for voluntary service. These persons, acting in committee or council, direct the policy and decide on the action to be taken in accordance with the powers conferred by Parliament.

It will be appreciated that since the membership of the County Council is representative of widely varying callings and professions, and is constantly changing from year to year, it is necessary to employ permanent officials, fully trained and experienced in local government work, to advise the Council and its committees on procedure and to deal with the vast amount of technical and clerical work involved.

I wonder how many of the younger generation, when considering their future careers, realize the infinite scope which local government work offers in almost every career of a professional or clerical nature, and how much added interest is to be gained by the knowledge that a local government officer is taking an active part in the government of his county and furthering the interests of the individual ratepayers.

In this section of the book it is therefore proposed to give some idea of the careers which local government affords.

CHIEF OFFICERS

The duties of the County Council are distributed amongst a number of chief officers who control the several departments of the Council's work. The principal officials are :—

  (i) the Clerk of the County Council;
  (ii) the County Accountant;
  (iii) the County Medical Officer of Health;
  (iv) the Secretary to the Education Committee;
  (v) the County Engineer and Surveyor;
  (vi) the County Architect;
  (vi) the County Valuer;
  (viii) the Director of Public Assistance;
  (ix) the Chief Officer of Public Control;
  (x) the Chief Officer of Local Taxation Licences Department;
  (xi) the Director of Agriculture and County Land Agent;
  (xii) the Clerk to the Mental Hospitals Committee;
  (xiii) the Medical Officer under the Mental Deficiency Act, 1913;
  (xiv) the Air Raid Precautions Officer.

In addition to the work of the County Council above referred to, you will have read in an earlier part that the Courts of Quarter Sessions sit at the Guildhall, and all the work connected therewith is dealt with in a separate office there under the control of the Clerk of the Peace, who is also the Clerk of the County Council.

The great majority of local government officials without professional qualifications have risen " through the ranks ", commencing in quite a junior capacity.

JUNIOR APPOINTMENTS

Most of the junior appointments are made from boys or girls of school-leaving age, and junior employees not otherwise qualified are required to have obtained the Matriculation or an equivalent Certificate. All persons appointed to the staff of the County Council are now required to pass a medical examination by the staff of the County Medical Officer's Department *before* entry to the service. This is necessitated by the Local Government Act of 1937, which provides that, subject to a short probationary period, all officers and servants on the permanent staff must, during their service with the Council, contribute to a superannuation scheme.

SUPERANNUATION

All new entrants to the service of the County Council contribute to the superannuation fund at the rate of 6% of their salaries or wages, and can retire from the service at 65 years of age or after 40 years'

service with a pension amounting to half their rate of pay (as averaged over the preceding 5 years), and receive in addition a lump sum of an amount which may equal as much as $1\frac{1}{3}$ years' salary or wages. A proportionately smaller pension is payable if retirement takes place earlier for reasons of ill-health, a death benefit is payable where an official dies before retirement, and in certain cases of voluntary retirement refunds of previous contributions are payable.

Generally speaking, the hours of duty consist of an 8-hour day, commencing at 9.30 a.m., with Saturday afternoons free; the annual vacation varies from two weeks in junior appointments to four weeks in the case of senior staff, and an extra day's holiday, in addition to Bank Holidays, is usually given at Easter and Christmas. There are certain modifications of these hours and holidays in some of the local offices and, of course, in schools and hospitals.

The choice of a career upon leaving school is far more carefully provided for to-day than it was formerly. In every secondary school there is a " careers " master or mistress equipped with up-to-date information about openings and the qualifications required for the various careers, who advises pupils needing guidance.

In order to give as detailed information as possible about the careers in the service, I will now refer individually to the work of each Department.

1. CENTRAL ADMINISTRATION

THE Department of the Clerk of the County Council is the central administrative department, and acts as the link between the other departments and the committees of the County Council, the Government Departments and the public.

The Clerk of the County Council is the chief administrative officer and legal adviser of the Council, and his responsibilities include acting as the clerk

to practically all the committees of the Council. He submits reports on all Parliamentary Bills and Acts of Parliament which may affect the functions of the Council and its committees. He has charge of the deeds and other legal documents and records of the Council, and is responsible for the whole of the legal work. The Clerk is responsible for all administrative work which is not specifically referred to any of the other chief officers, and is responsible for conducting the official correspondence of the Council on matters of principle.

There is a Deputy Clerk of the County Council and three Assistant Clerks (and of these three are also qualified solicitors), a staff of assistant solicitors, administrative assistants, committee clerks, conveyancing clerks, general clerks and shorthand-typists, in addition to cashiers, draughtsmen, etc. Non-professional entrants to the staff of this Department are principally recruited as junior clerks from the County secondary schools, and vacancies in the higher grades are usually filled by the promotion of those who have shown initiative and administrative ability.

Fully qualified solicitors are usually appointed, but from time to time opportunity has been afforded to a few of the more promising assistants to enter into articles of clerkship.

It need hardly be said that the work is exceedingly interesting and varied, since it covers every branch of the Council's activities, and includes the preparation of reports upon innumerable subjects for consideration by the various committees and the Council, attendance at committee and sub-committee meetings and the preparation of minutes and reports of such meetings, the issuing of various licences and registrations, in addition to correspondence so extensive as to necessitate the employment of five junior clerks, who are fully occupied sorting, opening, entering, distributing and despatching the incoming and outgoing and inter-departmental mails.

It is perhaps of interest to know that nearly all new junior clerks spend at least their first year in this section gaining an invaluable groundwork in the work of all Departments before being promoted to a " section " dealing with more specialized work.

The legal staff deal with the acquisition and sale of land, the preparation of leases for buildings and land, of agreements in respect of numerous matters, and of contracts for works and for the supply of materials and stores. They also represent the Council in Court actions, the majority of such cases being for the recovery of money owing to the Council or under Orders obtained in the local Courts, and the prosecution of offenders against certain enactments and bye-laws.

It will therefore be seen that the work is largely secretarial and legal in character, and that a considerable knowledge is gained of many Acts of Parliament affecting the Council's work, whilst acquiring the necessary experience for promotion to the higher grades.

You will have realized from Part II of this book the variety of subjects with which the County Council deals, with all of which the Clerk's Department is in intimate contact since, as previously stated, the Clerk of the County Council is responsible for the legal work of all, and acts as Clerk to practically all of the twenty Standing Committees of the Council, which are as follows:—

STANDING COMMITTEES OF THE COUNCIL

Agricultural Committee.
Air Raid Precautions Committee.
County Buildings Committee.
County Valuation Committee.
East Middlesex Drainage Committee.
*Education Committee.
Entertainments Committee.
Estates and Town Planning Committee.
Finance Committee.
General Purposes Committee.
Highways Committee.
Housing Committee.
Local Pension Committee.
Maternity and Child Welfare Committee.
Mental Deficiency Committee.
Officers and Staff Committee.
Parliamentary and Standing Orders Committee.
Public Health Committee.
†Visiting Committee of the County Mental Hospitals.
West Middlesex Drainage Committee.

* The Secretary of the Education Committee acts as Clerk.
† There is a separate Clerk.

A COMMITTEE ROOM AT THE GUILDHALL

Additional Committees

Joint Committee as to Thames Bridges.
(Composed of members of Surrey and Middlesex County Councils.)

Standing Joint Committee.
(Composed of magistrates and members of the County Council.)

The names of these committees mostly speak for themselves as to the services with which they deal. One, however, calls for explanation. The General Purposes Committee, as its name implies, deals with all matters which either affect several committees and upon which they each report to the General Purposes Committee, or with matters which do not fall within the duties of any other particular committee and, in fact, acts as a co-ordinating committee. It also directs the work of the Public Control, Architect's and Local Taxation Departments, issues licences to employment agencies and under the Pharmacy and Poisons Act, directs the registration of births, deaths and marriages and many other matters and, in addition, controls the appointment and salaries of the more senior and technical officers of the Clerk's Department.

These standing committees meet regularly each month to receive reports and to decide or further discuss all matters placed on the agenda by the Clerk.

SUB-COMMITTEES

To expedite consideration of the very great number of matters requiring attention, each committee delegates certain duties to various sub-committees, of which there are altogether about fifty. The sub-committees are given powers to decide certain matters, reporting their decisions to the next meeting of their standing committee—other more important matters they report upon for rulings by the full committee. The committee in its turn has power to make decisions on numbers of matters, reporting such decisions for the information of the County Council, but on important questions of principle and on matters of expenditure exceeding a certain amount the full committees have only power to make recommendations to the County Council which, at its monthly meetings, receives reports and recommendations from each standing Committee and considers whether or not the recommendations shall be adopted. It should again be mentioned here (see also Finance Dept. p. 121) that all recommendations involving expenditure of more than £50 have also to be submitted to the Finance Committee, which after careful consideration thereof submits an estimate to the County Council.

In addition to monthly meetings of the committees and their sub-committees, there are meetings of special committees and numerous conferences. In the last twelve months nearly 800 ordinary meetings were arranged, all of which were attended by one or more members of the staff of this Department. For these meetings agenda and reports are pre-pared, a minute book is kept of all proceedings and reports of the meetings are prepared for the consideration of the Council.

Instructions and decisions have to be recorded, and other officers and departments informed of those which require their attention.

The subjects discussed at these meetings naturally give rise to considerable correspondence, and also to interviews and conferences. There is also a great quantity of detailed work in connection with various forms of licensing and registration, such as explosives, employment agencies, theatrical employees, poisons and pharmacy, music, dancing and stage plays, cinemas, nursing-homes and other matters.

The Department keeps in constant touch with the borough and urban district councils both by letter and telephone, and very close co-operation is maintained.

Practically one-third of the staff of this Department consists of women, most of whom are shorthand writers and typists, with duties which include routine shorthand and typewriting of correspondence, draft reports, legal documents, duplication of innumerable agenda and reports, typing of resolutions, minutes of meetings and, in some cases, certain clerical duties. There are also comparatively few of the more senior women engaged on purely clerical and administrative duties.

2. FINANCE

THE County Accountant, who is the financial adviser of the Council, is responsible for the management of this Department. The work of the Department is not confined to "book-keeping", and is full of interest, on account of the new problems continually arising in all branches of the Council's works; a sound financial organization is, of course, essential to the administration of the County.

The majority of new entrants to the service are recruited from secondary schools, as referred to in the section dealing with the Clerk's Department, and the same scales of salary apply. The work of a junior is naturally of a routine character, but a certain amount of responsibility is incurred from the commencement. Useful characteristics in this Department are: an aptitude for figures (not necessarily great mathematical ability), accuracy, integrity and the necessary determination to get to the root of a problem.

The junior assistant is at once advised to continue his studies in book-keeping, commercial law and economics, preferably by working for the examinations of the Royal Society of Arts in book-keeping and commercial subjects. If he intends to reach senior administrative rank, the diploma of the Institute of Municipal Treasurers and Accountants must be his aim. Although no articles of clerkship are required, as in some other professions, he must first serve a qualifying period during which to grasp the elements of the subjects he must master. In addition to the subjects mentioned above, auditing, local government finance and the law relating thereto, income tax, rating and valuation, statistics, costing, banking and public finance and general commercial knowledge are included in the syllabus of the Institute. The examination fees are not high, and coaching organisations generally accept payment spread over the period of preparation.

The diploma is a key to financial posts with local authorities and accountancy assistants, auditors, deputies, borough and county accountants, and treasurers are usually recruited from men trained in the finance departments of these authorities. The Institute's examinations are open to both men and women, although at the time of writing no women have passed the final examination.

Women are principally employed in finance departments on secretarial work, shorthand, typewriting and duplicating, as well as accountancy machine work and calculating. Here the technical knowledge is not required to the same degree, although to any woman who has the flair for the work there is no bar to progress in the profession.

Recently, prominence has been given to the advantages of university training, and the acquisition of a diploma of public administration or a science degree in economics gives wider qualifications additional to the Institute diploma. London University is very accessible for Middlesex students wishing to become undergraduates.

3. EDUCATION

THE "man in the street" is aware, in a vague kind of way, that an "education authority" concerns itself with the schooling of the nation's children and, probably more clearly, that he pays an "education rate". The average man or woman probably does not realize that, in addition to administering the schools which they control, local education authorities have to administer a system of important social services which have grown up with the schools and are intended to promote the physical and social welfare of children and young persons, whether at school, at home or in employment.

TYPES OF EDUCATION AUTHORITIES

There are two types of education authority in this County. The County Council is an authority for both elementary and higher education—that is to say, it has powers and duties in regard to the provision and maintenance of schools giving children an elementary education, of which the majority are known as "public elementary schools", and further powers for the provision and maintenance of secondary, technical, commercial and art schools—that is to say, schools giving a more advanced or a more specialized form of education.

Certain of the boroughs and urban district councils are authorities for elementary education, but not for higher education. These latter authorities are often described as " Part III Authorities ", in reference to Part III of the Act under which they were constituted.

In the County of Middlesex the councils of the 12 following local districts are the authorities for elementary education, whilst the County Council is the higher education authority:—Acton, Brentford & Chiswick, Ealing, Enfield, Edmonton, Finchley, Hendon, Heston & Isleworth, Hornsey, Tottenham, Willesden and Wood Green; in the remaining 14 districts the County Council is the education authority for both higher and elementary education.

NUMBER OF SCHOOLS

In October 1937 there were in Middlesex 50 secondary schools, which were maintained or aided by the County Council, with a total roll of over 22,000 pupils. There were also 9 junior technical schools, 4 junior commercial schools, 9 schools of art, 10 technical colleges and polytechnics, all of which provided full-time instruction, and 78 institutes which afforded part-time instruction. The number of students taking advantage of these facilities was over 34,000. The number of elementary school departments maintained by the Middlesex County Council at the same date was 238, with nearly 80,000 boys and girls in attendance.

TEACHING AS A CAREER

These schools, of course, require a large staff of suitably qualified teachers. The staff of an elementary school consists of a head teacher and a number of assistant teachers, including teachers of handicraft subjects such as wood and metal-work and domestic subjects. In Middlesex vacancies for head teachers are usually filled by promoting head teachers of smaller county

schools or assistant teachers possessing suitable qualifications and experience. Candidates for appointment as assistant teachers in the Council's public elementary schools must be college-trained, certificated teachers.

The staffs of the secondary schools consist mainly of men and women teachers who have followed a three or four years' course at a university and have taken a degree in Arts, Science or some other University faculty. The non-graduate teachers in secondary schools are mostly employed on such special subjects as physical training, domestic science, handicrafts, art or music. In the absence of a degree, candidates are required to hold a recognized diploma as evidence of their ability to teach their special subject.

Vacancies for head teachers of secondary schools are advertised, and selected candidates are interviewed by a sub-committee representative of the County Council's Education Committee and the Governors of the school concerned.

In the technical schools a wider range of practical subjects is taught than in the secondary schools, and it is therefore natural that a larger proportion of the teachers are persons who, in addition to possessing a University degree, a diploma or some other evidence of a knowledge of the theory of their subjects, have had practical experience in industry or commerce. The evening institutes are staffed by teachers who are employed also in public elementary, secondary or technical schools, or by men and women with suitable qualifications and experience who are engaged in some branch of industry or commerce.

SALARY SCALES

The salaries of teachers employed in full-time public elementary, secondary, technical, art schools, etc., are regulated by standard scales of salaries, commonly known as the " Burnham Scales ", which have been adopted by committees representative of the teachers and the local education authorities, and have been accepted by the Board of Education,

THE SECOND COURT   *MIDDLESEX GUILDHALL*

which makes grants to local education authorities towards the cost of such salaries.

The scales are graded according to the area in which the teachers are employed. In Middlesex the scale applicable so far as teachers in public elementary schools are concerned is Scale IV; so far as teachers in secondary, technical, etc., schools are concerned the applicable scale is that prescribed for the London area.

The following are particulars of the Burnham Scales which are applicable to full-time assistant teachers employed by the Middlesex Education Authority:—

(1) *Elementary Schools*—Certificated Assistant Teachers, two years, college-trained:—

	Minimum Salary.	Annual Increment.	Maximum Salary.
Men	£192	£12	£408
Women	180	9	324

(2) *Secondary, Technical and Art Schools.*

Men:			
Graduate	£276	£15	£528
Non-Graduate	204	12	432
Women:			
Graduate	264	12	420
Non-Graduate	192	9	342

Part-time teachers in technical and art schools are remunerated according to the scale adopted by the local education authority and approved by the Board of Education for purposes of grant.

It is scarcely possible within the limits of this small book to give details as to the methods by which persons may secure entry to the teaching profession. Nowadays a course of study in a secondary school is an almost indispensable preliminary for entry into any branch of the profession, and intending teachers are advised to apply to a head teacher for information as to suitable courses of training and as to the financial assistance which is made available to them by the County Council as higher education authority.

ADMINISTRATIVE STAFF AND ORGANIZATION

On the administrative side of its work the Education Department offers many avenues of interesting and well-remunerated employment. There are, of course, many appointments of a clerical nature, either in the central office, in divisional offices or in the secondary and technical schools, where one or more clerical assistants are employed to assist the principal of the school on the clerical side of his work.

The conditions of such employment are the same, or approximately the same, as those for similar posts in other branches of the County Council's services, particulars of which were given in dealing with the Department of the Clerk of the County Council. Here it is only necessary to deal with appointments for which professional or technical qualifications are regarded as indispensable.

For the higher administrative posts a University degree or its equivalent and some teaching experience in at least one type of school maintained by local education authorities are essential. An officer who has had at least three years' teaching experience in a recognized school and who holds an office controlling the work of teachers in schools is eligible to become a contributor under the Teachers' Superannuation Acts, and therefore has an option of two superannuation schemes—the teachers' scheme administered by the Board of Education and the local authority's scheme.

The chief officer of the Education Department is the Secretary to the Education Committee, and the department is divided into a number of sections, each of which deals with certain aspects of the work under the control of an assistant education officer known as an Assistant Secretary. In order to secure closer co-operation with the local authorities, the schools and the public, it is necessary to maintain a number of local offices, called "divisional education offices", each under the charge of a "divisional organizing officer". A division may, in the case of the largest districts, consist of a single borough or urban district, or sometimes a number of smaller districts are combined for the purpose of educational administration. Like his colleagues at the head office, the divisional organizing officer is generally a University graduate with teaching experience, and is therefore in a position to discuss the problems of the schools from practical experience.

In most of the divisional offices there is a senior assistant, who is paid on a scale commencing at £350 per annum and rising, subject to satisfactory service, by annual increments of £20 to a maximum of £490. These posts are a useful training-ground for those anxious to secure administrative experience for higher grades.

SCHOOL ENQUIRY OFFICERS

The divisional officer's staff includes a number of "school enquiry officers" and "juvenile employment officers". Until recently, the former were known as "school attendance officers", as their duties were mainly limited to securing the regular attendance of children attending public elementary schools.

For two reasons less time is now spent in inducing parents (either by tactful persuasion or by threats of prosecution) to send their children to school regularly. One reason is that to the children of our generation the school has no terrors and is a very much happier place, and they are usually more anxious to attend than to miss school; so that the habit of "truancy" has almost disappeared. The other reason is that with the development of the social services the time of the "school attendance officer" is taken up much more with enquiries connected with the local administration of these services than with matters connected with school attendance. He is an important link between the parents and the education authority, and plays an important part in the education authority's welfare work for children.

In consequence of these changes the title of the office has been altered to " school enquiry officer " and the scale of remuneration has been improved, and is in most cases £250—£10—£350 per annum, with an allowance for travelling expenses which varies according to the size of the district in which he works and whether he uses a pedal cycle, a motor cycle or a small car in the discharge of his official duties.

Some education authorities employ a superintendent of school enquiry officers to organize the work and this officer, of course, receives a higher salary.

VOCATIONAL GUIDANCE

Under the Unemployment Insurance Acts most education authorities administer the Unemployment Insurance Schemes so far as juveniles—that is to say, persons under the age of 18 years—are concerned, and give advice on careers and vocations to children and young persons entering employment. This is now an important branch of an education authority's welfare work, and offers a most interesting and useful career for men and women interested in young persons and in industrial problems.

In recent years a number of university graduates have sought and obtained appointments as juvenile employment officers, and have been placed in charge of the bureaux through which this work is administered. The Middlesex County Council's salary scale for juvenile employment officers is as follows: £300—£15—£500 per annum (subject to a further recommendation on reaching £360 per annum).

AGRICULTURAL EDUCATION

There are other careers in the Education Department of the County Council open to young men and women of suitable education and experience. In the section concerned with agricultural education a specialist staff is employed to arrange lectures and classes on agricultural and horticultural subjects and to give advice in all branches of agriculture and horticulture. This staff in Middlesex consists of an organizer of agricultural education, a horticultural instructor and assistant instructors (two men and one woman) in horticulture and poultry husbandry.

PHYSICAL FITNESS

In recent years increasing attention has been paid to the development of physical education by means of gymnastics, games, swimming and similar activities of an outdoor or indoor character. These developments led to the appointment of a number of organizers and assistant organizers of physical training to give advice to teachers on suitable methods of physical training and kindred matters, and generally to improve and extend the physical education both of pupils in attendance at the various schools and of young persons who have left school. Both organizers and assistant organizers are suitably trained and qualified in their special subjects, and most of them have had experience as teachers of physical training in recognized schools. The salary scales for organizers and assistant organizers are as follows:—

	Minimum Salary.	Increment.	Maximum Salary.
Organizers :			
Men	£450	£25	£600
Women	400	20	500
Assistant Organizers :			
Men	300	15	400
Women	240	12	320

LIBRARY SERVICE

In Middlesex the County Council is the library authority in twelve of the county districts, and its duties are carried out by the Education Committee. The following salary scale indicates the various grades of assistants employed and the appropriate salaries.

Junior Assistants' Grade

Men.

£85 per annum (£75 if under 18) by annual increments of £15 to £160.

Women.

£85 per annum (£75 if under 18) by annual increments of £12 10s. to £147 10s.

Branch Librarians, Senior Assistants, and Secretarial Assistants at Headquarters

Men.

£160 by five annual increments to £250 per annum.

Women.

£155 by five annual increments to £230 per annum.

District Librarians and Departmental Assistants at Headquarters

District librarians have charge of a branch library and also supervise other branch libraries in the district. Departmental assistants at headquarters take charge of:—

1. Accessions Department,
2. Circulation Department,
3. Students' Book Service,
4. Inspection of Branch Libraries.

Salary Scales

Men.

£230 by annual increments of £20 to £330 per annum.

Women.

£215 by annual increments of £15 to £305 per annum.

Chief Assistant at Headquarters. (Man or Woman.)

£350 by annual increments of £20 to £490 per annum.

4. PUBLIC HEALTH

THIS is one of the largest Departments of the Council, although the administrative office at the Guildhall is comparatively small. The staff of this department comes into close contact with the ratepayers in the execution of its duties of safeguarding and improving the public health. The chief officer is the County Medical Officer of Health, who is responsible to the Public Health Committee for a very large staff of doctors, dentists, nurses and other specially trained officers, in addition to clerical staff. The hospitals, with their staffs of nurses, almoners, women clerks, etc., offer a wide choice of careers for women.

HOSPITALS

The County Council maintains the five large general hospitals (taken over from the Board of Guardians) and two sanatoria, in addition to dispensaries and convalescent homes. It provides a total of nearly 5000 beds for sick persons, and during the last year for which statistics are available nearly 50,000 persons were received and treated. Proposals are being considered for the erection of more hospitals to cater for the steady increase in the population of Middlesex, *estimated at more than 1000 persons each week.*

The care of the sick is not only a career for persons of high qualifications and skill, but is a vocation calling for the exercise of the best qualities from every person who devotes his or her life to it. The Middlesex County Council secures for its hospitals highly trained and experienced medical and nursing staffs, and also leaves no stone unturned in considering the comfort, health and happiness of the staff and patients at the hospitals. The hours of duty of the nursing staff have recently received particular attention, and have been reduced to 48 hours per week, although this has meant a considerable increase in the numbers of nurses employed. The probationers (that is, those who are received at the hospitals to train as qualified nurses) have a 48-hour week, including their lecture times.

It will be seen that the administration of these hospitals requires the services of a

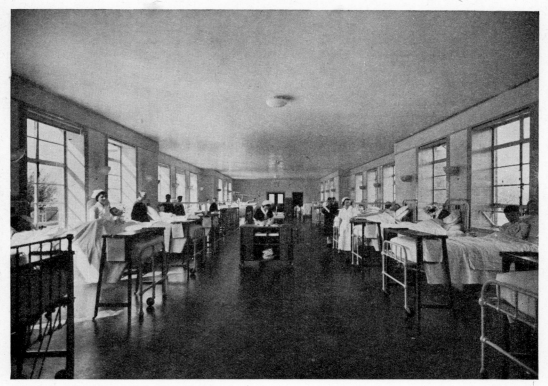

WARD AT HILLINGDON COUNTY HOSPITAL

great number of well-qualified persons, and these include—beside the medical superintendents in charge and many assistant medical officers—surgeons, physicians, pathologists, radiologists, radiographers, dentists, pharmacists and dispensers, and other specialists; matrons, sisters in all branches, midwives, staff nurses, assistant nurses, and probationer nurses; housekeepers, masseurs and masseuses, almoners, stewards, storekeepers and clerks, in addition to the domestic and manual staffs, so that in this branch of the Council's work there is a very wide choice of careers.

Medical Training

The necessary training for fully qualified medical men is lengthy and expensive for those who are not sufficiently brilliant to secure scholarships. Matriculation (or Schools Certificate with certain credits) is the usual preliminary to such training. In addition to this preliminary examination, students must pass or be exempted from a pre-registration examination in chemistry, physics and biology before they can be registered as medical students. Application may be made to the medical faculty of a University or medical school for admission to professional training at any time after 17 years of age. In general, the first two years of training for a medical degree or diploma are devoted to the professional scientific subjects, and in the following years the student enters a recognized hospital medical school for clinical studies.

Medical appointments in the Council's hospital service carry salaries varying from £350 (including emoluments) in the case of junior assistant medical officers to £1500 or more as a medical superintendent of one of the largest hospitals.

Nursing Training

In the nursing service it is possible to obtain full training and experience in

COUNTY GOLD MEDAL FOR NURSING

a county hospital. Usually probationer nurses commence their training between 18 and 30 years of age, but suitable candidates under this age may be accepted as " special probationers ", and employed chiefly in the nurseries and upon work of a less technical character during the early stages of training.

The period of training is four years. There is a three-months' preliminary period of training, at the end of which suitable candidates take an examination to qualify for the full course of training, which includes a preliminary State Examination, and concludes with the final State Examination for admission to the Nursing Register.

The County Council bears the cost of the examination fees of all probationers trained in its nurses' schools (provided it is their first sitting).

There is also an internal hospital examination in addition to the State examination, and the nurse obtaining first place receives a gold medal, and those obtaining second and third places receive silver medals.

Probationers receive an annual salary of £35 during their training, rising by £5 a year to £50, with board, lodging, laundry and uniform valued at £52 per annum. " Special probationers " under 18 years of age receive £25 per annum with the same additional benefits.

Upon passing the final examination for admission to the State Register, nurses are eligible for appointment as staff nurses, though they sometimes continue training to obtain certificates in special subjects such as midwifery, medico-psychology, tuberculosis, etc.

Nursing Salaries

The commencing salary of a staff nurse is £85 per annum, rising to £100, and slightly higher salaries are paid to nurses with the special certificates above referred to. The " emoluments " (additional benefits) of board, lodging, laundry and uniform are valued at £58 per annum.

Staff nurses can apply for appointments as ward sisters at salaries from £105 to £150, with emoluments valued at £71 10s. per annum.

Sisters in special departments, such as maternity, electrical, theatre, etc., receive appropriately higher salaries. Home sisters, housekeepers and sister tutors receive salaries of as much as £220 in some cases where a special diploma is held, with emoluments valued at £84 10s. per annum.

There are higher appointments as assistant matron, deputy matron and matron. The salaries of matrons vary according to the size of the hospital. The minimum salary in a very small hospital is £160 to £300, with residential emoluments valued at £215 per annum, and in the largest hospitals salaries run

WEST MIDDLESEX COUNTY HOSPITAL

INTERIOR OF NURSES' HOME

as high as £440 to £540 per annum, with emoluments valued at £260 per annum.

There are other appointments open to trained nurses. For those with special experience in tuberculosis work, dispensary nurses are required at salaries rising from £235 to £325 per annum, with allowances for uniform, laundry and travelling, and appointments of health visitors and school nurses are made at similar salaries.

This will give you a general idea of the careers in the nursing service, and further particulars as to training may be obtained from the County Medical Officer of Health.

Almoners

One other career may be mentioned— that of lady almoner. Almoners are not trained in the County service, but there is an Institute of Hospital Almoners, the main object of which is to select and train or arrange for the training of suitable candidates, to grant certificates to trained and qualified students and to recommend trained almoners to hospital authorities.

The duties of an almoner at a county hospital include the arrangements for the admission of certain patients. She interviews patients or their relatives at the hospital, and obtains particulars of their requirements and financial conditions. This information she enters in what is known as a " case-paper ", which she sends to the appropriate officer. She is responsible for collecting any Hospital Savings Association (or similar) vouchers accumulated by patients to meet the cost of treatment, and in certain instances acts as a relieving officer. She has considerable duties in connection with the out-patient department, and as a result of her inquiries arrives at a reasonable charge to be made for treatment according to the patient's means. She also is required to undertake such social welfare after-care and other work as may be found necessary.

It will be seen that this work requires women with special gifts of character and personality, in addition to careful training. Candidates should be between the ages of twenty and thirty-five, and the course covers a period of two years. This is divided up: firstly, four months' work in the offices of an efficient charity organization society, or similar organization, during which time instruction in practical social work is given; secondly, nine months under the direction of the London School of Economics, and thirdly, eleven months' work under the direction of an almoner at a hospital recognized as a training centre. The fee for training is fifty guineas, which covers the whole cost of lectures and practical training.

Hospital almoners in the County service are paid a minimum salary of £200 on appointment, rising to £250 per annum, with meals when on duty. Chief almoners in the largest hospitals receive salaries rising to £400 per annum.

Stewards

The steward of a hospital acts under the general control of the medical superintend-ent, and takes charge of the issue of all provisions and other articles (except medical) used at the hospital. He superintends the male non-medical staff and assists the medical superintendent in maintaining discipline. He is responsible to the County Architect for works of maintenance and to the County Accountant for keeping accounts and records. He keeps a record of all property at the hospital and reports each month on any matters which require consideration by the committee of management.

The salaries of stewards vary according to the size of the hospital; the lowest commencing salary in the smaller hospitals is £295 per annum, and in the largest £620, and the maximum salaries vary from £420 to £745 per annum.

Non-Professional Staff

Appointments on the male side of the hospital staffs include clerks, storekeepers, stewards, engineers and manual staff such as ambulance drivers, attendants, etc.

The hospital clerical staff is appointed at salaries on the lower scales applicable to the central administrative offices (see p. 232), commencing, for juniors, at £100 (£85 if under 18 years of age). The maximum salary is £400. The appointments are non-resident.

A certain number of women are engaged on the clerical staff both in the hospitals, dispensaries and the central administrative offices, at commencing salaries similar to the lower divisions in the clerical grading scheme already referred to.

5. MENTAL HOSPITALS

THE County Council is responsible, as you have read, for three large mental hospitals outside the County, Springfield Hospital at Tooting, and Napsbury and Shenley Hospitals near St. Albans. There is also a large " Colony " for mental defectives (that is, those who have never enjoyed normal mental faculties) at Shen-ley and one smaller institution for the same type of patient at Bramley House, Enfield.

The hospitals and institutions provide accommodation for approximately 7000 patients, and the care of these unfortunate people requires the services of a very large staff, including those with special professional qualifications for appointments such as medical superintendents, assistant medical officers, matrons, head male nurses, occupational therapy officers, in addition to the specialized, but less highly qualified appointments as stewards, clerks, dispensers, social workers, needle-room mistresses, kitchen superintendents, head laundresses, engineers, building foremen, farm bailiffs, head gardeners, and storekeepers.

In the nursing service at these institutions every opportunity is given to probationers to train by means of lectures, etc., in order to pass the Medico-Psychological Association's Examination, and thus qualify themselves for the higher-paid posts of matrons, assistant matrons and charge nurses.

In addition to the above-mentioned staff, there are many other well-paid posts on the clerical staff, and other manual and artisan appointments for cooks, laundresses, seamstresses, motor-drivers, porters, fitters, etc.

The salaries, wages and general conditions of service of the staffs of these hospitals and institutions are on practically the same basis as those of the hospital staffs administered by the Public Health Committee of the County Council, the details of which are set out in the preceding section. The work is in many ways very similar, but it will be readily understood that whereas in the public-health hospitals medical treatment is primarily of a physical or surgical nature, this kind of treatment in the mental hospitals is subsidiary to the psychological side of the treatment, and careers in this branch of the service must call for a high degree of sympathy, patience and understanding.

In the majority of cases persons appointed on the staff of one of the County's mental institutions are expected to live on the estate in which the institution is situated, and their salaries and wages include "extras", such as board, lodging, laundry and uniform.

All appointments are pensionable, subject to the usual medical examination, and the officers and staff are divided into two classes: first- and second-class officers. The first class consists of all those established officers and servants to whom is entrusted, in the usual course of their employment, the care or charge of patients. The second class includes all other established officers and servants.

Officers placed in Class I are eligible to retire at the age of 55, and in Class II at the age of 60, after having completed not less than 20 years' service. It will be seen that the strain of this particular work is recognized in the shorter qualifying period necessary for pension purposes.

6. PUBLIC ASSISTANCE

ADMINISTRATION

THIS is one of the newer departments of the County Council, and dates from 1930, when the Boards of Guardians (of which you have read in Part Two), which had for so many years been responsible for the administration of the Poor Laws, were dissolved, and the County Council was made responsible for practically the whole of their work.

The Department is mainly concerned with the relief of the poor, either by providing accommodation in institutions, or by the provision of weekly allowances to those living in their own homes. About 10,000 families at present receive such allowances. The administration of all this relief is primarily dealt with by the staff of the department, in accordance with regulations which have been framed for their guidance.

Contributions Towards Relief

Regulations have also been drawn up

providing for contributions to be made towards such relief by relatives who are liable in law to maintain the persons assisted. It will be appreciated that the nearer relatives of these poor persons should not be allowed to let the full cost of the relief provided fall upon other rate-payers who may already be voluntarily assisting their own poorer relatives. Provision is made so that those who receive relief and persons called upon to contribute, may appeal to a sub-committee of the County Council against decisions of the officers. This sub-committee meets at frequent intervals in different parts of the County which has, for this purpose, been divided into administrative areas.

The officers who deal with the granting of assistance are known as " adjudicating officers ", and the officers assessing the payments to be made by relatives are known as " area officers ".

Local Organization

For the purpose of easier administration the administrative areas above referred to are further divided into forty-six general relief districts, for each of which an officer known as a " relieving officer " is appointed.

Any necessitous person may apply for immediate assistance to the district relieving officer, whose services are available both day and night. This officer makes full enquiry into every case in his district, and in ordinary circumstances reports to the adjudicating officer, who decides the nature and amount of assistance to be given. In cases of emergency or sudden necessity the relieving officer may order immediate relief other than in the form of money—that is to say of food, clothing or accommodation.

If medical attention is required, the relieving officer calls in the services of another officer, known as the " district medical officer ". These officers are local doctors in private practice who are paid by the County Council according to the amount of service required of them. There are sixty such doctors engaged, and each year thousands of visits are made to patients' homes, in addition to as many visits by patients to the surgeries of the doctors.

Accommodation

The Council has several large institutions in different parts of the County in which reside numbers of old people who are unable to maintain or look after themselves in their own homes.

Then there are also the " casual wards ", which provide accommodation for " wayfarers ". Here they may rest for one or two nights and are fed. In return for this they are required to perform an allotted task before continuing their journey.

These casual wards are provided throughout the country, generally about fifteen miles apart, so that it is possible to " tramp " from one place to the next.

Care of Children

The department also has charge of a large number of orphan or deserted children. As many as possible are attached to private families, and allowances are made to their " foster mothers " for their keep and clothing. Other children who cannot be dealt with in this way are maintained until five years of age in nurseries staffed, as far as possible, by properly trained child-nurses, and children over that age reside in what are called " scattered homes ". The Council owns a large number of these homes, which are ordinary dwelling-houses " scattered " throughout the County. Each home is in charge of a foster-mother, and is run on the lines of an ordinary working-class family. The children attend the local elementary schools, and are encouraged to sit for the entrance examination to secondary and junior technical schools, and are allowed to join the Boy Scouts or Girl Guides.

To women who prefer domestic work and like to have the care of children, a position as foster-mother offers a very suitable means of livelihood, and much more congenial to some than either domestic service or industrial employment.

CHASE FARM INSTITUTION   STAFF RECREATION ROOM

Poor-Law Settlement

One section of the department deals with " settlements ". All persons have what is known as a " poor-law settlement " in some county, which means that in the event of their becoming destitute the council of that county is liable for their maintenance. Now, the cost of keeping a person for a long period, which may amount to the rest of his or her life, is a heavy liability, and the County Council may not refuse to give relief to a person who is destitute. It is very desirable, therefore, to find out in each case which county is the place of settlement so that the liability may be transferred. This is often a very complicated matter, as so many things which a person does during life alter his original " place of settlement ".

An idea of the volume of work carried out by the Public Assistance Department may be gained from the fact that over a million pounds a year is spent in the provision of this service in Middlesex.

THE DEPARTMENT AS A CAREER

To young men who enter institutions as clerks, there is a prospect of reaching the chief post of superintendent of an institution at a salary of £395/£600. A secondary education is the qualification, and promotion is earned by subsequent experience and aptitude for the work. Matrons of these institutions are usually recruited from the nursing profession.

Numbers of women are employed in looking after the old people, and to girls who have a liking for the work the posts of female attendants offer an alternative to either domestic or factory employment. Similarly, in the case of men attendants the work is more congenial than that of many an unskilled worker in industry.

For youths with secondary education who prefer interesting work with fewer clerical duties, the out-relief section offers further careers. Juniors entering this section gradually work their way through the successive stages up to the position of relieving officer, after which there are opportunities of promotion to higher positions, not only in Middlesex, but under other authorities. Certificates of efficiency in the duties of a relieving officer are granted, after examinations, by the Poor Law Examinations Board and these certificates are necessary for promotion to this office.

The scales of salaries of the relief staff are as follows :—

Relieving Officer's Clerk and Assistants—£100 by eight annual increments to £250 per annum.
Deputy Relieving Officers—£250 by annual increments of £12 10s. to £300.
Relieving Officers—£320 by annual increments of £15 to £440.

Inspection of Out-relief and Adjudicating Officers —£450 by annual increments of £25 to £500.

On the institutional side the salaries of the clerks, deputy and assistant superintendents correspond to those in Division 4, 3 and 2, up to £410 per annum, of the general clerical grading scheme set out on page 232.

Superintendents of institutions (non-resident) receive salaries according to the size of the institution. In the smallest the salary commences at £365 and rises to £395. There are four grades, and for the largest institutions the salary commences at £550 and rises by £25 per annum to £600.

Matrons in charge of institutions are paid on a residential basis, according to the size of the institution. The minimum salary in the smallest is £110, rising to £130, whilst in the largest it commences at £300, rising to £350. The emoluments—that is, residential benefits—in the small appointments are valued at £165 per annum, and in the largest they are valued at £255.

7. ENGINEERING AND SURVEYING

WHEN you have travelled out of Middlesex by car along those modern highways, such as the Barnet and Watford Bye-Passes, the North Circular Road or the Western Avenue, so different from the old roads in the County, perhaps you have wondered at these great engineering works, and what they involve. In one place a canal has been carried over the road, in others the roads are carried on embankments over viaducts or bridges. This work is one responsibility of the County Engineer and Surveyor, who is also responsible for the working and maintenance of the vast sewerage scheme for West Middlesex of which you have read earlier in this book.

This Department is, of course, mainly

a technical one and, in contrast with that of Public Health, it offers greater scope for men than for women. The usual minimum qualifications required in the higher posts are those of the Institution of Civil Engineers, the Institution of Municipal and County Engineers, the Chartered Surveyors' Institute or a University engineering degree. In order to obtain any of these qualifications except the University degree, it is necessary to enter into articles of clerkship as in the case of solicitors.

The junior positions on the staff, apart from clerical work, are those of engineering and surveying assistants, divisional and district surveyors, draughtsmen and clerks of works.

DRAWING OFFICE IN COUNTY ENGINEER'S DEPARTMENT

The junior professional grades commence at salaries of £165 per annum, and other grades receive salaries according to qualifications and experience up to £745 per annum. The Assistant Engineers receive salaries rising to £1000 per annum.

8. ARCHITECTURE

WHEN the County Council proposes to build a new school, hospital or other building, the County Architect is informed of the general requirements. He satisfies himself as to the suitability of the site, which involves a certain amount of surveying, and then designs an appropriate building and prepares what are known as sketch-plans and a rough estimate of the cost. When these have been approved, he proceeds with working drawings, and prepares a detailed specification of everything required in the erection of the buildings.

This work is very intricate and varied, requiring, in addition to the creative skill of the architect, the services of a staff of technical assistants and draughtsmen. Engineering knowledge is necessary in all branches, including fire prevention, steam, heating, electrical and fire installations, and in some cases also cooking and laundry

DRAWING OFFICE IN THE COUNTY ARCHITECT'S DEPARTMENT

installations. There may also be engineering work in connection with water purification, softening and filtration, refrigeration, lifts, pumps, telephones, and signals, the designing of reinforced concrete and steel structures, involving calculations of strains and stresses.

Advertisements stating the work to be carried out are then inserted in the press, and contractors apply for full particulars and specifications. They then submit sealed tenders to the Council, stating the price they would charge to carry out the County Architect's requirements. The lowest satisfactory " tender " is usually accepted, and a contract is entered into

with that firm. In the large works it is necessary to place more than one contract, and subsidiary or separate contracts are entered into for such things as the heating and lighting installations, and other matters involving the work of specialist firms.

A Clerk of Works is then engaged to watch the progress of the work, and he keeps a close check upon everything which is done, consulting the County Architect when necessary. As the work proceeds the builder is entitled to payment from time to time, according to the amount of work done, and the Architect has to check the value of such work and give him a certificate upon which the County Council makes a payment.

This is a general outline of the principal work of the Architect's Department, but it will be realized that progress is often delayed and variations in the original plan sometimes become necessary owing to unforeseen difficulties, and expensive delays may occur in obtaining delivery of some particular material or piece of machinery. The co-ordination of the work of the several contractors also requires very careful watching.

When the building is finished, the County Architect is responsible for the furnishings and fittings, and this is dealt with in close co-operation with the members of the appropriate Committees. He is also responsible, amongst other things, for the management of certain estates belonging to the County Council and for the maintenance and repair of the county buildings.

It will be appreciated from the above that the work of this department is one giving both wide and interesting scope for careers of a technical nature. The objective of most intending architects is membership of the Royal Institute of British Architects, usually referred to as the R.I.B.A. This body regulates examination requirements. There are three recognized stages in becoming a member: (1) as a probationer on passing a public examination, (2) as a student on passing the intermediate examination and (3) as an Associate on passing the final examination. For those desiring to qualify as Associates of the R.I.B.A., the pamphlet No. 5 of the Choice of Career series, published by His Majesty's Stationery Office, might usefully be studied.

A considerable number of unqualified assistants and draughtsmen are engaged in the Architect's Department. The junior grades commence at salaries of £165 per annum, and other grades commence at salaries according to the qualifications and experience of the assistant, and carry salaries up to £745 per annum. The Assistant Architects are paid salaries rising to £1250 per annum.

9. VALUATION

IN reading of the work of the County Accountant's Department, you have been advised to examine a rate demand note and to observe the references to assessment and rateable value. Every property in the County is valued and upon that value depends the amount each person has to pay in rates.

These values, representing the yearly worth of properties, are arrived at in the first instance by the rating committee of the twenty-six borough and urban district councils, and are subject to the approval of one or other of the assessment committees controlling the five areas into which the County is divided for this purpose. When approved, these lists of values are known as the " valuation lists ".

One of the principal duties of the County Valuer's Department is to ensure that no particular ratepayer pays more than his appropriate share of the expense of the local government service, and that other ratepayers do not pay less than their share—in other words, that there is a uniformity of assessment for rating purposes throughout the County.

The annual rateable value of all the property in Middlesex amounts to about £20,000,000, and there are over half a million separate assessments. You will therefore realize that the work entailed is very heavy.

The senior officers concerned with all these duties must have training and experience as surveyors and valuers. To become a surveyor it is necessary to obtain the professional qualification granted by the Chartered Surveyors' Institution, and normally it is necessary to serve a period of articled clerkship, usually of three years, to a chartered surveyor. If the pupil has not already obtained the Matriculation or the General Schools Certificate, he must pass a preliminary examination and then, after 18 years of age, become enrolled as a student of the Institution. The intermediate examination may be taken the following year. Then comes the final examination, after passing which the student may, if he is then engaged in professional work as a Surveyor, apply for election as a professional associate of the Institution. Professional associates who are upwards of 30 years of age may be elected as Fellows after five years approved experience as principals, responsible managers, or as technical officers in the public service.

Junior assistant valuers in the County Valuer's Department commence at a yearly salary of £175, rising to £275, assistant valuers rise to £400, senior assistants to £600 and principal assistants to £800 per annum.

In addition, there is a non-professional clerical staff employed at the head office, as in the case of other Departments at salaries in accordance with the scales set out on p. 232.

10. PUBLIC CONTROL

THIS Department is responsible for many important matters such as supervision of the purity of the food supply; verification and inspection of weights, measures and apparatus for weighing or measuring; the sale and storage of explosives (including fireworks); a record being kept of the sale of certain poisons; the verification of the accuracy of gasmeters; the destruction of rats and mice; and the supervision of registry offices and employment agencies.

Food Supply

People buying food are able to judge to a certain extent, or find out for themselves, whether the standard of food they are receiving is what they want or what they should have. But there are many things it is not possible for the ordinary purchaser to verify. Thus, an article of food may contain an undesirable ingredient, such as an unnecessary and harmful chemical preservative. It may have been deprived of part of its apparent value, as in the case of milk sold after some of the cream has been skimmed off, or whisky which has been excessively diluted with water. A cheaper type of food may be substituted for a more expensive article—*e.g.*, when margarine is sold as butter or a large haddock is sold as " hake ", or " real cream pastries " contain no dairy cream at all. Foreign produce, such as meat, poultry or fruit, may be sold as English produce at an unduly high price.

Protective Measures

Parliament has passed many Acts for the protection of the public in such matters, since householders would otherwise be at the mercy of manufacturers or salesmen employing such dishonest or harmful practices. It is a part of the duty of the County Council to enforce these laws, and this necessitates a staff of inspectors, analysts and other officers constantly at work on the Council's behalf.

One of the chief duties of the inspectors and their assistants is to enter a shop as an ordinary customer, take samples of food, make purchases, and see that statements on labels or show-cards are true. Sometimes they are able, with their special knowledge, to see or to find out

CHISWICK BRIDGE, UNDER CONSTRUCTION

for themselves that the law is being broken. For example, the inspectors can themselves apply tests to milk, and they frequently test the quality (as well as the quantity) of the milk supplied to schools in those attractive little bottles provided with a drinking-straw. Often, however, it is necessary that they should send a sample of food to the County Analyst for thorough examination in his laboratory.

The officers have to make themselves generally acquainted with the methods of the food trade, so as to be able to select the most suitable articles for their tests. It would, for example, be an obvious waste of public time and money if they were to buy numerous samples of a well-known brand of tea or beer—when they know that these proprietary articles are packed and sold in thousands all over the country and that one specimen is representative of the rest.

At times it is necessary for the County Council to prosecute vendors of unsatisfactory food before the magistrates. Sometimes the inspector is content to give advice or a word of warning to a shopkeeper who has unintentionally broken the letter of the law without doing much harm.

Public Analyst

The public analyst for the County of Middlesex is not a whole-time officer, but an analytical chemist in private practice. Some local authorities employ whole-time public analysts. For all prosecutions under the Food and Drugs (Adulteration) Act, in respect of the sale of unsatisfactory samples, a public analyst's certificate is required.

To become qualified as a public analyst, the diploma of Fellowship (F.I.C.) or Associateship (A.I.C.) of the Institute of Chemistry is necessary, together with a certificate granted by the Institute after an examination in the chemistry (including microscopy) of food and drugs and water. These examinations are difficult, and the qualifications can only be obtained by men and women who have had a long and advanced training and have become experts in analytical chemistry. Many public analysts also have University degrees in science.

Foreign and Imported Foodstuffs

Great Britain is so densely populated that a large proportion of the food supply has to be imported from overseas—often from countries where labour is cheap. Some of the foods which are imported are perishable and have to be stored in refrigerators or cold chambers on the voyage to this country. Meat—much of which comes from South America, Australia and New Zealand—is an example which will occur to everyone's mind. Butter and eggs are other examples.

Now, generally speaking, farmers in Great Britain cannot sell at a profit home-produced meat or butter or eggs or tomatoes unless they charge a higher price than is usually charged for imported produce. Many consumers are willing to pay a higher price for fresh produce than for food which has been frozen and has travelled on the ocean for some weeks. For these reasons, and because the average shopper cannot tell the difference between imported and home-grown produce, or between foreign and Empire produce, Parliament has made laws for the protection both of British farmers and of consumers who want to buy British food. These laws provide that the origin of certain kinds of food be marked or declared when the food is sold or exposed for sale.

As laws of this kind are apt to be evaded unless they are enforced, the County Council has power to protect the public through its inspectors. The marking regulations do not apply to all kinds of food, but they do apply, amongst others, to the following important articles—which are both imported from abroad and also, to some extent, produced in this country: meat, bacon, ham, poultry, butter, eggs, apples, tomatoes, oat products, and honey.

Inspectors themselves cannot always identify with certainty the origin of food of these kinds, but, with their special experience, they are able to do a great deal to prevent breaches of the law, and so to ensure that persons wanting English or Empire goods can know the origin of the food offered for sale before making their purchases.

Weights and Measures

If accurate weights and measures were not used in commercial transactions, there would be no confidence between buyers and sellers, who must be able to rely on a ton of goods being the equivalent of 20 hundredweight or 2240 pounds; and if a schoolboy wants to buy 2 ounces of chocolate, he ought to be able to rely on receiving not less than that weight. Tables of weights and measures would be useless if no steps were taken to see that the actual weighing and measuring appliances were accurate, so we have in this country a series of laws designed to secure that proper appliances are used, that they are not fraudulently used, and that purchasers of certain kinds of goods receive full weight or full measure.

Here we are faced with an example of the difference between the civil law and the criminal law. It is not usually a criminal offence (punishable by magistrates) to sell goods of short weight, unless Parliament has enacted that it shall be so. But Parliament has laid down in the

ANCIENT MEASURES, WITH MODERN MARKS IN FOREGROUND

Weights and Measures Acts that it shall be a criminal offence to sell short weight or short measure of *food*, or to sell short weight of coal or coke. It is not ordinarily a criminal offence to sell a load of hay or wood or a quantity of tobacco which is under weight, nor is short measure in petrol forbidden by the Weights and Measures Acts. The buyer of these articles must take his own steps to protect himself against loss, such as refusing either to accept the goods or to pay the full amount charged.

Verification of Weights and Measures

In Middlesex the same inspectors look after all these matters. Every weight, measure, weighing instrument or measuring instrument used in ordinary commercial transactions when goods are bought and sold must have been verified —that is, tested by comparison with the inspector's standard apparatus, and stamped as accurate by a qualified inspector of weights and measures. This statement applies to an enormous range of appliances—from tiny weights used by dispensing chemists or jewellers to weighbridges capable of weighing 50 tons or more; and from measures containing only a few minims to petrol pumps through which hundreds of gallons may pass in the course of a day.

One Middlesex factory makes about a million glass tumblers a year, each capable of holding half-a-pint, for use in public-houses, and each of them is verified by the County inspectors of weights and measures. The weighing equipment which the inspectors have at their offices includes fine chemical balances weighing only up to 10 grains, and weigh-bridges with a capacity of 30 tons. It is not enough that appliances shall be accurate when they are first made. Those who use them have to keep them in good condition and use them honestly.

The inspectors, therefore, have not only to verify all newly-made appliances for weighing and measuring but have to inspect, from time to time, appliances which are in use for trade. They must accordingly have a sound and extensive knowledge of the principles of mechanics and physics so far as these are embodied in the design of weighing and measuring machines, as well as of arithmetic and mensuration. Some of the automatic scales—such as those in which a travelling finger moves over a graduated dial—are extremely complicated pieces of mechanism. So are petrol-measuring pumps.

It may be asked, what limits of accuracy are laid down for weights and measures? The answer is that the Board of Trade, with the authority of Parliament, has made a code of regulations defining those limits of accuracy for new appliances and for appliances already in use, and the inspectors apply these regulations with reasonable strictness and reasonable discretion.

The inspectors have also to test the weight and measure of food sold or exposed for sale, and this means that they must often test purchases at shops. They have also to stop coal-carts conveying coal for delivery and weigh the loads of coal.

Qualifications of Inspectors

It will be seen that inspectors must have a thorough knowledge of the laws which apply to such matters, as well as a good deal of scientific knowledge and practical experience of trade methods. To ensure this, an intending inspector of weights and measures must pass a qualifying examination held by the Board of Trade. Full particulars may be obtained from a printed pamphlet sold by H.M. Stationery Office. The subjects of the examination are: (1) English composition, (2) Arithmetic and Mensuration, (3) Mechanics and Physics, (4) Weights and Measures Law, (5) Weighing and Measuring Practice, with an oral and practical examination in this subject. This last part of the examination is not easy, and there are many failures. The examination is held two or three times in each year but—and this is most important—no one may sit for the examination unless he is nominated as a candidate by a local authority, such as the County Council. Further, as the practical part of the examination could not be passed by anyone who had not actual and extensive experience in the verification and testing of appliances, and that experience cannot well be acquired except in the service of a local authority, nominations are in practice only given to men who have been employed by a local authority as assistants to the inspectors. No one should be persuaded to take a course of study for the inspectors' examination unless he is sure of a nomination.

Protection of Road Surfaces

Another duty of the inspectors of weights and measures is to see that the County roads are not used by excessively heavy motor-vehicles. The roads are made and kept in order by public money (as stated in Part Two), and individual users must not be allowed, through inconsiderate usage, to subject the roads to undue wear and tear. Moreover, excessive loading of vehicles may lead to danger in driving. Further, a firm of cartage contractors which obeys the law may find unfair competition from competitors who are willing to take the risk of overloading their motor-lorries, and are thus able to " cut " cartage rates. For these reasons there are laws limiting the weights of laden vehicles. To enforce those laws, inspectors have powers to stop vehicles and to cause them to be weighed on weigh-bridges or other suitable instruments. Much of the heaviest traffic uses the roads at night, so the inspectors have to be prepared to undertake this duty at any hour.

A new duty about to be undertaken by the Council is the inspection of road-

WEIGHTS AND MEASURES OFFICE   GREAT WEST ROAD, BRENTFORD

transport vehicles used to contain a measured quantity of sand or ballast, and the protection of purchasers against the supply of sand, ballast, etc., of short weight or measure.

So far, the public control duties of the County Council which have been mentioned relate largely to the protection of the health or purse of the public. Now we come to protection against certain dangers of injury through accidents.

Control of sales of Explosives, Poisons, etc.

Under this heading may be grouped the administration of the somewhat complicated laws and regulations relating to explosives (including fireworks) and poisons. The County Council's inspectors have to see that explosives are safely stored in places where there is the least possible danger of fire, and that fireworks are not sold to very young children. Also they enforce some of the laws regulating the sale, storage and labelling of poisons, to prevent the risk of accidents

or crimes and to enable sales of poison to be traced to the purchaser if the necessity should arise. It is not necessary to set out here precisely what the law requires, but some idea of the amount of work may be obtained from the fact that in Middlesex over 2000 shops are registered with the County Council for the sale of fireworks and over 2000 shops are similarly registered for the sale of poisons. All have to be visited by the county inspectors. (Pharmacies and chemists' shops do not require to be registered with the County Council or inspected by the Council's officers).

Inspection of gas-meters

About 100,000 gas-meters have also to be verified and stamped each year by the County Council's inspectors. Most of these are new meters, but some are repaired meters, and others are in use and are suspected of not registering correctly. The Board of Trade conducts a special qualifying examination for inspectors of

P

STANDARD WEIGHTS AND MEASURES

gas-meters. A " notice to candidates and syllabus of examination " may be bought from H.M. Stationery Office. As in the case of the examination for inspectors of weights and measures, candidates must be nominated by the County Council, and these nominations are only given to persons already in the Council's service. When there is a vacancy for a junior assistant in the gas-meter testing branch of the Public Control Department, a secondary schoolboy who has passed matriculation or some similar examination is usually appointed, on the understanding that in due course he will study for the examination with a view to becoming a qualified inspector, for which he has excellent opportunities of acquiring the necessary technical knowledge and practical skill.

Rat Destruction

Another branch of the Public Control Department, with a staff of about 15 men, deals entirely with the question of destroying rats and mice. Rats are a menace to health, and are amongst the worst carriers of germs of infectious diseases. They also cause great destruction to stores of food, to furniture and fabrics, to land (for example by undermining railway embankments) and houses, and seriously upset the nerves and health of many people.

Parliament has therefore decreed that occupiers of houses and owners of vacant land must take all necessary steps to destroy rats and mice and prevent infestation, and the Public Control Department ensures that these obligations are properly discharged. Special inspectors visit all places suspected or known to be troubled with rats and advise householders, without charge, how to get rid of them. The services of the rat-destruction staff of the County Council may be hired to exterminate rats and mice, multitudes of which are killed by them every year; the fees paid for their services amounting to nearly £3000 a year.

Many people think that it is the duty of the County Council to kill rats at the expense of the ratepayers. This is incorrect, except with regard to land and buildings belonging to the County Council. The methods of extermination adopted by the Council's rat-destroyers include the use of poisonous gases, setting traps of various kinds and laying poisons. The rat-destruction inspectors are able to give useful advice with regard to the protection of buildings, methods of storing food and disposing of refuse, and other miscellaneous advice on these matters.

Licensing of employment agencies

Persons who carry on for profit a servants' registry office or other employment agency must be licensed by the County Council, and must conform with a number of regulations for the protection of the public. Domestic servants are so scarce in comparison with the number required, that if there were no regulations, unscrupulous people might take unfair advantage of employers willing to pay commissions to agencies in respect of provision of domestic help. Also it has been found that singers, actors and dancers need to be protected against undesirable employment agents, who might, for instance, demand excessively high fees in return for introducing them to engagements at places of public entertainment. Similar regulations apply to agencies for the employment of clerks and nurses.

The inspectors in the Public Control Department of the County Council there-

WEIGH BRIDGE MECHANISM   WEIGHTS AND MEASURES OFFICE

fore keep all employment agencies under supervision, and undesirable agents find that they must either improve their methods or cease practising in Middlesex. (It should be explained that employment agencies are not controlled by general legislation applying everywhere, but by "local" Acts, passed by Parliament for particular counties or boroughs at the request of the local authorities concerned, and by local byelaws made by these authorities.)

CAREERS IN THE DEPARTMENT

And now with regard to careers in this department. The gas-meter staff and the rat-destruction staff confine themselves to their special duties. The other officers of the Public Control Department have to be prepared to deal with all the other subjects which have been mentioned. It will be realized that the ideal inspector has to be something of a lawyer, a detective, a chemist and an engineer. Anyone taking up this branch of work as a career needs alertness, keenness of observation, a good memory, self-confidence and a bent for mechanics, but perhaps the most important requisites of all are tact and courtesy, a sense of proportion and rigid integrity.

A young man wishing to get appointed to the staff should have acquired at school some elementary knowledge of chemistry, physics and mechanics, and should have passed Matriculation or some similar examination in those subjects. Vacancies on the staff do not often arise. When they do arise it is usual for the County Council to appoint, as assistants to the inspectors, young men who have the above qualifications.

No local authority appears to have appointed women inspectors of weights and measures. The reason is probably that inspectors have to be prepared to lift heavy weights when testing large weighing apparatus, are liable to have to work at all hours, and that much of their time is spent in walking from one shop to another carrying more or less heavy equipment. Good physical health and muscular strength are therefore necessary though inspectors frequently employ women to make test purchases on their behalf.

The work of the inspectors is varied and mainly interesting. Some of it is monotonous, as when about ten thousand half-pint tumblers have to be tested in one day. But normally this work is not allotted to any one officer more often than once in two or three weeks. The inspectors are generally out and about, but also have important indoor duties, such as verifying weights, scales and measures, and dealing with correspondence and other clerical work in their offices.

Some of the inspectors' time is spent at the Magistrates' Courts giving or waiting to give evidence, and many enjoy this side of the work.

The inspectors are vested with a good deal of personal discretion and responsibility, and often have to insist on compliance with the law, however much other people may object to complying with their instructions. At the same time, they have to remain courteous, even when dealing with people who may become unreasonable or provocative. The work is clearly not without its difficulties but an efficient inspector knows that it is worth while. In Middlesex, where many millions of pounds are spent every month on food and fuel, the services of these inspectors are invaluable to the ratepayer, since they secure protection for the public against certain forms of injury, protection for tradesmen from the unfair competition of law-breaking competitors, and ensure that purchasers of goods get better value for their expenditure.

The scales of salaries of the weights and measures staff are:—

Junior Assistants—£85 by 8 annual increments to £200 per annum.
Technical Assistants—£200 by 4 annual increments to £260 per annum.
Inspectors, Division II—£265 by 7 annual increments to £400 per annum.
Inspectors, Division I—£420 by 3 annual increments to £480 per annum.
Chief Inspector—£500 by 6 annual increments to £650 per annum.

11. LOCAL TAXATION

THIS Department was primarily concerned with licences issued on payment of taxes, the proceeds being applied locally—*i.e.*, paid to the General County Fund as part of its revenue. Since 1st January, 1921, however, it has been responsible also for the issue of motor vehicle licences and driving licences, and it is on this work that the greater part of the staff is engaged. It is interesting to note that the Ministry of Transport bears most of the cost of this latter branch of the work.

Local taxation licences on the one hand, and motor vehicle and driving licences on the other have no relation to each other, except that certain similar principles apply, but it is found convenient as a matter of administration for one department to be responsible for both groups of licences, consequently the staffs are interchangeable.

LOCAL TAXATION LICENCES

(*a*) Dog licences (to keep a dog).
(*b*) Armorial bearings licences (to wear or use a crest of any sort).
(*c*) Game licences (to kill game; to employ a gamekeeper, to deal in game).
(*d*) Gun licences (to carry or use a gun).

The above are all Local Taxation licences and are issued at some of the Council's local offices and at post offices, which pay to the County Council all money so received. It is the duty of the County Council to see that licences are obtained by all persons who incur liability to licence duty, and for this purpose a staff of inspectors is engaged working from offices at convenient centres in the County.

The inspectors' duties include calling on persons who have failed to renew licences, detecting cases where licences should have, but have not been bought, making " house-to-house " visits, preparing reports and conducting prosecutions in the Petty Sessional Courts. Registers of licence-holders are kept, and although this is not obligatory, reminder notices are sent out when licences expire.

The clerks engaged on this work have the opportunity of assisting inspectors in enquiry work, and can so qualify for posts as inspectors when vacancies occur.

MOTOR VEHICLE AND DRIVING LICENCES

In connection with motor-vehicle licences and driving licences, it is the duty of the Council to effect the registration and licensing of all motor vehicles in the County, and to issue driving licences to residents in the County.

The Department is divided into several sections, many clerks being given the opportunity of passing successively through each section; others, naturally, are placed where they are most suitable, but each section requires some knowledge of the work of the others. In fact, at the beginning of the day all sections combine to prepare the day's work.

The work includes allotting index marks and registration numbers (the index mark is the letters, the registration number the figures, appearing on a motor car's number plate) to new motor vehicles, issuing licences (the licence is the paper disc on the windscreen), and registration books (the owner of every vehicle is given a book containing particulars of the vehicle). Manufacturers, dealers and repairers are also issued with sets of number-plates known as trade-plates.

The Council has to satisfy itself that all applications for licences are correctly made, and it is here that knowledge, not only of motor vehicles but of motor

LOCAL TAXATION : CAR LICENSING DEPARTMENT AT MIDDLESEX HOUSE

vehicle law, is of first importance. This knowledge can be gained only by experience and reference to technical and law books which, on this subject, are very few, making it necessary for the officer himself to read and make notes from numerous Acts of Parliament and regulations.

Different types of vehicles are licensed (or tax is paid) on different bases as shown in the following table :—

Motor Cycles.	On cylinder capacity of the engine.
Invalid Carriages.	Now exempt from duty.
Hackney Carriages (i.e. Omnibuses or Taxicabs and Hire Cars.)	On seating capacity.
Tractors.	On unladen weight generally. Some special vehicles such as motor mowers pay a flat rate of 5s.
Goods Vehicles.	On unladen weight.
All other vehicles (chiefly private cars).	On horse power.

Considerable difficulty is found in deciding under which heading some vehicles should be placed, as not only has the construction and the ownership to be taken into consideration, but also the use to which the vehicles are put.

Exempt (or duty-free) licences are issued in respect of other vehicles, such as fire engines and ambulances.

It is estimated that 270,000 vehicles are kept in the County, and it will be realized that the work entailed in examining applications, issuing licences, keeping records and filing documents is enormous, while the keeping of accounts is a large and exacting task.

It is in this latter work that some aptitude for figures is essential. One section deals entirely with reports of alleged offences, and needs considerable knowledge of motor-licence law and police-court procedure.

Driving-licence law tends to become more complicated as the result of additional laws to make the roads safe for all users. The Council's duty in this connection is confined to the issue of licences and keeping of records of licences and endorsements.

A new driver is issued with a provisional licence, valid for three months, to enable him to learn to drive before taking the test conducted by the Ministry of Transport. Whilst holding a provisional licence the driver has to obey certain regulations, but when the test is passed the conditions are removed and the driver may apply for an annual licence.

Annual licences are divided into six groups, the groups indicating the type of vehicle the holder is entitled to drive. The type of vehicle on which the test is passed and the age of the applicant have to be taken into consideration when deciding from which of the six groups the licence may be issued.

CAREERS IN THE DEPARTMENT

The staff is in close contact with the public, and naturally each approaches the subject from a different viewpoint; a helpful attitude is therefore necessary. The work otherwise is almost entirely clerical, good handwriting and quickness at figures being necessary.

There are no professional examinations bearing directly on the work of the department, but those showing aptitude for legal or financial work are encouraged to fit themselves for senior positions. The legal work in particular offers great interest and scope for advancement. The higher posts, and those arising through the growth of the department, are normally filled by promotion. This department offers quite good prospects to those of average intelligence who show initiative and ability. A few shorthand typists are employed, but otherwise there are no special posts for women.

The salaries of the majority of the staff of this department are in accordance with the clerical grading scheme particulars of which are given on page 232.

The inspectorate are paid according to the following scale:—

Junior—£235 by six annual increments to £350 per annum.
Senior—£375 by five annual increments to £500 per annum.

12. AGRICULTURE

THIS is one of the smaller departments with a small staff. The principal technical officer is styled The Director of Agriculture and County Land Agent, but is usually known as "the County Land Agent", and is responsible to the Agricultural Committee. This Committee is a composite one with "co-opted members" under an approved Scheme (that is representatives of other bodies serving as members of this Committee) and is in this way representative of all branches of the agricultural industry.

The department deals with applications from farmers for advice and guidance on many matters. It has duties under several Acts of Parliament—for instance, the prevention of the growth and spreading of injurious weeds, the determination as to whether agricultural holdings are being cultivated according to the "rules of good husbandry", and the protection of farmers in connection with the quality of fertilizers and feeding stuffs which, by law, must contain no harmful substances.

The County Council owns several estates, amounting to over 1500 acres in all, and these are divided into nearly 150 small holdings, which are let to tenants. The control of these holdings is dealt with by this department.

Then there are duties under another Act of Parliament dealing with diseases of animals, and the services of a number of veterinary surgeons are engaged upon a part-time basis for the necessary work of inspection to prevent the spreading of infectious diseases.

As already stated, the work in Middlesex is carried on with a small staff and vacancies are rather infrequent.

SALARIES

REFERENCES to the salaries attaching to various specialized posts have been made under the headings of the main departments. It is not possible here to give tables of all the innumerable salary scales for professional staff with special qualifications, but the following tables show the rates of pay for non-professional clerical staff from the administrative assistants down to the junior clerks on probation :—

GENERAL SCALE FOR ADMINISTRATIVE ASSISTANTS

	£
Commencing	655
Intermediate Annual Salaries . . .	685
	715
	745
	775
	805
Maximum	835

SCHEME FOR GRADING NON-PROFESSIONAL CLERICAL STAFF

MEN

Temporary Junior Clerks—£75 per annum.

	Division 1.	Division 2.	‡Division 3. As from 1st April, 1939.	Division 4.
	£	£	£	£
Commencing salary .	515	350	260	100 †
Intermediate annual salaries .	540	370	275	115
		390		130
	565	410		150
			290	170
	590	430		190
				210
		450		230
	615	470	310	
Maximum salary .	640	490	330	250

WOMEN

Temporary Junior Clerks—£75 per annum.

	Grade 1.	‡Grade 2.	Grade 3.§ As from 1st April, 1939.	
	£	£	£	s.
Commencing salary .	355	260	100	0†
	375	275	110	0
			122	10
Intermediate annual salaries	395	290	135	0
			147	10
			160	0
			170	0
	415	305	185	0
			200	0
			215	0
	435	320	230	0
Maximum salary	455	335	250	0

‡ Any " stop " in this Division to be fixed at £290 per annum.
† £85 per annum, if under 18 years of age.
§ Entrants to this scale at salary below £135, " stop " at £160.

LIST OF ILLUSTRATIONS

233

LIST OF ILLUSTRATIONS

LIST OF ILLUSTRATIONS

Page references printed in heavy type indicate main references. Those printed in italics indicate references to the Schedule of Historic Monuments.

INDEX

PRINTED IN GREAT BRITAIN BY RICHARD CLAY AND COMPANY, LTD.
BUNGAY, SUFFOLK.